TUTORING PROGRAMS
FOR STRUGGLING READERS

TUTORING PROGRAMS FOR STRUGGLING READERS

The America Reads Challenge

Lesley Mandel Morrow
Deborah Gee Woo

Editors

Series Foreword by Louise Cherry Wilkinson
Foreword by Carmelita Kimber Williams

THE GUILFORD PRESS
New York   London

© 2001 The Guilford Press
A Division of Guilford Publications, Inc.
72 Spring Street, New York, NY 10012
www.guilford.com

Printed in the United States of America

This book is printed on acid-free paper.

Last digit is print number: 9 8 7 6 5 4 3 2 1

Library of Congress Cataloging-in-Publication Data

Tutoring programs for struggling readers : the America Reads Challenge /
[edited by] Lesley Mandel Morrow, Deborah Gee Woo.
    p. cm.—(Rutgers invitational symposia on education)
    "This volume is based on original papers presented by the authors at the
symposium on Tutoring Programs for Struggling Readers, March 16, 2000,
in New Brunswick, New Jersey, at the Rutgers Graduate School of
Education"—Series foreword.
    Includes bibliographical references and index.
    ISBN 1-57230-605-X (hardcover)
    1. America Reads Challenge (Program)—Congresses. 2. Reading—
United States—Congresses. 3. Tutors and tutoring—Training of—United
States—Congresses. 4. Tutors and tutoring—United States—Congresses.
5. Community and school—United States—Congresses. I. Morrow,
Lesley Mandel. II. Woo, Deborah Gee. III. Rutgers invitational
symposia on education series.

LB1573 .T83 2001
372.4'0973—dc21   00-063638

ABOUT THE EDITORS

Lesley Mandel Morrow is Professor at Rutgers University's Graduate School of Education and Coordinator of the Graduate Literacy Programs. She began her career as a classroom teacher, became a reading specialist, and received her PhD from Fordham University. She has done extensive research in the area of early literacy development and published numerous articles in national refereed journals. She also has published many monographs and textbooks. Dr. Morrow served as an elected member of the Board of Directors for the International Reading Association and received its Outstanding Teacher Educator of Reading Award. She also received the Excellence in Teaching, Service, and Research Awards from Rutgers University and Fordham University's Alumni Award for Outstanding Achievement. She served as a Principal Research Investigator for the National Reading Research Center and is presently an elected member of the Board of Directors of the National Reading Conference. She also initiated the America Reads program at Rutgers University.

Deborah Gee Woo is a doctoral student and teaching assistant in the Department of Learning and Teaching at Rutgers University. She has preprimary certification from the American Montessori Society and has taught in Montessori preschools for 6 years. Her master's thesis research study was incorporated in *Literacy Instruction in Half- and Whole-Day Kindergartens: Research to Practice,* coauthored with Lesley Mandel Morrow and Dorothy Strickland. She was engaged by the National Research Center on English Learning and Achievement at the State University of New York at Albany to assist in the investigation of the practices and beliefs of exemplary first-grade teachers. Ms. Woo is a contributing author to *Highlights for Children* magazine's Parent Involvement newsletter and a presenter at the National Reading Conference and the International Reading Association Convention. She was also the Program Coordinator for the America Reads: Project Literacy Tutoring Project at Rutgers for 3 years and the Assistant Director of the Rutgers Invitational Symposia on Education (RISE) conference, *Tutoring Programs for Struggling Readers: The America Reads Challenge.* Her dissertation study focuses on early literacy tutoring.

CONTRIBUTORS

Jodi Bolla is the District Coordinator for the Division of Language Arts/ Reading for Miami–Dade County Public Schools. Her primary responsibility is the coordination of the America Reads program, including overseeing all America Reads training and in-service activities. She received her bachelor's degree in elementary education from Eastern Michigan University. She holds a master's degree in TESOL from Nova Southeastern University, and master's degrees in both urban education and reading from Florida International University. She was a classroom teacher and Reading Leader prior to joining the district staff.

María Rosa Carbajo is Associate Professor of Educational Psychology at La Plata University (Buenos Aires, Argentina) and is a member of the Institute of Educational Research (National University of La Plata). Her research interests focus on cognitive and affective factors connected with school learning, especially centered on reading and writing. She works with the "Volunteer Tutors Programme: An Argentinean Experience" and is one of the translators of *The Reading Team*, by Lesley Mandel Morrow and Barbara J. Walker, from English to Spanish.

María Celia A. de Córsico is Professor of Educational Psychology at the National University of La Plata (La Plata, Argentina), where she is also Director of the Institute for Educational Research. Previously she taught educational research methodology and educational psychology at the National University of Buenos Aires and delivered several courses and seminars at other universities in Argentina, Brazil, Ecuador, Uruguay, and the United States. Professor Córsico is a member of the Argentinean National Academy of Education and is author of numerous articles and books. Her primary research interests are in the area of cognitive and noncognitive processes of school learning.

Margaret Doughty is the Executive Director of the Houston READ Commission, a mayoral commission dedicated to a vision of 100% literacy. As executive director, she is the leader of the largest urban literacy coalition in the United States. In 1992 and 1994, the commission was recognized by Leadership Houston with the Leadership in Action Award for its literacy achievements. Ms. Doughty has worked as a teacher, curriculum designer, trainer, and administrator, including service in the United Kingdom, Iran, United Arab Emirates, and Zimbabwe. She also serves on the Family-Centered Children Care Collaborative Governing Board and the Gulf Coast Workforce Development Board, was founding president of the National Alliance of Urban Literacy Coalitions, and has served as a member of the Texas State Board of Education's Task Force on Adult Education.

Ann J. Dromsky is a doctoral student and fellow at the University of Maryland at College Park, where she also earned her master's degree in reading education. She obtained her bachelor's degree in elementary education at St. Mary's College, Notre Dame, Indiana, and has held both elementary and middle school teaching positions. Her research interests center around the use of expository reading texts in the primary grades and early literacy comprehension. In addition to her academic work, she consults with Reading Is Fundamental in Washington, DC, on literacy intervention projects. She has published several chapters and contributes to *Literacy: Issues and Practices*, the Maryland State Journal of the International Reading Association.

Robert Exley is the Chairperson of Community Education at Miami–Dade Community College's (MDCC) Wolfson Campus. Dr. Exley received his AA degree from San Jacinto College in Houston, Texas, his BA and MS from the University of Houston–Clear Lake, and his PhD from the University of Texas at Austin. He served as the founding director for MDCC's nationally recognized Service–Learning Program. He also is a consultant with the American Association of Community Colleges (AACC) regarding leadership development, faculty training, and program evaluation strategies for AACC's national service–learning project and its newest collaboration with Microsoft, Inc., to provide information technology training programs throughout the country. He provides these same services for other colleges and universities.

Jill Fitzgerald is Professor of Literacy Studies at the University of North Carolina at Chapel Hill, where she has taught since 1979. She has published over 70 works, and she recently took a yearlong reassignment from her university position to be a full-time first-grade teacher. Her current primary research interests center on literacy issues for English-language learners. In 1998, her article "English-as-a-Second-Language Learners' Cognitive Reading Process: A Review of Research in the United States" won the American Educational Research Association's outstanding review of research award. She also won (with George Noblit) the 2000 International Reading Association Dina Feitelson Award for outstanding research in early literacy. She is currently Associate Editor for *Reading and Writing Quarterly* and serves on five editorial boards for national and international research journals, including *Journal of Educational Psychology*, *Reading Research Quarterly*, and *Journal of Literacy Research*.

Linda B. Gambrell is Professor and Director of the School of Education at Clemson University. She has coauthored books on reading instruction and written numerous journal articles. She also recently coauthored a chapter in the *Handbook of Reading Research* (Vol. 3) on literature-based reading instruction and has coedited the *Journal of Reading Behavior*, a publication of the National Reading Conference. Dr. Gambrell was a principal investigator at the National Reading Research Center, where she directed the Literacy Motivation Project. She has served as an elected member of the Board of Directors of the International Reading Association and as President of the College Reading Association and the National Reading Conference. In 1998, she was the recipient of the International Reading Association Outstanding Teacher Educator of Reading Award. Her current interests are in the areas of reading comprehension strategy instruction, literacy motivation, and the role of discussion in teaching and learning.

Marcia Invernizzi is an Associate Professor of Reading Education at the University of Virginia's (UVA) Curry School of Education, where she is also Director of the McGuffey Reading Center. She is the author of numerous articles in a variety of professional journals including *The Reading Teacher, Language Arts*, the *Elementary School Journal, Annals of Dyslexia*, and the *Journal of Reading Behavior*. Her current research interests focus on early childhood prevention programs and flexible ongoing reading interventions. She is a Center for the Improvement of Early Reading Achievement (CIERA) researcher, the Principal Investigator of PALS, the screening tool used for Virginia's Early Intervention Reading Initiative, and Project Coordinator for UVA's America Reads program. She is also cofounder of Book Buddies, which received the 1997 Virginia State Reading Association's Literacy Award for community service.

Michael J. Morand is an Assistant Vice President of Yale University, where he works to shape and execute the University's initiatives in support of community development in New Haven, Connecticut, including responsibility for coordinating the University's relations with the city and state governments and the public schools. He received his BA from Yale College and his MDiv from Yale Divinity School. In addition to his duties in the University, he serves as President of the Board of Directors of the New Haven Free Public Library, as Vice President of the Arts Council of Greater New Haven, and on the boards of a number of organizations in New Haven and the state. He served on the New Haven Board of Aldermen from 1990 to 1994.

Alicia Moreyra serves as District Director for the Division of Language Arts/Reading for Miami–Dade County Public Schools. Dr. Moreyra's teaching career encompasses kindergarten through the university level, with most of her time spent in elementary classrooms as a teacher and as a grade chairperson. For the past several years, she has taught university courses and conducted workshops at the local, state, national, and international level. She oversees language arts and reading in the nation's fourth largest school district, and she directs the America Reads consortium in South Florida.

Darrell Morris is Professor of Education and Director of the Reading Clinic at Appalachian State University in Boone, North Carolina. Upon receiving his EdD from the University of Virginia, he began his college teaching career at National-Louis University in Evanston, Illinois. There he established the Howard Street Tutoring Program, which has since become a model for volunteer tutoring programs throughout the country. Since moving to Appalachian State, he has directed the master's program in reading, researched the beginning reader and spelling processes, and helped school districts in six states set up early reading intervention programs. Dr. Morris is very interested in alternative ways of training teachers to work with struggling readers.

Lesley Mandel Morrow (*see* About the Editors).

Ronald J. Scherry has been an educator in Montana for 26 years. He was an elementary classroom teacher for 14 years and an elementary principal for the past 12 years, most recently at McKinley Elementary School, which was named a National 2000 Distinguished Title I School. At McKinley, Mr. Scherry implemented and managed the America Reads program, and with Barbara J. Walker and Lesley Mandel Morrow, he developed the America Reads training program. A facilitator and author of the Montana State Reading Standards adopted in 1998, Mr. Scherry has also received several state and national awards and recognitions. Nationally, he has presented at the Migrant and International

Reading Association Conferences. Mr. Scherry retired at the end of the 1999–2000 school year and is currently working as an educational consultant.

Jeanne Shay Schumm is Professor and Chair of the Department of Teaching and Learning at the University of Miami. She has authored numerous books and articles related to reading and the needs of diverse student populations. Dr. Schumm serves as program evaluator for a number of projects including the Miami-Reads Tutorial Project. Her primary research interests include multilevel instructional practices and phonological awareness.

M. Trika Smith-Burke is Professor of Educational Psychology at New York University (NYU), where she is currently working in the Department of Teaching and Learning and in the NYU Reading Recovery Project. Dr. Smith-Burke teaches literacy courses at the undergraduate level in the department and at the graduate level in the NYU Reading Recovery Project. Before coming to NYU, she taught as a primary teacher and a remedial reading teacher. She has served on numerous committees of the International Reading Association, the National Council of Teachers of English, and the Reading Recovery Council of North America, and is a past president of the National Reading Conference. Her current interests focus on language and literacy acquisition, the role of language and culture in teaching and learning, improving literacy instruction for the lowest-achieving children in the early grades, and institutional change and systems theory.

Barbara J. Walker is currently Professor of Reading at Oklahoma State University, where she teaches courses in literacy and coordinates the reading and math center. At Montana State University–Billings, she was coordinator of the reading clinic and worked with Ronald J. Scherry to develop the America Reads program utilizing work–study students. She is a coauthor with Lesley Mandel Morrow of *The Reading Team: A Handbook for Volunteer Tutors K–3,* as well as coauthor with Ronald J. Scherry and Lesley Mandel Morrow of its companion piece used for training tutors. Dr. Walker received the College Reading Association's A. B. Herr Award in 1997 for outstanding contributions to reading education and has served on the Board of Directors of the International Reading Association, the College Reading Association, and the Montana State Reading Council. She is the author of five books, including *Supporting Struggling Readers* and *Diagnostic Teaching of Reading: Techniques for Instruction and Assessment* (4th edition), as well as numerous book chapters regarding problem readers.

Deborah Gee Woo (*see* About the Editors).

Joshua Young is Director of Miami–Dade Community College's Center for Community Involvement where he oversees all service–learning and America Reads activities. He has a bachelor's degree in sociology from the University of Virginia and master's degrees in social work and public administration from Florida State University. He served two tours with the Peace Corps in Mali, West Africa, and Paraguay, South America, and he ran summer community service youth programs for four summers in the Dominican Republic with Visions International. He has been at Miami–Dade Community College since 1994.

SERIES FOREWORD

The profession of education was shaken to its roots nearly two decades ago, when national attention focused critically on education and on educators. Beginning with the highly publicized *A Nation at Risk* (1983), often contradictory criticisms, analyses, and recommendations on American education appeared from virtually every segment of contemporary U.S. society. Critics and friends have raised basic questions about our profession, including whether educators have met the challenges successfully that the students present, and, even more fundamentally, whether we are *able* to meet those challenges.

In this explosion of concern and ideas for educational reform, there has been a need for a national forum in which the problems of education can be examined in light of research from a range of relevant disciplines. Too often, analyses of complex issues and problems occur within a single discipline. Aspects of a problem that are unfamiliar to members of the discipline are ignored, and the resulting analysis is limited in scope and thus unsatisfactory. Furthermore, when educational issues are investigated by members of only a single discipline, there is seldom an attempt to examine related issues from other fields or to apply methods developed in other fields. Such applications may prove to be illuminating.

The national debate on educational reform has often suffered from myopia, as problems and issues are identified and analyses and solutions are often proposed within the limited confines of a single disciplinary boundary. In the past, national discussions have been ill informed or uninformed by current research, partly because there are far too few mechanisms or interdisciplinary analyses of significant issues.

In response to the call for educational reform in our country, the faculty of the Rutgers Graduate School of Education developed the *Rutgers Invitational Symposia on Education*, which is both a live forum at Rutgers and a published scholarly series. Taking a multidisciplinary and interdisciplinary perspective, the symposia focuses on timely issues and problems in education. Since there is an accumulating corpus of high-quality educational research on topics of interest to practitioners and policy makers, each symposium focuses on a particular issue, such as potential teacher shortages, ways to assess literacy skills, the optimal structure of schools, or the effects of cognitive psychology on teaching mathematics. Each volume in the series provides an interdisciplinary forum through which scholars interpret and disseminate their original research and extend their work to potential applications for practice, including guides for teaching, learning, assessment, intervention, and policy formulation. These contributions increase the potential for significant analysis and positive impact on the problems of educational improvement for American children.

The present volume, the 15th symposium, is dedicated to tutoring struggling readers. This volume is based on original papers presented by the authors at the symposium on *Tutoring Programs for Struggling Readers*, March 16, 2000, in New Brunswick, New Jersey, at the Rutgers Graduate School of Education. This topic, which focuses on a unique and increasingly significant educational program dedicated to improving students' literacy, could not be more timely. The America Reads Challenge is the first national voluntary literacy program; it will be implemented this year by every institution of higher education in the United States receiving federal funds. As we celebrate the millennium, we anticipate increased statewide testing of students' literacy skills, and perhaps the first national test in U.S. history—The Fourth Grade Voluntary Reading Test. In this context, the 15th symposium is an important contribution to our understanding and improvement of students' literacy learning.

It is with great pleasure that we contribute this volume to the *Rutgers Invitational Symposia on Education* series.

LOUISE CHERRY WILKINSON
Dean and Professor of Educational Psychology
Rutgers Graduate School of Education

FOREWORD

The Reading Excellence Act, introduced in 1997 and passed in 1998, implemented the America Reads Challenge as a literacy initiative for helping to promote reading success for students in kindergarten through third grade. As a result of this legislation, educators, parents, researchers, community leaders, and volunteers have forged a partnership for accomplishing the task of helping every child read by the end of third grade. This program, initiated by President Bill Clinton, was designed to have a wide impact on reading for children throughout the nation. One portion of the America Reads Challenge was to train volunteers and federal work–study students at colleges and universities to be tutors for children in need of help in reading from kindergarten through third grade.

I was pleased when I first learned about the America Reads Challenge in March 1997. I was asked to direct such a program at Norfolk State University where I am a professor. I saw this as a wonderful opportunity to involve university students in working with reading programs in the community. I was anxious to train work–study students to tutor children who needed help.

The University, with the help of the office of financial aid, hired work–study students from many different disciplines. We trained the students and matched them with children in local school districts to tutor. Adler (1999) states that successful tutoring programs are those that screen tutors, train and monitor tutors, carefully match children and tutors, and maintain close relationships between sponsoring colleges and local school districts.

We realized that the tutors were not to take the place of expert teachers in the classrooms, but were to serve as mentors in helping children to read. We focused on preparing tutors with strategies to increase the reading ability of the students they tutored, and also on providing tutors with strategies to help children enjoy reading. The motivation to want to read and the development of reading skills can be synergistic and can build on each other.

According to research, successful literacy programs help children develop their language skills, knowledge of relationships between letters and sounds, understanding of phonemic awareness, comprehension strategies, writing, and independent reading skills. Therefore the components of our tutoring lessons included reading aloud, shared reading, language experiences, guided reading, shared writing, phonics, phonemic awareness, comprehension strategies, and independent reading.

Many colleges and universities signed on to the list to be America Reads institutions. Soon there were training manuals, tutor handbooks, and articles written detailing what works and what's best in providing tutor training and materials. The International Reading Association developed books and articles to assist in program implementation (Morrow & Walker, 1997). The U.S. Department of Education provided a Web site for the America Reads projects that were sprouting up across the nation. There was a necessity for resources and materials for the preparation of tutors, as well as materials for program implementation.

Since 1997, the America Reads Challenge has made great strides in helping thousands of children throughout this nation to read. Carol Rasco, the director of the America Reads Challenge, states: "We are witnessing a time of unparalleled activity to get more children on the road to reading. An unprecedented pro-literacy movement, focused on children under age nine, is sweeping through thousands of communities across the nation. A common strategy has emerged for reading success. We must start early by preparing young children to read, and we must finish strongly by providing excellent instruction and community support in the primary grades."

The present book is written for the express purpose of assisting those involved with America Reads programs and other tutoring programs for struggling readers. It is coming at a very important time for those interested in starting new programs. It is the first publication of its kind to describe established America Reads programs from many parts of the country. These programs show how colleges and universities can collaborate with public schools and community agencies in promoting reading achievement among children. The evaluation studies included show what effects these programs have had throughout the implementation of the America Reads Challenge, and what we have learned about the tutoring of reading by volunteers. This book also gives examples of exemplary tutoring models for early intervention in reading instruction, for the prevention of reading difficulties. This text helps educators to refine existing programs, to add new components to them, and to start new programs. The book also includes vignettes from personal experiences of tutors, which give descriptive insights into the tutor–tutee learning process.

The guidelines for federal work–study funds call for all colleges and universities receiving such funds to have some type of reading tutoring program, so more institutions are going to be looking for available information for their immediate use. The present volume is ideal for those interested in developing tutoring programs for early intervention in reading for young children. Lesley Mandel Morrow and Deborah Gee Woo have put together a useful and informative book for starting such programs and refining existing programs.

CARMELITA KIMBER WILLIAMS
President (2000–2001), International Reading Association
Professor, Norfolk State University

REFERENCES

Adler, M. (1999). *The America Reads Challenge: An analysis of college students' tutoring.* Ann Arbor: Center for the Improvement of Early Reading Achievement, University of Michigan.

Morrow, L., & Walker, B. (1997). *The reading team: A handbook for volunteer tutors K–3.* Newark, DE: International Reading Association.

Rasco, C. (1999). *Ideas at work: How to help every child become a reader.* Washington, DC: U.S. Department of Education, America Reads Challenge.

ACKNOWLEDGMENTS

We would like to acknowledge the many people who worked on this book as part of the *Rutgers Invitational Symposia on Education* (RISE). We thank Louise Cherry Wilkinson, the Dean of the Graduate School of Education at Rutgers, for her inspired idea for the RISE conference related to this text on tutoring programs for struggling readers. Special thanks go to Carol Rasco, codirector of the conference and the national director of the America Reads Challenge initiative, for her support of the RISE project. Our appreciation is likewise extended to Frances Bond and her colleagues in the U.S. Department of Education for assistance in planning and coordinating the conference. Of course, we thank all the authors for their excellent chapters. Thanks also to David Muschinske, Director of Continuing Education at Rutgers; his assistant, Jana Curry; and Joyce Carlson and Joan Melillo, who helped coordinate the conference part of the RISE project. We offer particular thanks to Michelle Rosen, assistant director of the RISE conference, for pulling all the details together. We thank Chris Jennison, Senior Editor at The Guilford Press, for supporting the project, and we sincerely appreciate the work of the production editor, Anna Nelson. Finally, to all the universities, administrators, principals, teachers, tutors, parents, and children involved in the many programs described in this text, we are extremely grateful.

CONTENTS

TUTORING PROGRAMS
FOR STRUGGLING READERS

INTRODUCTION
TO TUTORING ISSUES

Deborah Gee Woo
Lesley Mandel Morrow

For as long as there have been readers, there have been struggling read-ers. Researchers and practitioners of literacy instruction have generated an enormous quantity of literature related to teaching reading, writing, and language arts. Although the debate on best practices for delivering literacy instruction in the classroom continues, there is evidence to sup-port the effectiveness of individualized or one-on-one tutoring for those students at risk for reading failure.

Guided by these findings and by the National Assessment of Educa-tional Progress (1994), which reported that 40% of fourth graders in the United States did not attain a basic level of reading achievement, Presi-dent Clinton and his administration proposed the America Reads Chal-lenge in 1996. The Congressional response, the America Reads Challenge Act of 1997, is part of a national, bipartisan effort to address the issue of ensuring that every child can read independently by the end of third grade. The effort is multifaceted, with families, schools, and the community en-gaged as integral components.

One important aspect of the America Reads Challenge is the utiliza-tion of volunteers to serve as literacy tutors for children in kindergarten through third grade. Universities and community groups throughout the country have created numerous tutoring programs in a variety of formats. Some successful programs involve volunteers from the business commu-nity, retirees, or parents; some utilize participants in the AmeriCorps or Volunteers in Service to America (VISTA) programs; and others employ college students who are recipients of federal work–study grants. What-

1

ever the configuration of the tutoring program, evaluation indicates that tutors must receive some form of training and supervision to be effective (Wasik, 1998a; Juel, 1996).

Recent changes in government policy mandate that colleges and universities participating in the federal work–study program establish and maintain a tutoring initiative to assist children in their local community. These new tutoring endeavors will naturally turn to the established models for guidance in creating management and training protocols to ensure the quality of programs.

This introductory chapter reviews the research literature to answer the following questions: (1) Does tutoring work? (2) How effective are volunteer tutors? (3) What guidelines are recommended for tutoring programs, based on literacy research? It then provides an overview of the contents of this book.

DOES TUTORING WORK?

Tutoring as a mode of training and teaching has a long history. From the philosophical dialogues conducted by Socrates and his students, to the intellectual and moral discipline identified with Oxford and Cambridge Universities in England in the 16th century, to the private tutoring conducted at Cambridge's Trinity College in the 19th century, the tutoring relationship combined task-oriented training with the affective elements of friendship (Rapoport, Yair, & Kahane, 1989). The word "tutor" is derived from the Latin *tueri* and originally meant "one who protects, guards, cares for" (Rapoport et al., 1989, p. 16). This definition highlights the duality of the tutorial relationship and its particular significance. In the ideal situation, not only is the tutor committed to specific academic goals, but also there exists a personal bond of trust and caring.

The effectiveness of tutoring has been examined in a number of studies. In a meta-analysis of findings from 65 evaluations of school-based tutoring programs, Cohen, Kulik, and Kulik (1982) determined that there was a positive effect on academic performance and attitudes of those being tutored. The size of these effects was significantly related to certain features of the programs: Larger tutoring effects were observed in more structured programs, as well as those of shorter duration. Moreover, the teaching and testing of lower-level skills produced larger effects, as did the teaching of mathematics rather than reading. Finally, effects were stronger when assessment involved locally developed tests versus nationally standardized instruments.

Benjamin Bloom (1984), upon review of several studies that compared student learning outcomes under three different instructional methods identified as "conventional," "mastery learning," and "tutoring," coined the phrase "the 2 sigma problem" (p. 4). This referred to the finding that on final achievement measures, the average student with a "good" tutor scored about two standard deviations above the average of the control class. This finding prompted Bloom to search for a method of group instruction that was as effective as "good" tutoring (i.e., tutoring conducted by a professional teacher).

In a review of five tutoring programs, Wasik and Slavin (1993) found that one-to-one reading instruction was very effective when undertaken by certified teachers. Two programs that utilize highly skilled professional tutors and paraprofessionals and have been extensively studied are Reading Recovery® and Success for All.

Reading Recovery is an early intervention program for first graders who have been referred by their classroom teachers. The creator of the program, Marie Clay (1985), designed a test battery that identifies those children who would benefit most from the program; the assessment measures are also used as diagnostic tools to implement instruction (Clay, 1993a). Once children are accepted into the program, each child meets individually with a rigorously trained Reading Recovery teacher daily for a maximum of 20 weeks. Children are discharged from the program either when they have reached a prescribed level of competence (about second-grade reading level), or when their Reading Recovery teachers decide that they are not benefiting from the program and that other avenues should be explored (Clay, 1993b).

Reading Recovery was first tested in New Zealand, where the program originated. DeFord, Lyons, and Pinnell (1991) report that in initial field testing, the majority of the children who had been involved achieved average reading levels upon completion. A longitudinal study done in Ohio showed that after 2 years, children who had been in Reading Recovery scored consistently higher on readings of leveled text than a comparison group who had received other early intervention in reading (DeFord et al., 1991). M. Trika Burke-Smith provides a more expansive description of the Reading Recovery model in Chapter 11 of this text.

In Success for All (Slavin, Madden, Karweit, Dolan, & Wasik, 1992; Slavin, Madden, Karweit, Livermon, & Dolan, 1990), tutoring is a part of a comprehensive school-based reform system designed for high-poverty districts. In contrast to Reading Recovery, in Success for All tutoring is integrated with a school's reading program. All teachers in a Success for All school receive training in the Success for All curriculum. The lowest-achieving children within the target grades receive one-to-one tutoring from either teachers or paraprofessionals. Most of the tutoring services are provided to the low-achieving first graders and can be considered preventative measures (Wasik & Slavin, 1993).

Research on Success for All in nine school districts showed that first graders in the program, on the average, scored 3 months ahead of control groups in individually administered and standardized reading tests. Fifth graders were a year ahead of their counterparts on similar measures (Slavin, Madden, Karweit, Dolan, & Wasik, 1996).

HOW EFFECTIVE ARE VOLUNTEER TUTORS?

Barbara Wasik (1998a), in a review of 17 volunteer tutoring programs in reading, reached several important conclusions. The first finding of interest was the lack of documentation regarding the effect of one-to-one tutoring by adult volunteers on reading achievement. Of the 17 programs reviewed, only the Howard Street Tutoring Program and the School Volunteer Development Project utilized rigorous experimental designs. Darrell Morris presents the Howard Street model in detail in Chapter 9.

Second, Wasik (1998a) determined that the difficulty in conducting experimental research in school and community settings stems from the logistics of creating a control group of students who are denied services for the purpose of pre- and posttest comparisons. Without such a comparison between treatment and nontreatment groups, it is difficult to make a determination that year-end gains are due to the tutoring intervention.

Finally, when Wasik (1998a) analyzed the 17 programs together, four similarities emerged that provide insights into volunteer tutoring. The common features include (1) the presence of a coordinator/supervisor who possesses expert knowledge on the reading process to provide guidance; (2) the presence of a prescribed structure in the tutoring sessions that includes similar basic elements; (3) training for tutors that varied in amount and quality across programs; and (4) the lack of coordination between classroom instruction and the tutoring program.

Juel (1996) suggests a number of reasons for the positive effects of one-to-one tutoring. In the focused one-to-one setting, the learner is less distracted by the bustle of the classroom. He/she is able to remain engaged with materials and the learning process for longer periods of time. In addition, individualized instruction allows the student to receive appropriately leveled materials and immediate feedback at the right time for the maximum benefit. This is especially critical for early literacy development and young readers.

Children who struggle with reading in first grade are very likely to continue to do so unless adequate intervention is provided (Clay, 1979; Juel, 1988; Lundberg, 1984, cited in Juel, 1996). The two reasons noted for this by Juel (1996, p. 271) are that "children who are struggling with word recognition sometimes become mired in extremely unproductive hypotheses about how print works," and the "phenomenon that has been labeled the 'Matthew Effect' (Stanovich, 1986) can be at work." In this latter phenomenon, experiencing difficulties in learning to read often results in the development of a dislike for reading, which leads to an avoidance of reading, which cycles back to more difficulties. Immediate feedback in context in a tutorial situation can help to ameliorate this effect. In addition, trained tutors are able to intervene via scaffolding and modeling to reduce the tangle of unproductive hypotheses that can impede progress.

WHAT GUIDELINES ARE RECOMMENDED FOR TUTORING PROGRAMS, BASED ON LITERACY RESEARCH?

Although there are ongoing controversies within the field of literacy pedagogy, Gambrell and Mazzoni (1999, pp. 14–19) delineate eight common-ground principles for best practices in literacy:

1. Learning is meaning making.
2. Prior knowledge guides learning.
3. The gradual-release-of-responsibility model and scaffolded instruction facilitate learning.
4. Social collaboration enhances learning.
5. Learners learn best when they are interested and involved.
6. The goal of best practices is to develop high-level strategic readers and writers.
7. Best practices are grounded in the principle of balanced instruction.
8. Best practices are a result of informed decision making.

Because reading is a meaning-making process, it is essential that children be helped to make sense of what they read (Clay, 1991; Goodman, 1997; Morrow, 1997). Comprehension is an interactive process involving prior knowledge and information found in the text (Vacca, Vacca, & Gove, 1995). To activate this process, young children need to learn to retell stories, respond to text, and evaluate what they have read (Morrow, 1997).

Questions that scaffold comprehension can be divided into three categories: literal, inferential, and critical. On the literal level, retellings of stories help children to recall what they have read and to sequence events. Inferential and critical comprehension are considered higher-level thinking skills (Morrow, 1997; Rubin, 1997). Even emergent readers can engage in discussions that require them to make predictions and evaluate stories (Morrow, 1997). Relating literature to real life helps children to make connections between books and their own personal experience.

The young reader also needs to develop concepts about books. Questions and discussions about a book's cover, title, author, and illustrator help children to internalize the parts of a book (Morrow & Walker, 1997). Directed reading and thinking activities (Morrow, 1997; Rubin, 1997) set a purpose for reading by posing questions before reading that ask readers to look for specific information as they read. Pictures are used before, during, and after reading with young children to clarify the text (Clay, 1991).

Reading and writing support one another. According to Pearson and Stephens (1994), by reading children learn to write, and by writing children learn to read. For emergent readers, writing gives them the opportunity to match letters with their sounds. When children are encouraged to sound out words as they write them, their awareness of sound–symbol correspondence is increased. Moreover, writing about reading increases comprehension of the text. Morrow (1997) states that rewriting "helps a child develop language structures, comprehension, and a sense of story structure" (p. 211).

Interactions between adults and children support both reading and writing development. As Teale (1982) says "by being engaged in activities which have literacy embedded in them and in which the reading or writing, and the oral language which accompanies them, are played out in the social interaction between the child and the more experienced, literate person, the child is able to participate in the activity itself, gradually internalize the social relationships, and thereby develop personal competencies in reading and writing" (p. 563). Attempts at writing need to be purposeful, valued, and recognized as meaningful. Children learn to write by being exposed to print, and adult modeling provides opportunities for children to learn the conventions of writing. Writing also presents opportunities for more explicit skill instruction.

These principles are to be found in many successful tutoring programs. Wasik (1998b) closely examined four programs that have been evaluated as effective, in order to determine the common components that are essential for successful tutoring. Three of the four programs—Reading Recovery, the Howard Street Tutoring Program, and Book Buddies—are described in Part III of this text and share seven of the elements. The eighth component is derived from evidence on the Success for All program. The list includes the following (Wasik, 1998b, pp. 565–569):

1. A certified reading specialist needs to supervise tutors.
2. Tutors need ongoing training and feedback.
3. Tutoring sessions need to be structured and contain basic elements, particularly rereading a familiar story or text, word analysis, writing, and introducing new stories.
4. Tutoring needs to be intensive and consistent.

5. Quality materials are needed to facilitate the tutoring model.
6. Assessment of students needs to be ongoing.
7. Schools need to find ways to ensure that tutors will attend regularly.
8. Tutoring needs to be coordinated with classroom instruction.

OVERVIEW OF THIS BOOK

The primary purpose of the present text is to assist those who are initiating tutoring programs and to share ideas among those who are refining existing ones. It was conceived as a response to this need to disseminate information and resulted from the *Rutgers Invitational Symposia on Education,* cosponsored by Rutgers University and the U.S. Department of Education, that addressed current issues related to early literacy interventions in general and America Reads tutoring programs specifically. Within each chapter, the authors have made an effort to describe the tutoring framework of the particular program being described, its basis in theory, and the challenges posed in its implementation.

The book has been organized into three parts. In Part I, separate chapters describe five established America Reads tutoring programs that exemplify different tutoring models. Part II includes three chapters describing research studies that demonstrate the effects of the America Reads experience on tutors, students, and teachers. In Part III, exemplary models of early literacy interventions that have been evaluated and shown to have a positive impact on student achievement—namely, Reading Recovery, the Howard Street Tutoring Project, and Book Buddies—are presented.

Part I: Established America Reads Tutoring Programs

In Chapter 1, "America Reads Tutoring: Communities Working Together," Barbara J. Walker and Ronald J. Scherry demonstrate how collaboration between a university and a public school began the America Reads tutortraining project for the entire state of Montana. Much of the chapter focuses on the initial tutoring program development and the subsequent implementation of the tutoring program at McKinley Elementary School in Billings, which included work–study students. From the work–study program, tutor-training procedures were developed that were used to broaden the range of tutors to include community members from a local hospital and other volunteer groups. The training program was refined again as the summer included a school-based program in Pryor, Montana, where tutors were supported by work–study funds, Native American tribal funds, mission school funds, and private donations. During the following year, the training model was expanded to include a training-of-trainers section, and statewide training seminars were implemented.

The chapter includes qualitative data from the McKinley School program and from the work–study program. Tutors were interviewed to ascertain the impact of tutoring on their perceptions of literacy and children. Descriptive data on students at the McKinley site demonstrate the effects of a tutoring program on reading achievement. In conclusion, the chapter focuses on the successful implementation of the statewide training-of-trainers program for America Reads in Montana, and the stages at the community level that preceded its implementation.

Chapter 2, by Margaret Doughty of the Houston READ Commission, is entitled "The Voices of Houston Reads to Lead!: Building an Urban Literacy Coalition through America Reads." Issues discussed in this chapter include a brief history of the need for community collaboration; how Houston built its partnership; why the partnership works; what is involved in school–community collaboration; why such collaboration only succeeds when it is built around the family; stories that made a difference; learning from mistakes; the role of volunteers; best-practices exchanges with other cities; who the struggling readers are in Houston; how the coalition assists at an individual level; the role of AmeriCorps, VISTA, other volunteer groups, and federal work–study students in the citywide effort; celebrating Houston Reads to Lead!; practical tips for collaborative community thinking; hands-on ideas for getting started; and photographs of unlikely learning partners.

In Chapter 3, Joshua Young, Jodi Bolla, Jeanne Shay Schumm, Alicia Moreyra, and Robert Exley describe "The South Florida America Reads Coalition: A Synergistic Effort." The Miami–Dade County (Florida) metropolitan area has developed one of the nation's most ambitious, successful, and collaborative America Reads efforts. With over 220 federal work–study tutors, an extensive orientation and training program, a parental involvement component, a Buddy Reading project that targets high school and community volunteers, and a research-tested tutoring curriculum that provides one-on-one tutoring sessions to struggling first graders, much has been accomplished in only 2 years with minimal resources. This chapter describes the progression of this project—how four universities and the local school district formed an America Reads coalition; how federal work–study tutors have been recruited, trained, and supported; and how the initiative has grown in scope and quality. The chapter focuses on lessons learned that will help other colleges, universities, and communities respond successfully to the America Reads Challenge. In addition, the chapter shares the impact that America Reads has had on the college student tutors—an unanticipated, but powerful and important, outcome.

In Chapter 4, in "America Reads and Comprehensive Neighborhood Revitalization: The Yale–New Haven Experience," Michael J. Morand describes a collaborative effort between the community and an involved university. Yale University and the New Haven (Connecticut) Public Schools joined together through the America Reads Challenge to promote literacy with a comprehensive program in a local elementary school. Yale's involvement began when its president, Richard C. Levin, responded to the direct appeal of President Clinton to college and university presidents throughout the nation. Yale has a strong tradition of allocating federal work–study funds for off-campus community service, and it recognized America Reads as an opportunity to focus these funds in a strategic way that would strengthen its growing partnerships with New Haven.

Yale's program has the goal of providing a trained college student tutor for each of 70 children at all achievement levels in the third grade at the Timothy Dwight Elementary School, which is located in a neighborhood immediately west of Yale's main campus. The university and the neighborhood share a community of interests, both geographically and in terms of their goals of sustaining a vibrant area with strong education, economic development, affordable housing, and public safety. America Reads in New Haven is thus part of an overall comprehensive plan for neighborhood revitalization. This chapter describes how Yale and the New Haven Public Schools established their literacy tutoring program, designed its daily operations, recruited and trained tutors, and sustained it beyond the first year.

In Chapter 5, "A Tutoring Program for Struggling Readers in Argentina," María Celia A. de Córsico and María Rosa Carbajo describe a tutoring program they designed based on an America Reads model. Reading difficulties are among the main factors in grade repetition and school dropout in Argentina. Inspired by the work of Lesley Mandel Morrow and her coworkers at Rutgers University, the chapter authors and their colleagues at the National University of La Plata developed an adaptation of that work to the sociocultural environment in Argentina. University students in educational sciences have been trained for the tutoring program implementation. Favorable attitudinal changes and some improvement in children's reading performance have been registered.

Part II: Evaluation Studies of America Reads Tutoring Programs

In Chapter 6, "The Effect of an America Reads Tutoring Program on Literacy Achievement and Attitudes of Teachers, Tutors, and Children," we describe an America Reads Challenge tutoring project that involves federal work–study university students tutoring children in kindergarten through third grade in an urban school in the northeastern United States. In addition to a description of the tutor-training program, training materials, and the components of the tutoring session, the results of a research study are included. Inquiries were made in the following areas of interest: (1) enhancement of tutored students' achievement in reading and writing; (2) attitudes of teachers, tutors, and children toward the tutoring program; and (3) literacy strategies used by tutors to help with literacy development.

In Chapter 7, "America Reads: A Close-Up Look at What Two Tutors Learned about Teaching Reading," Jill Fitzgerald presents research results detailing the learning of two America Reads tutors. One tutor had a supervisor who was experienced in teaching reading; the other tutor's supervisor was inexperienced. Striking differences between the tutors were found in what and how they learned about teaching reading. Implications are drawn for tutorial training and policy.

In Chapter 8, "America Reads: Literacy Lessons Learned," Ann J. Dromsky and Linda B. Gambrell focus on the effective elements of an America Reads tutoring program. Information is provided about essential features of tutor training, instructional practice, and school-based support that facilitate student learning.

Part III: Exemplary Models of Early Literacy Interventions

In Chapter 9, "The Howard Street Tutoring Model: Using Volunteer Tutors to Prevent Reading Failure in the Primary Grades," Darrell Morris begins with a summary of the few research studies that support the use of volunteer reading tutors in the primary grades. Next, the Howard Street tutoring model is described. Tutoring methods and materials are covered, along with a detailed plan for providing the volunteer tutors with ongoing training and supervision. Because close supervision of volunteers by a reading specialist is the key to a successful tutoring program, the chapter closes with a research proposal for training reading teachers how to provide such supervision. Such training of school-based supervisors is necessary if the concept of volunteer tutoring is ever to fulfill its promise.

In Chapter 10, "Book Buddies: A Community Volunteer Tutorial Program," Marcia Invernizzi describes the Charlottesville (Virginia) Book Buddies program, detailing the history of its development, and outlining its growth and refinement over an 8-year span. Research on the effectiveness of the program is summarized, and efforts to replicate the program in challenging urban settings are described. The chapter ends with conclusions regarding the potential impact of volunteer tutorials on the reading development of children at risk, and the ramifications of long-term community involvement in the education of all children.

In Chapter 11, M. Trika Smith-Burke discusses "Reading Recovery: A Systemic Approach to Early Intervention." As we have briefly noted earlier, Reading Recovery was designed and developed by Marie Clay as an early intervention program for children at risk of literacy failure in first grade. This chapter describes the complex design of the program, including the instructional component, the staff development model, the implementation model, and the monitoring and alternative evaluation design. It also discusses some of the key factors in the success of the program, as the key studies on the program are reviewed. The complexity and inclusiveness of the design, an emphasis on learning at all levels, a built-in capacity to incorporate new understandings from research and from individual teachers, and the clear outcome of student success for all components contribute to Reading Recovery's potential for systemic impact by significantly reducing the number of children who are encountering the most serious difficulties in learning to read and write.

Our intention in preparing this text has been to provide some insight into the tutoring process from a number of perspectives. We hope that those of you who are contemplating the establishment of a tutoring program, as well as those already engaged in one, find inspiration and practical help in the authors' work in this field. Learning to read is a complex process, and dedicated, trained, well-supervised tutors can provide opportunities for young readers to practice and hone their skills in a supportive setting.

REFERENCES

Bloom, B. S. (1984). The search for methods of group instruction as effective as one-to-one tutoring. *Educational Leadership, 41*(8), 4–17.

Clay, M. M. (1979). *Reading: The patterning of complex behaviour.* Portsmouth, NH: Heinemann.

Clay, M. M. (1985). *The early detection of reading difficulties* (3rd ed.). Portsmouth, NH: Heinemann.

Clay, M. M. (1991). *Becoming literate: The construction of inner control.* Portsmouth, NH: Heinemann.

Clay, M. M. (1993a). *Observation survey of early literacy achievement.* Portsmouth, NH: Heinemann.

Clay, M. M. (1993b). *Reading Recovery: A guidebook for teachers in training.* Portsmouth, NH: Heinemann.

Cohen, P., Kulik, J. A., & Kulik, C. (1982). Educational outcomes of tutoring: A meta-analysis of findings. *American Educational Research Journal, 19,* 237–248.

DeFord, D. E., Lyons, C. A., & Pinnell, G. S. (Eds.). (1991). *Bridges to literacy: Learning from Reading Recovery.* Portsmouth, NH: Heinemann.

Gambrell, L. B., & Mazzoni, S. A. (1999). Principles of best practice: Finding the common ground. In L. B. Gambrell, L. M. Morrow, S. B. Neuman, &

M. Pressley (Eds.), *Best practices in literacy instruction* (pp. 11–21). New York: Guilford Press.

Goodman, K. S. (1997). Miscues: Windows on the reading process. In K. S. Goodman (Ed.), *Miscue analysis: Applications to reading instruction.* Urbana, IL: Educational Resources Information Center.

Juel, C. (1988). Learning to read and write: A longitudinal study of fifty-four children from first through fourth grade. *Journal of Educational Psychology, 80,* 437–447.

Juel, C. (1996). What makes literacy tutoring effective? *Reading Research Quarterly, 31,* 268–289.

Morrow, L. M. (1997). *Literacy development in the early years: Helping children read and write* (3rd ed.). Needham Heights, MA: Allyn & Bacon.

Morrow, L. M., & Walker, B. J. (1997). *The reading team: A handbook for volunteer tutors K–3.* Newark, DE: International Reading Association.

National Assessment of Educational Progress. (1994). *America's report card.* Washington, DC: U.S. Government Printing Office.

Pearson, D. P., & Stephens, S. (1994). Learning about literacy. In R. B. Ruddell, M. R. Ruddell, & H. Singer (Eds.), *Theoretical models and processes of reading* (4th ed., pp. 22–43). Newark, DE: International Reading Association.

Rapoport, T., Yair, G., & Kahane, R. (1989). Tutorial relations: The dynamics of social contract and personal trust. *Interchange, 20,* 14–26.

Rubin, D. (1997). *Diagnosis and correction in reading instruction.* Needham Heights, MA: Allyn & Bacon.

Slavin, R. E., Madden, N. A., Karweit, N. L., Dolan, L., & Wasik, B. A. (1992). *Success for All: A relentless approach to prevention and early intervention in elementary schools.* Arlington, VA: Educational Research Service.

Slavin, R. E., Madden, N. A., Karweit, N. L., Dolan, L., & Wasik, B. A. (1996). *Every child, every school: Success for All.* Newbury Park, CA: Corwin.

Slavin, R. E., Madden, N. A., Karweit, N. L., Livermon, B. J., & Dolan, L. (1990). Success for All: First year outcomes of a comprehensive plan for reforming urban education. *American Educational Research Journal, 27*(2), 255–278.

Stanovich, K. E. (1986). Matthew effects in reading: Some consequences of individual differences in the acquisition of literacy. *Reading Research Quarterly, 21,* 360–406.

Teale, W. H. (1982). Toward a theory of how children learn to read and write naturally. *Language Arts, 59,* 555–570.

Vacca, J. A. L., Vacca, R. T., & Gove, M. K. (1995). *Reading and learning to read.* New York: HarperCollins.

Wasik, B. A. (1998a). Volunteer tutoring programs in reading: A review. *Reading Research Quarterly, 33,* 262–292.

Wasik, B. A. (1998b). Using volunteers as reading tutors: Guidelines for successful practice. *The Reading Teacher, 51*(7), 562–570.

Wasik, B. A., & Slavin, R. E. (1993). Preventing early reading failure with one-to-one tutoring: A review of five programs. *Reading Research Quarterly, 28,* 178–200.

Part I

ESTABLISHED AMERICA READS TUTORING PROGRAMS

Chapter 1

AMERICA READS TUTORING: COMMUNITIES WORKING TOGETHER

Barbara J. Walker
Ronald J. Scherry

Dear Mr. Scherry,

I would like to take this opportunity to thank you so much for the great opportunities I have experienced this past year tutoring for the America Reads program. It was my privilege to tutor. As you can imagine, most volunteers are quite apprehensive starting out. I can confidently say I fit nicely into that category! There seemed so much to remember at first, but then I found us getting into the swing of things and actually accomplishing goals. My student was wonderful to work with—very bright and eager to learn. I have to admit I was devastated the last day of tutoring. Shocked was more like it, actually! Somehow we had lost track of time and fully expected there to be another month. . . .

I look forward this fall to a continued partnership with McKinley students and staff. THANK YOU AGAIN FOR A WONDERFUL OPPORTUNITY. The America Reads program definitely made a difference in my life!

—ADMINISTRATIVE COORDINATOR
Deaconess Billings Clinic Psychiatric Services

Volunteers at the McKinley Elementary School in Billings, Montana, continually comment on the wonderful opportunity that tutoring presents. We had no idea of the magnitude our project would eventually have when we started it in 1997. That was the year after President Clinton issued his America Reads Challenge urging all citizens to work to ensure all children read well and independently by the end of third grade. He challenged the nation to mobilize a million volunteer tutors to meet this goal. In Montana, we were ready to take up the challenge. The two of us—Ronald Scherry, the principal of McKinley Elementary School, and Barbara Walker, the chair of the America Reads committee for the International Reading Association—paired up to develop the format and organization that would later be implemented throughout Montana. Beginning on a small scale in the fall of 1997, we revised and added to a program that would be at the core of the Montana America Reads initiative. By the fall of 1999, through the steady efforts of many volunteers, we had conducted approximately 40 training workshops. There were 220 trainers in 37 counties in Montana, resulting in 645 America Reads volunteer tutors who were working with over 2,000 students statewide. Although Montana is a rugged state spread out over many miles, it was still possible to provide coordinated training for a large cadre of volunteers— training that was based on research in literacy tutoring. This chapter describes how the Montana America Reads initiative grew into such a collaborative effort.

DESIGNING A TUTORING FORMAT

Initially, we developed the tutoring program on a small scale. We used what we knew about literacy learning to develop our program. We knew that Juel (1996) found one common characteristic of successful programs to be a manual providing a structured format for tutors to implement consistently at each session. We set out to find out what such a structured format might include.

Studying tutoring is difficult because of the constraints of schools and their policies, as well as variations in attendance of both tutors and children. However, several researchers and program directors have managed to summarize some research results from volunteer tutoring programs. Juel (1996) reviewed hours of videotaped tutor sessions. Doing this, she found that the successful tutors kept children engaged in reading and writing activities longer than the less successful tutors. In addition, she found that those tutors whose students gained the most kept their students *actively reading*, rather than talking a lot or letting students do nonreading activities. Therefore, we looked for components of tutoring that would keep students and their tutors engaged. We used five of the components described in *The Reading Team* (Morrow & Walker, 1997) and pilot-tested these at McKinley Elementary School. We began in the fall of 1997 by training four work–study students from Montana State University–Billings (MSU-B) and placing the tutors with students in second through fourth grades. Eight students were tutored in the fall of 1997.

Through the research, we knew that three components (reading in connected text, writing, and word study) were frequently used by other tutoring programs (Juel, 1996; Wasik, 1998). Based on this information, we used four elements (reading old favorites, reading together, word study, and writing together) to form the core of the tutoring program for the state of Montana. We added a fifth element, called "summarizing success," as the final component. The following paragraphs explain these elements.

Reading Old Favorites

Old favorites like *The Little Red Hen* are selections children have already heard and know well. Reading something familiar provides an opportunity to read connected text and a familiar context for figuring out words. In a study using easy-to-read and familiar stories in a restructured Chapter 1 program that included daily rereading of familiar text, it was found that 77% of at-risk first graders reached the primer level, while only 18% reached that level in a traditional Chapter 1 program (Hiebert, Colt, Catto, & Gary, 1992). When children reread material they know well, they practice reading and notice features about print and meaning. This experience, then, begins the session with a series of successful reading experiences that increase motivation and support active reading. This component also helps develop the mentoring relationship between a tutor and a child. As young children read these books aloud, tutors can support reading by prompting the children to think about words, or they can simply read along with the children until the children have gained confidence to read alone.

Reading Together

For young children, literacy emerges out of reading and writing with others. Usually mothers, fathers, grandparents, aunts, and uncles read with young children, supporting their literacy attempts. This type of experience is emulated by the shared reading approach, where the teacher and children read stories together. As a tutor and a child read together, the child repeats what the tutor reads. This type of reading with a young child is powerful. The tutor models what reading sounds like. As the child reads alone, the tutor offers support for attempts and gives hints so the child can read fluently. In a research review, Leslie and Allen (1999) found that modeling and scaffolding while reading connected text were characteristic of all early interventions. In fact, when training in the Reading

Recovery program, teachers spend a year learning how to model and scaffold young children's reading. The Reading Recovery approach has consistently demonstrated improved reading strategies in children receiving instruction (Center, Whedall, Freeman, Outhred, & McNaught, 1995). Although most volunteers' training is not as extensive, they can learn to prompt children as they read text (see discussion later in this chapter). This supportive beginning of an unfamiliar selection is continued throughout this phase by stopping to discuss what is happening. Finally, the child reads the new selection alone with support from the tutor.

Both of the first two elements of the volunteer tutoring program focus on reading connected text. A balance is maintained between reading familiar text and reading something new; this allows the children to refine their reading strategies in a familiar context while learning new strategies in more challenging text. Next, the program focuses on word study to extend the knowledge of strategies for figuring out new words.

Talk about Words (Word Study)

The tutoring program also includes a word study activity, where the tutor and child discuss features of words as well as their meaning (Juel, 1996). Research tells us that the most important part of words to study are the onset or the beginning of the word, and its rime, which is the ending word pattern (Adams, 1990; Bradley & Bryant, 1985). Children develop this knowledge about words through reading a lot, having tutors talk about rhymes, and writing rhymes (Snow, Burns, & Griffin, 1998). For volunteer tutors, focusing on beginning word sounds and on how words rhyme is most appropriate.

In the Montana program, both the tutor and the child select an interesting word from that day's session. This word is written on a chart entitled "Words: Bridging the New and the Known" (Morrow & Walker, 1997). Then both the tutor and the child tell why their word is interesting, define what it means, and point out some key features like the rhyme in the word. Finally, they use the word in a sentence.

Writing Together

Writing encourages children to think about how words are put together to form a meaningful message. By writing together with children, tutors can demonstrate how to communicate ideas in writing. They provide a powerful model of how writing works when they share writing with their students. Likewise, writing stretches children's knowledge about words. When people write, they have to think about how words are formed and their consistent letter patterns. In fact, early writing with invented spelling helps students notice how words are spelled and their sound patterns (Snow et al., 1998).

In our program, we suggest three different ways that a tutor and a child can share in the writing process. We recommend written communication, where the tutor first writes a question to the child; then the child writes a response and another question to the tutor. In this way, the tutor models written conventions for the child, as well as purposeful writing. We also suggest "I write, you write" stories. In this approach, the tutor and the child take turns writing sentences in a story. Again, the tutor provides a model, and the child can use the model and extend it further. Finally, for a young child, we recommend writing side by side in separate journals. In this experience, the tutor models the enjoyment and celebration of the writing process. As reading together does, writing together provides a powerful model for children and helps reading and writing develop together.

The third and fourth components of the volunteer tutoring program work to balance a young child's knowledge about words both in and out of context. The isolated word study focuses on the pattern of letters within words, while writing together focuses on using that word knowledge in written communication. Both of these aspects advance the child's knowledge of the conventions of printed language.

Summarizing Success

In a final short activity, the child summarizes what has been accomplished during the session, to help the child talk about what he/she did well. By talking about what went well, the child will be motivated to engage in the activities that promote literacy. This concrete record of accomplishments helps children take charge of their literacy as they describe their progress in reading and writing.

Using all these components at each session provides a consistent structure that promotes engaged readers. Tutors know how to proceed with each session and look forward to discussing old favorites and new stories; learning through writing and word study; and summarizing the session.

BUILDING A COMMUNITY TEAM

Establishing a Corporate Partnership

From this beginning, materials and procedures were developed for implementing the program in a school setting. As we were looking for community partners to expand the number of tutoring pairs, Scherry began discussing with the staff of Deaconess Billings Clinic (a medical facility) ways the staff members could become involved with their community. Through these discussions, Deaconess Billings Clinic, which is located near the school, decided to adopt McKinley Elementary as its neighborhood school and to become a sponsor of the America Reads program. As a sponsor, the clinic provides volunteer tutors by allowing its employees work release time to tutor at McKinley. It also provides funding for training materials, as well as space at the clinic to conduct training workshops.

Training more than three tutors at a time demanded that the procedures for training become more standard. The draft training materials were quickly modified for group use. In January 1998, we trained 12 Deaconess Billings Clinic employees and an additional 3 MSU-B work–study students. In the spring semester of 1998 these tutors, along with the tutors from the fall semester, worked with 28 students in grades K–3 at McKinley. From interviewing the tutors near the end of the school year, we found that they felt they profited as much from tutoring as the children in the school did. The coordinator of human resources at the clinic said, "When I walk out of there, I'm just smiling. I think everybody should be able to read fluently, and it feels wonderful to think that we're making progress." The manager of oncology services said that one of the highlights of her week was spending 30 minutes helping a first grader with his reading. She also mentioned that the training helped her become a better tutor. She said, "It provided specific guidelines that can help both

Dr. Nicholas J. Wolter, CEO, Deaconess Billings Clinic, tutoring McKinley first-grade student Ashley Hernandez. *Billings Gazette* photo by Larry Mayer.

the reader and the tutor achieve success." Both of these individuals enjoyed working with the teachers and said that it increased their understanding of what teachers deal with every day.

As we trained tutors and implemented the program at McKinley, we saw a real need to develop a specific training procedure to follow and details about how to implement, organize, and manage the volunteer tutor program at the school level. The tutors who came from Deaconess Billings Clinic asked important questions that we had not considered. They were nervous about what to do when they couldn't tutor, what to do in emergency situations, how to keep the students engaged, and how to know whether they were making a difference. So we began writing *Training the Reading Team* (Walker, Scherry, & Morrow, 1999), and used draft versions of this material for training volunteers.

Extending Training to Community Groups

Training for volunteers is imperative. It only took one group of community volunteers to convince us of that. We were lucky to have college students, nurses, physicians, and hospital administrators in those first training sessions, as they were sufficiently knowledgeable to ask the significant questions. We realized that we needed to prepare them for the close personal relationships they would develop with the children. We began with 10 hours of training spread over at least two sessions within a 2-week period. During the 2 weeks between sessions, each volunteer made a visit to the school, observed in classrooms, and met classroom teachers. This gave the tutors a concrete picture of where they would be tutoring and the approximate age of the students.

As we developed the training program, we realized that we needed to include activities demonstrating how to interact with a child in a instructional setting. The research also suggested that tutor–child interactions are a crucial aspect of a successful volunteer program (Juel, 1998). Thus we began to develop training sessions about the interactions that a tutor can provide by having tutors pair up during training activities and participate in the type of activities they would be doing with the children. Our training program, therefore, emphasized—and continues to emphasize—tutors' becoming literacy mentors by actively listening to children read and offering support when they became confused.

Much of this training was and is based on the research of Lev Vygotsky (1978), who described the "zone of proximal development." This zone occurs between what a novice can do alone and what can be done in collaboration with a more skilled individual. Learners can move to a more complex level of learning with the support of experienced individuals. As more experienced readers and writers, the tutors offer support to the children. In this type of scaffolding, the support is collaborative and interactive in nature. Looking for an analogy to teach this concept to volunteers, we decided upon the "coaching" metaphor. In reality, tutors are much like coaches as they work with children. They model how the process works; they support the children's attempts with encouragement; and they celebrate the children's successful reading. In an analysis of videotapes of lessons, Juel (1996) found that these aspects were used by successful tutors but not by the less successful tutors.

Like young athletes, young readers need models of what readers do, because environments rich in literacy models facilitate reading development (Braunger & Lewis, 1998). As a coach models new plays for a young athlete, so a literacy tutor models new strategies for a young reader. We have suggested that when tutors discuss stories, they use "I statements" to describe how they themselves actually thought about the story or figured out a word (Walker, 2000a). For example, they can easily say, "I was just thinking that the lamb might be the reason Mary is in trouble," to indicate how they are thinking about the story. This is called "thinking aloud" and is a powerful way to provide a model for young readers. Thinking aloud helps tutors share their literacy by talking about their own strategies.

As all coaches know, much learning comes from making mistakes. However, young children get discouraged when they make mistakes. A tutor can model a light-hearted attitude toward making mistakes by saying, "Oops, that didn't make sense. Now what were we reading about?" Using these types of statements helps children understand that reading is not a perfect process, but rather a process of predicting and checking their understanding.

Besides modeling, tutors coach thinking by prompting or giving hints when children stumble as they read. According to Juel (1998), the tutors in her study who were able to give students clues created higher learning. Likewise, research has shown that parents who learn to give children clues can increase children's reading (Walker, 2000b). Support involves pausing to let the students figure out a word and prompting by giving hints about how to figure out words. Because of the one-to-one situation, tutors can provide immediate support as the children are reading. Leslie and Allen (1999) found that in many intervention programs, teachers or tutors scaffold multiple strategies for figuring out words. When training tutors a quick way to remember is to use the "three P's" of tutoring, which are "pause," "prompt," and "praise."

1. *Pause.* A tutor can respond by pausing to give a child time to think. Waiting for 5 seconds before prompting is essential to supporting literacy. This wait time gives the child time to work out a miscue and correct it. It also indicates to the child that the tutor believes he/she can figure it out.

2. *Prompt.* If the child is unsuccessful, the tutor can prompt the child to help him/her figure out the meaning. We have trained our tutors to encourage the child to reread the sentence to think about what might fit. If the child still can't figure out the word, then the tutor may say, "Read the sentence again, think about the meaning, say the beginning sound, then make a real word and keep reading to see if the sentence makes sense." In this prompt, the child can use the other words in the sentence *and* the beginning letter sound to figure out the unknown word. The meaning of a sentence plus the pictures on a page can also help children figure out a word. The more clues children use to figure out words, the more likely they are to say the word and become independent, fluent readers (Morrow & Walker, 1997).

3. *Praise.* Finally, when the child does figure out what went wrong, the tutor can praise the child's efforts. In our program, we have generated phrases as examples of specific praise. Responses like "Great work," "I like the way you corrected," "Look what you read," and "Good thinking!" are ways to celebrate successes. Providing personal support for attempts to figure out words and reading connected text is a key role that a tutor plays as a child reads. Juel (1998) found that giving praise was a critical factor separating successful tutors from less successful tutors in her study. A tutor's recognition of success is extremely important. We have demonstrated, and have had volunteers practice, interactions like the following.

TUTOR: Wow! Look what you just did!

CHILD: (*Laughs.*)

TUTOR: You read that whole book all by yourself!! Give me five.

CHILD: (*Slaps tutor's hand and smiles.*)

To provide an opportunity for discussing success at the end of each session, the tutor and child complete the "Look What I Did" sheet from *The Reading Team* (Morrow & Walker, 1997). This sheet helps the tutor talk about the child's success at each session. Together, the tutor and child record the books they read, note the topic of their writing, and indicate what they might work on the next time. This monitoring and celebration of completed work contributes to motivation and student success (Braunger & Lewis, 1998).

Ongoing Management of Volunteers

Now that we liked the training format for the tutoring session, we needed procedures for ongoing management of volunteers. In order to implement and manage the volunteer program, we developed a planning model outline and site management forms to ensure good communication, consistency, and sustainability. In developing our program for America Reads, we utilized the steps set forth in *Training the Reading Team* (Walker et al., 1999). We end each training session with discussions of general rules about dress during tutoring and school rules when coming to and leaving the building. For effective management of volunteers at McKinley, volunteers sign in, wear America Reads badges while they are in the building, and sign out. Scheduling, training, management, and communication with staff and tutors are carried out by the site manager (a Volunteers in Service to America [VISTA] volunteer), a certified teacher, and the principal (Scherry), who is a reading specialist. This orientation is usually completed by the designated coordinator or the reading specialist. These supervisors discuss responsibilities for being on time, attending all sessions, and being prepared for the tutoring session. We particularly emphasize the crucial importance of completing the "Look What I Did" sheet, so that coordinators can create new packets for the next session. Providing a regular routine that is easy for volunteers to follow is important because tutors at McKinley come from many segments of the community. They include employees of our corporate sponsor (Deaconess Billings Clinic), MSU-B work–study students, parents, and volunteers from service organizations.

Tutoring packets are prepared by work–study students and our parent room manager under the supervision of our site coordinator. Our parent room manager and our librarian continually assist in the inventory and management of books that are appropriate for the different types of readers in the program. Having enough easy and familiar books is essential for a tutoring program. A significant aspect of the McKinley tutoring program has been the acquisition of easy-to-read books that are predictable in nature. Deaconess Billings Clinic has donated money to buy a substantial collection of such reading materials. When tutors enter McKinley, they check in and receive a packet of materials for the day's session. After they tutor, they check out and return the packet with the "Look What I Did" sheet completed. With this sheet as a guide, each tutoring packet is replenished after each tutoring session with reading materials that are at the fluent and instructional reading levels of each child.

During the 1998–1999 school year, 87 tutor–student pairs worked together, with over 850 hours of volunteer service given to the program at McKinley Elementary School. According to the John's Informal Reading Inventory, the average improvement for students who were in the America Reads program for the entire year was a year and a half. Therefore, their reading progress did improve with the support of volunteer tutors, since it was more than the normal growth of one year. This meant that 87% of the students were reading at or above their grade level. In addition, the students' motivation to read also improved on pre–post testing: On the Motivation Interview (Gambrell, 1993), 95% of the students reported an increase in motivation. Increased motivation influences students' desire to read independently when tutors are not available. We see this as a positive attribute of the America Reads program. Thus, as these tutors interacted with the children, the staff, and the principal, they became valued members of our team and contributed to the literacy success at McKinley School.

DEVELOPING THE MONTANA AMERICA READS INITIATIVE

On April 13, 1998, State Superintendent of Schools Nancy Keenan held a joint press conference with Harris Wofford, chief executive officer of the Corporation for National Service, to announce the opening of the Montana America Reads Office within the Montana State Office of Public Instruction. June Atkins, a literacy specialist, was appointed as the Montana America Reads director. In her opening remarks, Keenan implied that Montana students do read well and demonstrate proficiency on reading tests. However, Keenan was concerned that there were fourth graders who scored below where they should be. She challenged the America Reads program to target reading skills of early elementary students in Montana. We all knew we had to move our model beyond McKinley Elementary School to affect more children in Montana.

Moving beyond McKinley Elementary School

As we began to discuss our model at state meetings, we were asked to participate in other Montana volunteer literacy programs. Using the knowledge we had gained at McKinley, we accepted invitations to work in other areas around Billings. The summer of 1998 provided three opportunities for expanding the program.

Pryor Summer Program

By spring 1998, we had begun to expand the America Reads program in the Billings area. We set up a summer reading program in the Pryor community, based on the McKinley reading team model and the Read, Write, Now program (U.S. Department of Education, 1996). St. Charles Elementary School had made a strong commitment to this project and was committed to providing individual summer reading tutoring for Native American students who were experiencing difficulty in classroom reading. We began collaborative planning to involve as many partners as possible. Work–study students who had been involved at McKinley Elementary School spent their summer tutoring on the Crow reservation in Pryor, Montana. We also trained teachers and Native American aides to be reading tutors, and we extended training for the Title I teacher so that she could manage the program during the year. We involved high school students who were attending a private Catholic high school by giving them tuition fee waivers for completing the training and participating as reading tutors in the summer program. Three additional students were paid through tribal funds to be reading tutors in the summer program. The training sessions and subsequent supervision helped refine the training manual.

Montana State Reading Council Leadership Workshop

Supporting the Montana Reads program, the Montana State Reading Council voted to take a leadership role in promoting and sustaining the Montana America Reads initiative. At their summer leadership retreat, local reading council leaders were trained as volunteer trainers at a special session. This has provided the state with a cadre of trainers who have an extensive understanding of the reading process and of how children learn to read and write. They are able to provide training for other trainers and volunteer reading tutors, who are located in small towns all across the state. This has assured needed support for volunteers throughout Montana.

Retired and Senior Volunteer Program

During the summer of 1998, several other organizations became involved in volunteer reading tutoring. One organization that is strong in rural parts of Montana is the Retired and Senior Volunteer Program (RSVP), which recruits older citizens to provide service in their communities. When some of its volunteers heard about our program in Billings, they wanted to know more about the training needed to become volunteer reading tutors. At the end of the summer and during the fall, we trained RSVP tutors in Roundup and Miles City. We found that we could include information for trainers of trainers and for site supervisors by having them complete another 5 hours of the training program. We trained the RSVP directors at both sites, the Roundup Elementary School principal, and a reading specialist in Miles City. They oversaw the expansion of the program in the Roundup and Miles City areas. This was funded by a grant received by the Roundup and Miles City RSVP organizations. We used *The Reading Team* (Morrow & Walker, 1997) format to train tutors, and a draft version of *Training the Reading Team* (Walker et al., 1999) to train the trainers and site supervisors.

Further Expansion

As we began the 1999–2000 school year, Ron Scherry provided the training for nine new sites in Yellowstone County and VISTA volunteers from eight sites outside Yellowstone County. These trainings were again funded by Deaconess Billings Clinic. The project that had begun as a simple collaboration between a university work–study program and an elementary school had begun to influence other sites beyond the Billings area. The sites had grown, as well as the commitment of Deaconess Billings Clinic, which became a steady and consistent member of the collaborative team.

Going Statewide

The Montana America Reads office organized a statewide partnership with Governor Racicot's America Reads Commission, the Office of Community Service, the Montana office of the Corporation for National Service, the Montana Campus Compact, the Montana State Reading Council, and the Office of Public Instruction. The Office of Public Instruction, under the direction of June Atkins, administered 14 Montana America Reads AmeriCorps and VISTA member placements to oversee the implementation of America Reads sites throughout Montana. At the heart of the Montana America Reads program is the idea of creating a cadre of trained volunteer reading tutors along with trainers of volunteers. These latter trainers, as noted above, are essential in organizing and managing the various Montana sites and enhancing the sustainability of the program throughout the state.

This statewide partnership received an America Reads training contract from the Northwest Regional Educational Laboratory. The essential elements identified by the partnership were much the same as we had in our initial efforts at McKinley School. The partnership articulated these exceptionally well as follows:

- A strong partnership between the school and the community
- A well-defined, site-based management plan
- A comprehensive program of volunteer tutor recruitment
- A comprehensive tutor-training model

- A comprehensive training for trainers and site managers
- Training materials
- Training expertise

Training expertise and a comprehensive training program emerged as the most immediate needs. Montana America Reads drew on our expertise as well as that of the Montana State Reading Council. Scherry was asked to provide training statewide utilizing the reading team model, and as a result little time was lost in developing training materials.

Throughout 1998–1999, training workshops for volunteer tutors and trainers were provided at four regional sites (Great Falls, Billings, Havre, and Missoula); the training materials developed at McKinley and Montana State University–Billings were used. Once trained, these individuals trained volunteers in local areas. Included in the trainings were Montana State Reading Council members, teachers, administrators, VISTA participants, AmeriCorps members, federal work–study students, college and university students, high school students, RSVP members, and other community and business volunteers.

A "best-practices" conference was held in Helena in the spring of 1999 to promote sustainability and replicability of the project. This conference brought together selected Montana America Reads trainers and supervisors from around the state to discuss and share practices that were working and difficulties that were being encountered. The conference included representatives from the colleges and universities involved in the project, the Montana Campus Compact, and the Montana State Reading Council, as well as VISTA volunteers, teachers, and administrators.

June Atkins—who, as noted earlier, is the America Reads coordinator for the state of Montana from the Office of Public Education—has been a key broker in providing leadership among all the partnerships. By the fall of 1999, in addition to the four regional training workshops, approximately 35 training workshops had been held by trainers who were trained at the regional workshops. We now had 220 trainers in 37 counties, and 645 America Reads volunteer tutors had been trained. Over 2,000 student–tutor pairs were working in the program statewide. We felt that we had accomplished the main goal of the Montana America Reads initiative, established by the Montana America Reads tutoring partnership, which was to build a cadre of trainers who would continue to provide sustainability for the project for future years.

Providing a consistent training model, and training trainers and volunteer tutors in regional workshops across the state, has done much to promote the initiative. Members of the Montana State Reading Council will continue to work in partnership with school districts across the state to maintain the project's sustainability by providing follow-up training for volunteer tutors and trainers. Many who have been trained with this model have commented that this was just what they were looking for to help them in implementing their projects. Through the training sessions, trainers learn how to structure a tutoring session and how to implement and manage a volunteer tutoring program. Volunteer tutors learn the steps involved in a structured tutoring session, and this enables them to provide consistency for the students they are tutoring. They also learn the essentials of a well-constructed tutoring session and some essential literacy instructional strategies. Tutors have expressed appreciation for the training and have stated that they like the structured tutoring session components.

The elements in *The Reading Team* (Morrow & Walker, 1997) provide an easy-to-follow tutoring model. The scripted training materials in *Training the Reading Team* (Walker et al., 1999) provide trainers with the materials needed to conduct training sessions. The school management techniques, materials, and forms have assisted in the implementation and organization of reading tutor programs at the various school sites.

We have been excited to see the America Reads program expanding in Yellowstone County and other parts of the state (see Figure 1.1). From its small beginnings in one school, the program has developed into a statewide collaborative effort that can be sustained throughout Montana. We have surmounted the distance and wide-open spaces of Montana to create an America Reads program that provides a consistent for-

●   Billings—Site for Collaboration among Mckinley School, Billings Deaconess Hospital and MSU-Billings

★   Location of Trained Trainers

FIGURE 1.1. Montana America Reads Project.

mat and ongoing training of tutor and trainers. This project demonstrates the power of the Montana America Reads initiative to amass volunteers from all walks of life to contribute to the literacy needs of Montana's children.

REFERENCES

Adams, M. J. (1990). *Beginning to read: Thinking and learning about print.* Cambridge, MA: MIT Press.

Bradley, L., & Bryant, P. (1985). *Rhyme and reason in reading and spelling.* Ann Arbor: University of Michigan Press.

Braunger, J., & Lewis, J. P. (1998). *Building a knowledge base in reading.* Portland, OR: Northwest Regional Educational Laboratory.

Center, Y., Whedall, K., Greeman, L., Outhred, L., & McNaught, M. (1995). An evaluation of Reading Recovery. *Reading Research Quarterly, 30,* 240–263.

Gambrell, L. B. (1993). *The impact of Running Start on the reading motivation of and behavior of first-grade children.* College Park: University of Maryland, National Reading Research Center.

Hiebert, E. H., Colt, J. M., Catto, S. L., & Cury, E. C. (1992). Reading and writing of first-grade students in a restructured Chapter 1 program. *American Educational Research Journal, 29,* 545–572.

Juel, C. (1996). What makes literacy tutoring effective? *Reading Research Quarterly, 31,* 268–288.

Juel, C. (1998). What kind of one-on-one tutoring helps a poor reader? In C. Hulme & R. M. Joshi (Eds.), *Reading and spelling: Development and disorders* (pp. 449–472). Mahwah, NJ: Erlbaum.

Leslie, L., & Allen, L. (1999). Factors that predict success in an early literacy intervention project. *Reading Research Quarterly, 34*(4), 204–223.

Morrow, L. M., & Walker, B. J. (1997). *The reading team: A handbook for volunteer tutors K–3.* Newark, DE: International Reading Association.

Snow, C., Burns, M. S., & Griffin, P. (1998). *Preventing reading difficulties in young children.* Washington, DC: National Academy Press.

U.S. Department of Education. (1996). *Read, Write, Now.* Washington, DC: U.S. Government Printing Office.

Vygotsky, L. S. (1978). *Mind in society.* Cambridge, MA: Harvard University Press.

Walker, B. J. (2000a). *Diagnostic teaching of reading: Techniques for instruction and assessment* (4th ed.). Upper Saddle River, NJ: Merrill/Prentice-Hall.

Walker, B. J. (2000b). *Supporting struggling readers* (2nd ed.). Markham, Ontario, Canada: Pippin.

Walker, B. J., Scherry, R. J., & Morrow, L. M. (1999). *Training the reading team: A guide for supervisors of a volunteer tutoring program.* Newark, DE: International Reading Association.

Wasik, B. A. (1998). Volunteer tutoring programs in reading: A review. *Reading Research Quarterly, 35,* 266–292.

Chapter 2

THE VOICES OF HOUSTON READS TO LEAD!: BUILDING AN URBAN LITERACY COALITION THROUGH AMERICA READS

Margaret Doughty

My name is Dewey Stovall. I am a 70-year-old student at the Houston READ Commission's Palm Center Family Literacy Center. I was born in Shongaloo, Louisiana, on March 2. Growing up with seven other kids, money was not something that my father had a lot of. Times were tough. I will never forget the day my father told me that I couldn't continue to go to school. My brother and I had to go to work in the fields. The wood we chopped for sale was our only source of family income.

My reading and math skills were limited. I couldn't write very well. I struggled to make ends meet. Making matters worse, I couldn't help my children with their schoolwork.

Today, however, my life has turned 180 degrees!! I can read my Bible, write a letter to my sister, and calculate my monthly income. I have not only become a lifelong learner, but I am now committed to family literacy and helping others. I help young mothers learn to read so that they may help their children. As my mother always said, "If you had a kindness shown to you, pass it on. It was not yours to keep. Pass it on. Let it travel down in years until it wipes someone's tears, and then in heaven the deed appears. Pass it on."

My "adopted granddaughter" is Patricia Brantley. Patricia is in her first year of school. I am helping her learn to read. I realize that I can change her life through the power of reading.

Dewey Stovall and his "adopted granddaughter," Patricia Brantley and her mother.

THE RIGHT TO READ

On a visit to the Palm Center Family Literacy Center in Houston's Third Ward, it is a pleasure to hear the loud buzz of learning as small groups of parents chat in an English conversation session. They are talking about "building a bridge to the school" and discussing how to understand what is being learned in their children's classrooms. A smaller group of mothers are making shoebox libraries, while one parent is sitting on a rug with four preschoolers, talking about a stack of caterpillar books. Two children are reading together behind a pile of giant building blocks; other children are sitting at the table with their Literacy AmeriCorps learning partners, organizing sentences that describe pictures they have cut out of magazines donated by the Time to Read program. All the books have come from a community book drive and from the First Book or Reading Is Fundamental programs.

Houston is the third largest city in the United States, with an adult illiteracy rate as high as 78% in some neighborhoods. The program at Palm Center is part of Houston's response to the America Reads Chal-

Family Literacy Program members gather together to celebrate reading in the Sharpstown Center.

lenge—the Houston Reads to Lead! program. Our city believes in the right to read, and our goal is to achieve total community engagement in the literacy issue.

BUILDING AN AMERICA READS COALITION

In 1997, educational and community leaders in Houston took a long and thoughtful look at the gap between our vision for our children's education and the reality of urban illiteracy. There was a need to see the whole picture: Many high school graduates couldn't read their diplomas, and preschoolers with nonliterate parents were starting kindergarten already behind their peers.

We adopted the slogan "With literacy and justice for all." The way to make change was for our community to embrace a vision of 100% literacy. The San Jacinto Girl Scouts and the Houston READ Commission headed the initiative to bring community partners together to initiate a dialogue around the literacy vision and to determine how to implement the America Reads Challenge. The Girl Scouts described increasing evidence that reading skills had been dropping. Carolyn Johnson, program direc-

Family members read together at the Kandy Stripe Academy.

tor, told of girls' having difficulty reading the requirements for earning badges, and she offered the full commitment of her organization to support a literacy initiative.

Concern about literacy rates in Houston had preceded the America Reads Challenge by several years. The Houston READ Commission was formed in 1989 by the mayor and city council in response to the publication of shocking adult illiteracy statistics for the greater Houston area. When local nonprofit neighborhood organizations came together in 1994 to discuss the issue and to explore whether the U.S. Department of Education could help create a new community partnership, the READ Commission provided the glue to cement a new partnership. Mayor Lee P. Brown joined the effort, saying, "I want Houston to reach the promised land of 100 percent literacy. Literacy should be available and attainable for every Houstonian." In 1995, 29 community organizations representing over 500,000 Houstonians met together for many long sessions to plan around this mission: *As members of the greater Houston community, we will ensure all families develop a joy of reading by helping them to acquire strong literacy skills.*

During an evening meeting in a room full of flipcharted goals, we agreed that family literacy was the intervention strategy most likely to succeed, and that the goals of the America Reads Challenge could fit into a local collaborative effort to encourage and promote reading. The

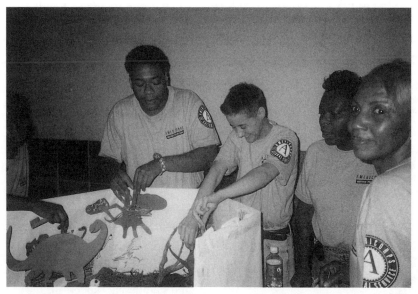

AmeriCorps puppeteers entertain children attending the Martin Luther King Read-a-thon.

Houston Reads to Lead! project was created. We called the U.S. Secretary of Education's office and invited Secretary Riley to our kickoff as the first city in the United States to take up the America Reads Challenge. The secretary responded. His was the outside support needed to encourage and bond this new local initiative. The structure chosen for Houston Reads to Lead! was a traditional one, involving working with a steering committee (representing adult and family literacy organizations), volunteer groups, ethnic organizations, youth service providers, the city, libraries, school districts, religious congregations, and the business community. Committees plan and execute activities as described in Table 2.1.

WHAT MAKES THIS COALITION WORK?

How is Houston Reads to Lead! different from typical education initiatives? First, community engagement is a driving goal for this program. There can never be too many partners! Also, the partners share a common belief that the issue of illiteracy is solvable, and that with everyone working together, the job can be done. The concept of urban literacy coalitions (bringing a multiplicity of stakeholders together around an

TABLE 2.1. Committee Structure of Houston Reads to Lead!

Committee	Goals and responsibilities
Steering Committee	• To oversee the operation of Houston Reads to Lead! • To develop strategies to share the joy of reading within the greater Houston area
Council of Service Providers	• To provide information and reports on citywide Houston Reads to Lead! programs and projects • To implement the America Reads Challenge in local programs • To provide input to the Steering Committee
Marketing Committee	• To generate publicity for Houston Reads to Lead! activities • To plan marketing, information, and fundraising support for the operation of Houston Reads to Lead!
Membership Committee	• To build adequate and appropriate outreach to serve the community • To increase the numbers of Houston Reads to Lead! sites
Training and Materials Committee	• To train trainers and learning partners • To review and evaluate current training materials • To perform research and to develop additional training materials and methodologies

issue) is a powerful force for social change. Many networks falter for lack of coordination, so the Houston READ Commission has donated a paid project coordinator and a small team of Volunteers in Service to America (VISTA) participants to the project. Another driving goal is long-term sustainability. We have committed ourselves to this project as an ongoing, integral part of our community education plan.

A framework was needed to connect the various family literacy support programs into one flexible, yet unified, approach. We used the U.S.

Department of Education's Read, Write, Now and Ready, Set, Read as our models to link all the diverse efforts together. As a result, we can now say with a loud voice that every child and every parent in the city of Houston can have access to educational equality and literacy. The U.S. Department of Education assisted us with this effort by sending thousands of packets for the volunteers and program leaders, as well as providing consultants who helped facilitate the conversation among representatives of different programs.

Each program partner has trained with our training team, but no group has been asked to change its current operations or structure. This new component is flexible enough to be a complete, new, stand-alone project, but it can also be—and has been—a valuable addition to previously existing family or community-based projects.

The idea that "learning partners" be recruited to help foster a joy of reading has been the real focus of the effort. In the beginning, there was much discussion about a tutoring model. There was concern that the Houston Reads to Lead! learning partners should not *teach* reading, but should promote and encourage an enthusiasm for reading. A clear distinction was made to clarify the fact that teaching reading must be a school-based classroom activity and that learning partners must act as a support mechanism to help children succeed in school.

Volunteers in training for Read, Write, Now.

The first learning partner training took place in a packed AMC Theatre. The learning partners ranged in age from 8 to 68 and included Girl Scout troops, Literacy AmeriCorps volunteers, and retirees. Trainers from the U.S. Department of Education provided the training in a number of tutoring techniques. With a goal to encourage children to read for half an hour a day, the learning partners saw demonstrations of ways to keep children engaged, encouraged, and excited. Techniques included paired reading, popcorn reading, choosing books according to a child's interest and reading ability, fun comprehension activities, and vocabulary building. After the training, each participating organization was responsible for pairing readers and learning partners. "I've Been Matched" forms were forwarded to the Houston READ Commission for tracking. Some learning partners felt nervous about embarking on their tutoring, and practiced first in small groups until their confidence had built. The overwhelming response of the tutors doing the training was that the learning partners really appreciated the one-on-one interaction and enjoyed the reading experiences.

Houston has a strong coalition of community-based literacy organizations, coordinated by the Houston READ Commission, the mayor's coalition for literacy. It is Houston's "underground school district"—a safety net that stretches under the traditional school system and helps those who fall through the cracks in that system. It is encouraged and supported by the traditional education system. But, despite all good intentions, the coalition stumbled as it grew. Some groups worked harder than others and resented that their efforts were not matched. Communication with so many partners was a problem. The need to make decisions by consensus, yet to act quickly on opportunities, created further problems, and there was friction between the year-round community programs and the school district program (which was only offered in summer school). But we all shared the same vision, believing that every child has a right to read and every child should expect to have a literate parent.

A systematic approach was needed at this point, if we were to maintain momentum and sustain the Houston Reads to Lead! program. In education, the pendulum swings back and forth, but we were determined that this project would be integrated into the school system over the summer and into the network of community programs year-round. Our community partners came together to build a framework for sustainability. This framework is built around three key principles:

- Create opportunities for ongoing reading activities with every school and community-based partner.
- Build community support and awareness to maintain every effort.
- Don't just talk about it—do it!

Communication tools became a critical link in the process of sustaining the coalition. A bimonthly newsletter was developed, supported by Compaq and Texaco, and a partnership was formed with the editor of a local children's newspaper, *Kid'n Around.* Circulation of meeting notes, and regular celebrations bringing all partners together, also facilitated communication.

STRONG READERS MAKE STRONG LEADERS

The business community has taken a strong leadership role in Houston Reads to Lead!, under the guidance of William Melendy of AMC Theatres. Melendy says,

"The corporate partners play a key role in this community coalition. Not only do they provide the needed funding and financial support, they provide a key leadership role. Corporate leadership comes in many different forms: by lending support with facilities for training and committee meetings, by providing learners and their partners

Carolyn Johnson, chair of Houston Reads to Lead!; William Melendy of AMC Theatres, chair of the Houston Reads to Lead! Marketing Committee; and Julie Perea of the Houston READ Commission, coordinator of Houston Reads to Lead!.

with incentives that motivate them to be the best they can be, and by using relationships with media and other corporations to get the word out. Today's new readers are tomorrow's new leaders in the business world. With that in mind, what company would not want to support literacy?"

The Houston Independent School District (HISD) is responsible for the in-school development of Houston Reads to Lead!, especially as it is connected to the 4-week summer school offered by the district. Phyllis Hunter, HISD's reading manager, says,

"HISD is proud to be a part of Houston Reads to Lead!! In the HISD, we believe that every child has the right to learn to read on grade level. It is the new civil right! In collaboration with America Reads and Houston Reads to Lead!, our students have an opportunity to practice reading, acquire new words and write about their reading by participating in Read, Write, Now. This past summer [1999] over 11,000 children participated in this program. In Houston, we are working diligently to meet the America Reads Challenge."

Collaboration needs nurturing. Julie Campbell of Interfaith Ministries believes that only by working in partnership can we make a difference. Campbell says,

"In keeping with the mission of America Reads—marshaling the resources of entire communities, school and libraries, religious institutions, universities, college students, and senior citizens to work together with teachers and parents to teach our children to read— Interfaith Ministries for Greater Houston has mobilized congregations to promote the love of reading for Houston area families. For too long, institutions from various sectors of the community have worked independently, often resulting in duplication of services as well as gaps in services. America Reads has provided an avenue for these various groups to collaborate to ensure that every child learns to read."

A good example of this collaboration occurred at one of our Read, Write, Now sites: the St. James Episcopal Elementary School, which is located directly behind Turner Middle School. The Turner students were escorted to St. James on Tuesday afternoons for their Read, Write, Now sessions. However, since there was a fence dividing the two schools, the students had to walk around the block past a liquor store, where there were often men hanging around. St. James recognized this problem and made arrangements to have a gate put in the fence so that the children

Carol Rasco, director of the America Reads Challenge, with Julie Campbell of Interfaith Ministries, celebrating at the Festival of Reading.

Houston Reads to Lead! leaders with Barbara Bush and Margaret Doughty announcing the book drive results—33,000 books.

could safely walk directly from Turner to St. James. This gate continues to serve as a symbol of the breaking down of barriers.

MEASURING SUCCESS AND ASSESSING IMPACT

The following information comes from the Literacy AmeriCorps Youth Reading Survey and from an HISD survey of English-speaking versus bilingual students. These surveys show the tremendous impact of volunteers in the community.

Youth Reading Survey

Methodology

In response to the America Reads challenge, many Literacy AmeriCorps members are placed in programs where they work with children. In order to monitor their effectiveness, Literacy AmeriCorps staff, with the assistance of educational research consultants from Project STAR (Support and Training for Assessing Results), designed a survey to measure members' impact on young readers. This survey consisted of 12 sentences, to which the young respondents answered "Yes" or "No," depending on whether the sentence applied to their own behavior or attitudes. The 12 sentences are listed in Table 2.2.

The intent of this survey was to elicit responses that would demonstrate the respondents' sense of how their reading habits had been influ-

TABLE 2.2. Youth Reading Survey Items

Item #	Sentence
1	I like to read more now than before.
2	I spend more time reading.
3	I need less help with reading.
4	I know more words.
5	I visit the library more often with my family.
6	I have a library card.
7	It is easier to read.
8	I understand more of what I read.
9	I look at the pictures for clues to the story.
10	I like to talk about books I have read.
11	I like to read out loud.
12	I like to tell or write my own stories.

enced by their participation in the America Reads program, in which Literacy AmeriCorps members serve as tutors. Items were included to measure the level of a child's reading activity ("I spend more time reading" and "I like to read out loud"), the level of a child's reading skill ("I know more words," "I understand more of what I read," and "I look at the pictures for clues to the story"), and a child's awareness of reading resources ("I visit the library more often with my family" and "I have a library card").

Administration and Results

The survey was administered by the Literacy AmeriCorps members directly. Members distributed the surveys among their learners, who returned the surveys to the members when they were completed. In all, information from 82 surveys was submitted to the national coordinator, who then tabulated the responses. (See Figures 2.1 and 2.2.)

HISD Survey of English-Speaking versus Bilingual Students

A further survey identified information from English-speaking as compared with bilingual (primarily Spanish-speaking) students (see Table 2.3). The HISD conducted this survey.

The need for Spanish materials and books has been evident since the onset of the program.

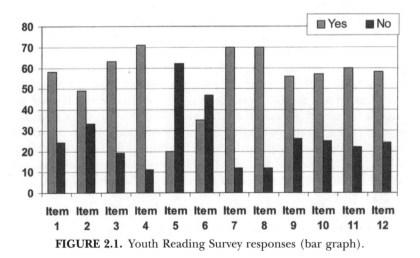

FIGURE 2.1. Youth Reading Survey responses (bar graph).

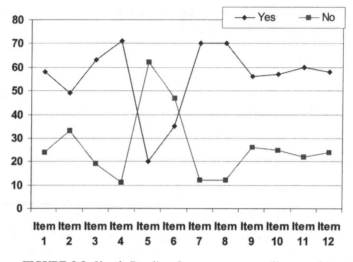

FIGURE 2.2. Youth Reading Survey responses (line graph).

GETTING BOOKS INTO THE HANDS OF CHILDREN AND PARENTS

At the beginning of summer, there are never enough books for all the families, so we have a citywide children's book drive. In 1999, 33,000 books were collected and donated to 77 different Houston Reads to Lead! partners. We believe it was the biggest ever children's book drive for new and gently used books. B'nai Brith and a collaboration of business and community groups put out fliers and announced collection sites around the city. Texaco produced information sheets and fliers; Greensheet and Motorola trucks collected and delivered books; Cynthia Cooper, three-time Women's National Basketball Association Most Valuable Player and national basketball champion, was spokesperson for the event. Half Price Books was a major donor. It cannot be overstated that to attain the vision of 100% literacy, there can't be too many partners—but there must also be good coordination and collaboration. To celebrate the success of the book drive, Barbara Bush, our nation's leading family literacy advocate, visited a learning center, met with the Houston Reads to Lead! partners, and read to children outside (near a "reading tree" she had planted some 5 years earlier).

The Houston Reads to Lead! program is a wonderful example of the exciting things that happen when a city truly mobilizes its resources to bring literacy to all its citizens.

TABLE 2.3. HISD Survey Items and Results

As a result of the program:	Student responses (%)	
	Yes	No
English-speaking students only		
I like to read more now than ever.	87	13
I spend more time reading.	70	30
I need less help with reading.	63	37
I know more words.	94	6
I enjoy reading with a partner.	89	11
I have a library card.	51	49
I have visited the school library this summer.	44	56
It is easier to read.	92	8
I understand more of what I read.	94	6
I look at the pictures for clues to the story.	79	21
I like to talk about books I have read.	86	14
I like to read aloud.	62	38
I like to tell or write my own stories.	72	28
Bilingual students		
I like to read more now than ever.	98	2
I spend more time reading.	70	30
I need less help with reading.	61	39
I know more words.	96	4
I enjoy reading with a partner.	60	40
I have a library card.	37	63
I have visited the school library this summer.	97	3
It is easier to read.	96	4
I understand more of what I read.	80	20
I look at the pictures for clues to the story.	87	13
I like to talk about books I have read.	58	42
I like to read aloud.	92	8
I like to tell or write my own stories.	100	0

HOW BROAD IS THE MISSION?

In many of our inner-city neighborhoods, grassroots organizations support local families by providing literacy, homework support, and after-school programs for parents and children. Often these activities are included in a broader community mission along with, perhaps, a food pantry, counseling, job search activities, and immigrant services. Liem Ngo, from a community-based organization, remarks,

> "Our program, Research & Development Institute [a Vietnamese community program], has been grateful to participate in the Houston Reads to Lead! program. We distributed a variety of books to our students, both adults and youngsters, in our literacy programs and encouraged them to read more. Part of the curriculum of our Summer Youth Program was geared toward helping young people better their reading skills. On July 30, 1999, we brought groups of families from the sites where our tutoring programs are held, along with kids from the Summer [Youth] Program, to attend the Festival of Reading at [an] AMC Theatre. All of them had a wonderful time. We look forward to continuing our cooperation in this worthwhile endeavor of promoting literacy in Houston."

A young boy reads his favorite story to his mother.

THE SPIRIT OF VOLUNTEERISM AND COMMUNITY SERVICE

Houston Reads to Lead! provides materials and training to support both the staff and the volunteers in the program. Volunteers are recruited through the citywide literacy helpline and by individual program partners. They are tracked by the Houston READ Commission and trained by the training team, either in large community training sessions or on site. We could not have managed without help from local AmeriCorps programs—Literacy AmeriCorps and Serve Houston. In both programs, members were trained as Houston Reads to Lead! learning partners and assigned to over 40 school- and community-based sites. "The AmeriCorps volunteers have built the program capacity—without their dedication and hard work, we would not have achieved so much," says Claudia Salinas, Literacy AmeriCorps coordinator. As the program grew, each organization became responsible for recruiting its own volunteers. The Literacy AmeriCorps and Serve Houston members were all provided with additional training to equip them to work in community family literacy sites, and Serve Houston members were provided with sessions to help them prepare for after school site tutoring. In addition, community volunteers signed up, as well as the peer tutors enrolled by the school system for the summer program. VISTA volunteers have assisted with planning and program coordination.

Literacy AmeriCorps member reads to children.

Rod Paige, the HISD's superintendent, says, "Literacy is the most basic, and I think the most important skill a person can have in these days of high technology. Teaching the illiterate to read, then, is one of the greatest services we can give an individual." In the HISD during the summer program, hundreds of sixth graders were trained as learning partners for first graders, building the skill of both age groups and introducing the spirit of service to sixth graders—a spirit that exemplifies the program as a whole, from the makeup of the committees to the trainers and the volunteers supporting the project.

A project goal has been to build on the strengths of current programs as well as to build new programs. Leveraging opportunities, resources, and national initiatives has been one way to do this. The Houston Reads to Lead! volunteers contacted the office of the America's Promise organization and made a commitment to recruit 20,000 learning partners by the year 2000. This goal was accomplished in the summer of 1999. General Colin Powell, the head of America's Promise, wrote this letter:

> Let me take this opportunity to congratulate the City of Houston. I am confident that Houston's spirit will inspire the community to meet the goal of 100% literacy. Houston is a fine example of how communities are keeping America's Promise. Keep up the good work!

HELPING PARENTS BREAK THE CYCLE OF ILLITERACY

Community-based organizations target families with parents that need help with literacy skills. The high dropout rate in Houston, as well as the large numbers of adult learners in basic skills, General Equivalency Diploma, and English as a Second Language programs (over 100,000 adult learners in 1998), indicate the need for family literacy. Breaking the cycle of intergenerational illiteracy in our city is critical to success. The mayor's coalition for literacy has 135 participating community-based organizations. These groups struggle for funding and value the role of the coalition in collaboratively trying to make change and access resources.

In community family learning centers, parents take part on a daily basis in activities that will assist them in helping their children to enjoy reading and to succeed in school. Houston Reads to Lead! focuses on families in greatest need. At Kandy Stripe Academy, a preschool program, Ready, Set, Read is the basis for the daily story time with learning partners. At the Sharpstown Center, parents and children come together for reading celebrations sponsored by Reading Is Fundamental. Parents with very limited literacy skills learn to read children's books with their tutors, and then enjoy sharing their learning as they read these books to their children.

Mayor Brown and Stephanie
Johnson celebrate Houston
Reads to Lead!'s success.

AmeriCorps member
Madison Ledet takes time
out to read.

One of the many differences between the Houston program and others has been the focus on family literacy. Parents in learning centers are invited to sign up as learning partners for their own children. Initially this is a daunting prospect for some parents, who not only find it difficult to cope with their own limited literacy, but are intimidated by the prospect of helping their children read as well. Each center provides a training session for the Read, Write, Now program for parents and includes extra tips for encouraging children to read, ideas on choice of books, and discussion about fitting reading into a hectic daily schedule. Books are provided at each center so that parents can choose books according to the interests of their children, and so that they can practice reading with the literacy tutors before in turn becoming the learning partners to their children. Only when parents feel confident they can read a book do they read it with their children. Once the process begins, though, most parents are encouraged and begin taking more and more books home. The training is then expanded to include activities and strategies for parents with preschool children, using the Ready, Set, Read materials.

A father and his little girl reading together during parent-and-child time at Kandy Stripe Academy.

FALLING INTO THE POTHOLES—AND CLIMBING OUT OF THEM

Building an urban literacy coalition is very hard work. It's hard to build, hard to maintain and hard to sustain. The Steering Committee of Houston Reads to Lead! is the first to let people know it is not easy. We have learned from past mistakes, from poor judgment, from lack of trust, and from plain hard-headedness. Sometimes it has felt as though we were the Three Little Pigs and the Big Bad Wolf was constantly at our door, huffing and puffing to blow our house down. These are some of the lessons we have learned:

- *Communication.* Every partner needs to be involved in the planning and development process.
- *Respect.* All partners must feel valued and know that they are important to success.
- *Money.* Competition for funds breaks collaborative spirit. Developing a sharing philosophy is challenging and requires community trust, but it must be accomplished to succeed.
- *Governmental funding restrictions.* Because many grants require applications to flow through local education agencies, community-based programs do not have direct access to resources. Despite good work and track records, programs are frustrated by non-collaborative attitudes of traditional school systems.
- *Turf issues.* Building a spirit of trust and cooperation that breaks down turf barriers is challenging and time-consuming, but partnerships must embrace a mutuality of goals and a shared vision.
- *Creativity and flexibility.* Changing things that don't work well is hard, but change brings forward movement.

Julie Perea, the Houston Reads to Lead! coordinator, says, "Sometimes it's a bit like walking on eggshells, but most of the time it's exciting to be working with such committed people." We can see the impact we are having and can document participants' changes in attitudes about reading.

One example of collaborative success was that schools were opened for summer school for 4 weeks, but the children had no access to books because school libraries were closed during this time. The Houston Reads to Lead! Steering Committee asked the district to open the libraries, and appreciated the superintendent's agreement to do so. In another example, most public schools were closed in the evenings, and there was a charge to community organizations to cover the costs of the janitors' salaries when schools stayed open. Slowly but surely, a more flexible attitude has permeated the system, building new school–community partnerships. With funding from the Reading Excellence Act, these issues are being overcome.

PROGRAM BENEFITS

The Houston Reads to Lead! model has provided the following:

- A framework for citywide family literacy tutoring
- A training program that can be adapted to most organizations
- A method of tracking participation across programs
- A structure for shared decision making
- A bridge between community organizations and schools
- A partnership process to encourage business support
- A low-cost/low-maintenance tutoring program
- The opportunity to develop and sustain the program into the future

WE BELIEVE WE CAN, AND WE CELEBRATE OUR SUCCESS

The Houston Reads to Lead! partners are committed to their role of leadership and dedicated ongoing effort: "You can't stop till the job is done," says Jan West of the Urban League. The role of the city in supporting the initiative is critical. City Council member Bruce Tatro believes that "education is the most important issue facing our workforce as we head into the 21st century." In addition, Tatro wants to "facilitate an environment that aggressively promotes the importance of literacy to the surrounding community. Public awareness and celebrity spokespersons are critical to success. People need to know this is an important issue in our city."

Celebrating reading is another driving goal of the program. At the Festival of Reading, hundreds of parents and children swarmed around the learning booths at an AMC Theatre. Reading games, quizzes, challenges, and book walks lined the walls. Fifty organizations set up booths with fun free reading activities, and Southwestern Bell provided underwriting to cover the transportation that brought Houston Reads to Lead! families from every part of town. Stopping to talk to the representative of the American Bible Society, a mother selected an easy-reader Scripture with her son; a small girl beamed with delight as she shook hands with Spot the Dog (Chris Drew, chair of the First Book Advisory Board, representing B. Dalton); Miss Frizzle (Amanda Gorman, coordinator for

City Council member Bruce Tatro describes the role of the city in supporting Houston Reads to Lead!, with the support of King Henry (of the Renaissance Festival).

the Family-Centered Child Care Collaborative) frisked in and out of the crowd, greeting and directing people to puppet shows and theater productions. Groups of children representing the enormous wealth of diversity in Houston gathered in the food court to share the goodies in their sacks and read to each other. Scholastic Book Services set up a photo booth with Clifford, the Big Red Dog, and the city and county library system booths were busy with excited readers. Barbara Gubbin, director of Houston Public Library, said, "The partnership with Houston Reads to Lead! has encouraged our community to come together. The city has embraced the Power Card [library card], and hundreds of children are enthusiastically reading."

At one booth a sign read, "Spelling Is S-W-E-E-T," and as children put quiz letters together, Greg Erwin stirred an enormous pot of cotton candy. As he twirled it around a cane for a mom with her two children, he talked about his company's involvement.

"As our law firm approached its 75th anniversary, we wanted to give something back to the community that had provided us so many opportunities over the years. As lawyers, words, language, and ideas are our stock in trade. Support for literacy immediately came to mind. We could not have found a better partner to help us support family

Greg Erwin and Sharon Sample make cotton candy for young readers.

literacy in Houston than the Houston READ Commission. In addition to sponsoring the 'Great Grown-Up Spelling Bee' and underwriting the first Houston citywide children's book drive, our firm 'adopted' the Bayland Learning Center. Over a third of our lawyers and staff are trained as learning partners in the literacy program provided at the Bayland Learning Center. We are proud to be a part of the Houston Reads to Lead! team to share the joy of reading in Houston."

WHERE DO WE GO FROM HERE?

Houston Reads to Lead! is constantly growing, adapting, and improving. There is still a long way to go. Challenges for the future include building partnerships with other school districts in the greater Houston area. The first step to formalize this has been taken by the creation of a School District Advisory Board. Another challenge is in the area of accessing community family literacy funding to maintain and support community-based programs whose mission is to support the reading success of children, especially by assisting parents with limited literacy skills in the context of family literacy programs. There are several federal funding streams

A parent and child enjoying a story.

A parent and children sharing books.

that can support this important work, including the Reading Excellence Act funding. The long-term goals for the future are to build the capacity of the program to include more children and families, and to raise the awareness of the importance of literacy throughout our community. The Marketing Committee has planned an awareness campaign to kick off in the spring of 2000, and it has a marketing plan that includes four major annual community events. Also a public awareness campaign is under way and includes radio, television and print ads with the tags "Did you read with a child today?" and "Read with us." The campaign aims for 100% engagement of all Houstonians in the effort to improve literacy levels. Four community events that are now annually established activities are: the Martin Luther King Day Read-a-thon, the Book Drive, the Festival of Reading, and Read across America Day. Long-term success will depend on sustained, improved daily individual program implementation, well-coordinated program administration, and access to sufficient funding. The American Reads Challenge has provided the impetus for this collaboration, and local effort provides the willpower to make it happen. Ongoing success will sustain the effort, because our city believes in the right of every child and parent to be able to read.

Chapter 3

THE SOUTH FLORIDA
AMERICA READS COALITION:
A SYNERGISTIC EFFORT

Joshua Young
Jodi Bolla
Jeanne Shay Schumm
Alicia Moreyra
Robert Exley

> In all my years in the field of education, I've never seen such
> a wonderful example of collaboration.
> —JEANNE SHAY SCHUMM
> *Professor and Chair*
> *Department of Teaching and Learning,*
> *University of Miami*

In South Florida, we embarked on our America Reads journey in the spring of 1997. It's hard to believe how far we've come; what an amazing experience this has been; and how this program has truly touched the lives of thousands and thousands of children, tutors, teachers, and parents in Miami–Dade County, Florida.

In 1996 we accepted a challenge from President Clinton and the U.S. Department of Education, asking Americans to get involved in helping children read well and independently by the end of third grade. What has evolved is a vibrant, far-reaching, synergistic program that has united disparate groups in Miami–Dade County around this important goal. The infrastructure we have created trains, places, and supports some 220 Federal Work–Study (FW-S) tutors from four different colleges and universities at 43 elementary schools and community sites. Each week, almost 1,800 children receive individual instruction from these tutors. In addition, many of the schools are implementing parental involvement workshops, and hundreds of volunteers—high school students, retirees, community members, and parents—have stepped forward to lend a hand and participate in the America Reads Challenge. We are truly changing our community, one child at a time, and there is nothing more important.

Much of our success stems from the fact that from the beginning this project has depended on a coalition built on a foundation of sharing, joint ownership, collaboration, and the energy of committed individuals. This coalition brought together the nation's fourth largest school district, its largest community college, three local universities, the AmeriCorps VISTA (Volunteers in Service to America) programs, and the local public broadcasting station's *Ready to Learn* program.

THE MAGIC OF CONVERGING EVENTS

As we look back upon our success, three seminal factors laid the groundwork for America Reads and allowed the program in South Florida to flourish.

Leadership from the Top

There is no greater gift you can give a youngster than the gift of reading. America Reads means what it says. Through this vitally important grassroots initiative, Miami–Dade Community College students are making a genuine commitment. They are helping to make America Reads a reality.
            —EDUARDO J. PADRÓN
                District President, Miami–Dade Community College

America Reads came to Miami when President Clinton asked Miami–Dade Community College (M-DCC) District President Eduardo Padrón to join his College and University Presidents' America Reads Steering Committee. This request struck a responsive chord with Padrón. Not only is the Miami–Dade County metropolitan area one of the poorest in the nation (15% of the population lives below the poverty line), but its illiteracy rate is also among the highest. South Florida is a region of recent immigrants; 60% of residents have a first language other than English, and almost a quarter of the student population in K–5 is classified as "limited-English-proficient."

Padrón was also extremely concerned about the high number of underprepared students entering M-DCC. Students were coming to college without having mastered basic reading and writing skills in high school. Each year, for example, almost 70% of entering students needed to take at least one remedial (high-school-level) course. Padrón was convinced that America Reads would be a long-term solution to reducing the number of underprepared students in K–12 and eventually in higher education.

America Reads challenged every college and university to take half of its increased FW-S monies (increased by 34% in 1997) and use it to place college students as America Reads tutors. Padrón took this message to heart and committed $400,000 a year of FW-S funds to the America Reads Challenge (50% of M-DCC's $800,000 FW-S increase). Clearly, much of our success with America Reads is due to the commitment and leadership of Padrón.

"A Book in Every Child's Hands": The Local School System Steps to the Plate

My involvement with America Reads has been the highlight of my professional career.

—ALICIA MOREYRA
*Director, Division of Language Arts/Reading,
Miami–Dade County Public Schools*

The second factor that had a major impact on our success was the support and involvement of Miami–Dade County Public Schools (M-DCPS). Now that the funds to hire tutors had been obtained, new questions arose: What would these tutors do? What curriculum would they use, what training and support would they receive, and where would they do their tutoring? M-DCC approached the local experts in the Division of Language Arts/Reading at M-DCPS to ask for direction and assistance. Two dynamic educators whose professional lives were devoted to helping children read responded enthusiastically to this request for help by taking leadership roles in the newly formed coalition and by marshaling the school system's resources to support the program.

The first of these visionaries, Norma Bossard, was at that time the director of the Division of Language Arts/Reading. (Bossard was later stricken with cancer and died in June 1999.) Her lifelong dream was to have "a book in every child's hands." Under Bossard's leadership, the school system was about to initiate a districtwide "comprehensive reading plan" that would change the way reading was taught and make it the number one priority in the elementary system. She immediately threw her support behind America Reads and asked one of her supervisors,

M-DCC District President Eduardo Padrón (third from left) with M-DCC VISTA members. Others, left to right: Rachelle Martinez, Carrie Lambert, Peaches Tyson, Shannon Robinson, and Erick Munoz.

Alicia Moreyra, director of the M-DCPS Division of Language Arts/Reading (center, holding America Reads manual), with two of her district reading specialists who help coordinate America Reads: Margie Stutz (left) and Jodi Bolla (right).

Alicia Moreyra (now the division's director), to head up the America Reads project.

Moreyra was, and is, a highly respected team builder who believes strongly in the power of one-on-one intervention strategies; she quickly recognized the potential of America Reads. She assembled a team of reading specialists to (1) gather information on other effective programs, (2) review what the research said about successful tutoring programs, (3) develop a tutoring curriculum that would match the needs of both tutors and children, and (4) develop training and in-service modules.

Applying the Lessons of Service–Learning Programs

Miami–Dade Community College's history of commitment to community made America Reads a natural extension of our mission. The fact that we had a premier service–learning program in place, known for its quality of leadership and reliability, paved the way for America Reads to be successful both within the college and within the community. America Reads was not only the right thing to do, but a natural and necessary collaboration between M-DCC and M-DCPS.

—Robert Exley
Founder, Service–Learning Program, M-DCC;
Chair, Department of Community Education, M-DCC

The third factor that led to our success was that M-DCC already had in place a service–learning infrastructure that was well suited to building and supporting an America Reads program. M-DCC had initiated its formal Service–Learning Program in 1994 with help from the Corporation for National Service (CNS). The college was well versed in effectively managing the complex logistics of placing and supporting up to 1,400 service–learning students each semester with several hundred community agencies. It had also forged strong relationships with the local school system.

High-quality service–learning programs depend on successfully overseeing several key factors, including training faculty and agency hosts, preparing students before they begin their service, providing ongoing support, helping students reflect on and learn from their experiences, and recognizing students and agency partners. As we began planning for America Reads, we made a commitment to replicate the following service–learning "best practices":

- *Training.* Both tutors and tutoring site personnel must receive preservice orientation and training.
- *Ongoing support.* Both tutors and tutoring site personnel must receive ongoing support to answer questions, address unforeseen problems, and ensure program quality.

- *In-service training.* Tutors must regularly be given the opportunity to reflect on their experience and receive additional training.
- *Evaluation.* Data gathering and program evaluation are essential components in assessing program effectiveness and identifying areas for improvement.
- *Recognition.* Tutors and tutoring site personnel must be recognized for their hard work and contributions to the program.
- *Partnership building/collaboration.* Multiple partners must contribute their expertise, resources, and commitment, and the workload and project management must be shared.

SYNERGY: WORKING TOGETHER FOR THE INDIVIDUAL AND COMMON GOOD

Forming the Coalition

Miami–Dade is so unusual because the program is so well orchestrated. The schools and the universities work closely, and the commitment is strong.

—Marsha Nye Adler
*Director of America Reads, Higher Education,
San Francisco State University*

Realizing that America Reads was an initiative with the potential to have a significant impact on the well-being of South Florida's children, two officials in the M-DCC Service–Learning Program—the director, Joshua Young, and the founder, Robert Exley—worked with the M-DCPS reading supervisor, Alicia Moreyra, to identify a number of possible America Reads partners and to organize an exploratory meeting. Invitees included representatives from three local universities, a number of college and K–12 reading teachers, an elementary school principal, leaders of several community tutoring programs, a coordinator from Big Brothers/Big Sisters, and a number of school system representatives (including personnel involved in after-school care, community involvement, adult education, Title I, and early childhood education).

This group began meeting monthly to hash out myriad issues related to the development of such a complex project—tutor student ratios, site selection, amount of training needed, recruitment of tutors, logistics of placing and supporting tutors, training of personnel at host sites, and so on. Gradually the program began to take shape. The college and university partners were primarily responsible for identifying all personnel issues related to managing FW-S tutors, while the M-DCPS Division of Language Arts/Reading took the lead in curriculum development, training, site selection, and ensuring the effectiveness of the tutoring process.

Members of the South Florida America Reads Coalition. The people pictured represent M-DCC; Barry University; the University of Miami; Florida International University; WLRN Public Television; Communities in Schools of Miami; and the M-DCPS Division of Language Arts/Reading, as well as the M-DCPS Afterschool Care and Adult Education Departments.

The remaining coalition members each shared their expertise and provided ongoing feedback. For example, the representative from Big Brothers/Big Sisters developed a "Tutor Check-In Form" that provided a means of monitoring tutor progress every 2 weeks. Other partners emphasized the importance of training and providing ongoing assistance to personnel at each of the sites that would be using America Reads tutors.

At our monthly meetings, coalition members reported their progress for discussion and feedback. As each partner stepped forward with tangible and significant contributions, a sense of excitement and energy blossomed into an even stronger commitment to the goals of America Reads. We all felt that we were part of something very special that would enhance the lives and well being of everyone involved.

Several additional factors contributed to the coalition's success. M-DCC secured a grant from the CNS Learn and Serve program that provided funding to help purchase materials (manuals, tutor supply boxes, alphabet cards, tutoring materials, etc.) and pay M-DCPS trainers for occasional evening or Saturday sessions. This invaluable support from CNS has continued in years 2 and 3 of our America Reads project.

M-DCC also contacted the CNS state office and submitted a request for VISTA members to be assigned to the coalition. M-DCC agreed to administer the program, and M-DCPS made a commitment to provide reimbursement for the VISTA members' work-related mileage (a requirement of the VISTA program). To make sure that all coalition members were supported, M-DCC placed VISTA volunteers at each of the college/university partners. Six VISTA members were recruited in both 1998–1999 and 1999–2000, and they have been essential to coalition activities. In 1998, M-DCC and M-DCPS applied for an America Reads training grant that was one of 61 funded by the U.S. Department of Education to improve tutor training. This grant provided funds to develop a training video and workbook, create a Buddy Reading program, initiate a parental involvement curriculum, and offer a series of countywide training events.

What Are the Tutors Going to Do?: Developing the Curriculum

One of the outcomes of the coalition meetings was the need to assemble a writing team consisting of district reading specialists and teachers. Initially there was no money to pay the writers for the summertime work on this project, but so committed were they that they agreed to volunteer their time. Quite by chance, Moreyra, who led the writing team, ran into a colleague who shared her belief in the mission of the America Reads challenge. This individual secured funds through the Area Center for Educational Enhancement to pay the writing team for the time spent developing the tutorial curriculum, as well as to print the first 500 copies of the finished manuals.

The writing team spent several weeks reviewing research conducted by a variety of nationally known reading specialists, such as Connie Juel, Marcia Invernizzi, and their colleagues (Invernizzi, Juel, & Rosemary, 1996–1997; Johnston, Invernizzi, & Juel, 1998; Johnston, Juel, & Invernizzi, 1995); Marie Clay (1993a, 1993b); and Keith Topping (1987, 1988, 1989). The reviewers paid special attention to the similar characteristics and elements of success in each tutoring model. The team members then met to discuss their findings and begin drafting a curriculum that built on the best aspects of these model programs. Each draft was carefully reviewed, discussed, and then field-tested at several local sites with struggling first-grade readers. Those trial runs served to assist the team in streamlining and further refining the tutorial model. After 6 weeks, the team emerged with a final curriculum and began planning how to train FW-S tutors, site coordinators, first-grade teachers, and other district personnel.

America Reads tutor Cristina Bautista, a FW-S student from Florida International University, tutoring a first grader at Silver Bluff Elementary in Miami.

Throughout the process of creating a new curriculum—writing, testing, revising, and testing again—the team members felt a common energy that propelled them forward. The results of their time spent working together were (1) a user-friendly curriculum guide designed to meet the needs of both tutors and struggling readers (including English as a Second Language students); (2) a complete training component, which included a comprehensive new tutor-training module and a series of three tutor in-service sessions; and (3) training modules for the site coordinators and first-grade teachers that included both beginning- and end-of-year sessions.

The curriculum the writing team developed is a one-on-one in-class intervention model that targets first-grade preemergent readers and provides 30-minute tutoring sessions two to four times a week. The curriculum's foundation is a lesson plan that consists of four steps (see Figure 3.1). The first step is rereading familiar materials, which includes not only reading a "little book" for emergent readers, but also the rehearsal of a "chunk" of text. This "chunk" is a small piece of text from something the entire class is working on, and it serves to build a connection between the classroom and the time spent in tutorial. Linking these two experiences serves to increase the amount of successful interactions in class, helps develop the tutored student's self-esteem, and allows the student to demonstrate his/her developing abilities.

Level I: Early Emergent Reader Plan

Early Emergent Reader Plan	Activity/Names of Books	Time: 30 min.	Observations
Rereading Familiar Materials — 1. Read class "chunk." — 2. Reread yesterday's book. — 3. Record book title in Book Log.		5 min.	
Exploring Words and Sounds (Phonics) **Word Bank:** — 1. Read Word Cards. — 2. Record known words. — 3. Make new Word Cards. — 4. Match unknown words to text. — 5. Select one Word Bank Activity. — 6. Select one Phonics Activity.		10 min.	
Writing to Read — 1. Choose a page. — 2. Read the word or words on the page. — 3. Draw a line for words heard in the sentence. — 4. Elongate the sounds heard in the word. — 5. Write the sounds heard in the world. — 6. Acknowledge attempt. — 7. Pick one Writing to Read Activity.		5–7 min.	
Reading New Material — 1. Introduce new story. — 2. Read new story with support. — 3. Read new story alone.		5 min.	

FIGURE 3.1. Example of 30-minute lesson plan—tutors complete this form during each session.

The remaining three steps are 10 minutes of exploring words and sounds (phonics), 5 to 7 minutes of writing to read, and 5 minutes of reading new material. Each time a tutor meets with a student, the tutor completes a lesson plan outline like the one shown in Figure 3.1. This outline gives the tutor the pacing and structure needed to ensure consistent and effective instruction. Over time, the completed lesson plan outlines become valuable documentation of the student's literacy development. These completed forms are also used as springboards for discussions among the reading coordinator, classroom teachers, and tutors. In addition to the lesson plan, tutors complete word bank forms and book logs during each session to build a record of each child's progress.

In order to select which children would benefit most from the tutoring, the writing team also developed an assessment instrument based on the work of Marie Clay (1993a, 1993b) and Connie Juel and her colleagues (Invernizzi et al., 1996–1997; Johnston et al., 1995, 1998). The instrument consists of five sections designed to assess alphabet knowledge, concept of print, phonemic awareness, word recognition, and oral reading and comprehension. Depending upon the section, there are several forms for administration that include individual, small-group, and whole-class forms. The results of each student's score on each section are recorded on a class roster. Included as part of this roster are subtest areas and determined levels of mastery. Placement of student data on the roster gives the teacher a comprehensive profile that indicates areas of strength and weakness for each individual student as well as the whole class. After completing the entire assessment and roster, the teacher and reading coordinator work together to select the children most in need of tutoring.

FROM PLAN TO ACTION: RECRUITING, TRAINING, AND IMPLEMENTING

Quality versus Quantity: Selecting Schools and After-School Tutoring Sites

Very, very good program—extremely beneficial, I think, for both tutors and students.

—ADMINISTRATOR FROM A SOUTH FLORIDA AMERICA READS SITE

Although practically every school and after-school site in Miami–Dade County wanted America Reads FW-S tutors, we made a conscious decision to focus on quality versus quantity, to ensure that each tutoring site would receive the tutors and support it needed. We prepared a "Request for Proposals" and sent it to all eligible elementary school principals. Selection of the 37 elementary schools was based on the following criteria:

Primary Considerations

- Reading scores below the 40th percentile
- Not already using a specialized "purchased" reading program
- Responded to "Request for Proposals" to demonstrate administrative commitment

Secondary Considerations

- Proximity to college/university locations
- Equitable countywide distribution
- Preexisting partnerships with college/university service–learning centers or colleges of education

Realizing that many students take classes in the morning and need to work in the afternoon, and that most after-school programs are in dire need of trained staff and structured activities, M-DCC identified six community tutoring programs that were involved in the M-DCC Service–Learning Program and had an infrastructure strong enough to support the America Reads program. These 6 sites, combined with the 37 elementary schools, resulted in a total of 43 America Reads tutoring sites.

Recruiting Federal Work–Study Tutors

I was a teacher in my country, and when I came to the U.S., for different circumstances, I started my major in office technology; however, as a result of the America Reads program I want to return to my first dream, to become a teacher again.
—Tutor with the South Florida America Reads Program

In order to qualify for an America Reads job, college students had to be eligible for FW-S funds and had to be taking at least 6 credit hours. Each of the four colleges and universities recruited tutors by using a combination of strategies that included the following:

- Presentations to education and honors classes
- Referrals from work–study coordinators in the financial aid office
- Recruitment from the office of student employment
- Targeted marketing to service–learning students
- Word of mouth

Phillis Wheatley Elementary School's reading coordinator, Patricia Monroe (on left, in uniform), with two of her tutors, Joanel Avrilien and Jacqueline Caldwell. In front of them are several first-grade America Reads children.

- Flyers
- Referrals from tutoring sites
- Paying a higher hourly rate for America Reads than for other work–study jobs

Orienting and Training Personnel at Tutoring Sites

If you have students with reading difficulty, this program is one of the best as far as helping them.

—ADMINISTRATOR FROM A SOUTH FLORIDA AMERICA READS SITE

For elementary schools to receive America Reads tutors, we required that each school send its reading coordinator and at least one first-grade teacher to a 4-hour training session. Each school also had to send an administrator for the first 2 hours of the session. Community tutoring sites were asked to send their on-site coordinators. The training was so well received that all first-grade teachers from the participating schools were also trained in 1997. Additional support and training are provided in the following ways:

- *Video/workbook review.* Each site is given an 18-minute instructional video that demonstrates the curriculum, and a workbook that is used in conjunction with the video to ensure mastery of key concepts.
- *Periodic site visits.* The M-DCPS Division of Language Arts/Reading periodically sends one of its reading specialists to visit schools. In addition, VISTA members also visit the tutoring sites at least two times each semester.
- *End-of-year evaluation meeting.* Each site sends its reading coordinator and a first-grade teacher to an end-of-year 4-hour debriefing session to critically examine the overall program and identify areas that need improvement. VISTA members also produce an evaluation of each site to help determine eligibility for participation the following year.

Making Engineering Students into Effective Tutors: Tutor Orientation and Training

It gives kids the chance to work with a person on a one-to-one basis. This strengthens their vocabulary, phonics, and writing abilities. I have noticed a great boost in some kids' self-esteem. It makes me proud to know that I am making a difference.

—TUTOR WITH THE SOUTH FLORIDA AMERICA READS PROGRAM

Tutors are required to attend 12 hours of orientation and training each year. This training is hosted by the college/university campuses and is facilitated by a reading specialist from the M-DCPS Division of Language Arts/Reading (except for the initial orientation, which is led by the college/university coordinators and/or by VISTA members). The training program is set up as follows:

- *Initial orientation.* Two-hour overview of program. Review of expectations, procedures, and rationale.
- *Pre-service training.* Four-hour instruction in the tutoring curriculum, including various types of hands-on practice with the model.
- *In-service sessions.* Two-hour training sessions every 6 weeks to review curriculum, teach new skills, and reflect on successes and challenges.

In addition to the structured orientation and training, tutors also receive ongoing support in the following ways:

- Monitoring and guidance from host site reading coordinator/ supervisor and first-grade teacher.
- VISTA members call tutors, visit tutoring sites, and are available on campus.

America Reads orientation session at Florida International University. The university's FW-S coordinator, Adelfa Ukenye, speaks to new tutors.

- College/university coordinators (volunteer center, student employment office, or financial aid office) are available to handle questions or concerns.
- Tutors must complete regular progress reports every 2 weeks and review these with their reading coordinator prior to submitting them to their college coordinator.
- Reading coordinators are expected to hold biweekly meetings with all tutors at their sites.

WHAT DOES SUCCESS LOOK LIKE?: PROGRAM EVALUATION DESIGN

The format is excellent in that it provides review, phonics, reading, and writing! It is the best thing to come along in quite a while!
    —FIRST-GRADE TEACHER FROM A SOUTH FLORIDA AMERICA READS SITE

Realizing that it was critical to document and evaluate the impact of our America Reads project, Jeanne Shay Schumm, a professor of reading and chair of the Department of Teaching and Learning at the University of Miami, worked with the coalition to create a comprehensive evaluation plan. This evaluation plan was implemented in both year 1 (1997–1998) and year 2 (1998–1999) of the project. The guiding question that shaped the evaluation process was "What does success look like?" The coalition identified six indicators to gauge success. The first two success indicators were improved student achievement in reading and spelling. The other four indicators were satisfaction of key stakeholders with tutor training, with tutoring materials and methods, with logistical procedures and tutor performance, and with M-DCPS student assessment and selection procedures. The coalition identified four primary stakeholder groups: first-grade students, college and university tutors, school administrators, and teachers.

Data were collected from several sources to measure success. Student data included pre- and posttests on all assessment instruments included in the America Reads training manual. In addition, a student survey was designed to tap first-grade students' perceptions of the tutoring program. Surveys were developed both for teachers and for college and university tutors. Surveys included demographic information about the respondents, as well as items tapping their perceptions about program components and resources, overall program perspectives, and open-ended comments. A telephone survey for school principals was designed to gather administrators' perceptions of America Reads.

The quantity of stakeholder data collected was similar in both years. In year 2, for example, data for 1,110 first-grade students were collected; a total of 166 school-based personnel (28 reading coordinators and 138 classroom teachers) and 116 tutors responded to surveys; and 35 principals or their designees were interviewed.

These data were analyzed to compare years 1 and 2 and to answer the evaluation question: "What would success look like?" Findings, broken down by the six indicators identified by the coalition, are summarized below.

Improved Student Achievement in Reading and Spelling

The America Reads program had a strong impact in the academic achievement of my students and helped with their self-esteem.
    —First-Grade Teacher from a South Florida America Reads Site

In both years 1 and 2, there was significant improvement in all student academic measures from pretest to posttest (letter recognition, letter production, concepts of words in print, phonemic awareness and phonics, word recognition, and story reading). Moreover, tutors and school-based personnel provided compelling testimony to the overall progress of students who participated in the program. Approximately 1,800 children received individualized tutoring in reading each week at 43 sites across South Florida during the project's first 2 years, and this continues

Children in the America Reads program at Silver Bluff Elementary in Miami.

in year 3 (1999–2000). In some schools, close to half the first graders have received instruction from America Reads tutors.

Three major limitations in the student data should be noted: lack of a control group, lack of a standardized measure of achievement, and teacher administration of measures. Plans are in place to address these limitations as much as possible in year 3.

Satisfaction of Key Stakeholders with Tutor Training

Satisfaction with tutor training on the part of both tutors and school-based personnel was generally high in year 1 and improved in year 2. School personnel rated the quality of training 4.26 (on a 5-point scale, where 5 was "high") in year 2, up from 3.77 the previous year. Tutors rated the quality of training 4.94, up from 4.21 in year 1. Tutors also reported satisfaction with in-service training, with a significant increase in quality reported in year 2 (3.73 in year 1, 4.17 in year 2).

Satisfaction of Key Stakeholders with Tutoring Materials and Methods

The tutoring manual was highly endorsed. The manual provided a structure that helped solidify the program. Methods and materials were cited as primary strengths of the program. Some school sites were challenged initially in setting up materials, but most recognized that once the system was in place, it was ready for the future. The America Reads project is highly materials-centered. Access to the materials and coordination of materials were achieved at most school sites in the first year, despite limited set-up and preparation time. Satisfaction with the materials and methods increased from year 1 to year 2 among all categories of key stakeholders. For example, school personnel rated the quality of the tutoring instructional program as 4.37 in year 2 (up from 3.94 the previous year), and tutors rated it 4.39 (up from 4.25 in year 1). School personnel also strongly endorsed the importance of one-to-one attention.

Satisfaction of Key Stakeholders with Logistical Procedures and Tutor Performance

The America Reads tutors were very special to my students. The students were able to learn a lot and experience a feeling of "I am special." They were kind and gentle with the students, and the students looked forward to their turn to be tutored. The program helped me a lot and I'd like to see it continued.

—First-Grade Teacher from a South Florida America Reads Site

The task of matching the schedules of schools and of undergraduate students is daunting. Space limitations at most public schools also provide a challenge to tutorial programs. Some administrators found tutor turnover and attendance to be problematic. When these factors are kept in mind, even moderate satisfaction with logistical procedures for a project of this scale would be amazing. Overall, both tutors and school-based personnel reported satisfaction with logistical procedures. The most dramatic improvements from year 1 to year 2, according to reading coordinators and teachers, were in procedures for interviewing tutors at the schools (4.25, up from 2.55 in year 1), and paperwork (3.91 in year 2, up from 3.26).

Satisfaction with tutor performance was generally high. School-based personnel rated the preparedness of tutors as 4.25 (up from 3.88 in year 1) and felt the effectiveness of tutors increased from year 1 to year 2 (4.11 to 4.21). One area of ongoing concern is tutor reliability. Although school-based personnel rated tutor reliability as the most important program component (4.92 in year 2), this area received the lowest quality rating in year 2 (3.67, down from 3.79 in year 1). A few recommended better screening of tutors; others suggested using only education majors.

Satisfaction of Key Stakeholders with M-DCPS Student Assessment and Selection

It has helped me pinpoint where my students need help.
—First-Grade Teacher from a South Florida America Reads Site

Teachers reported that the assessment information was helpful in identifying students' needs, both for tutoring and in the classroom (4.35 in year 2, 4.16 in year 1). Although some teachers reported that the assessment and selection procedures were somewhat cumbersome and time-consuming, the overall consensus was that they were worthwhile and effective.

Overall Conclusions

The America Reads program is an excellent resource for the first-grade students that were identified at the beginning of the school year. Hopefully, it will stay on for many years. Thank you on behalf of the children, who will be the ultimate winners in the future. A literate community is very important. Thank you again and again.
—First-Grade Teacher from a South Florida America Reads Site

The findings from years 1 and 2 indicate that the South Florida America Reads tutorial project is a high-quality program that should be continued and expanded. Students, teachers, reading coordinators, tutors, and principals were all enormously supportive of the program and its impact on meeting the reading instructional needs of students in the school district. Both tutors and school-based personnel strongly felt that America Reads is a high-quality program that should be continued (tutors reported 4.90 in both years, and the school-based personnel's mean response was 4.64 in year 1 and 4.71 in year 2). Overall, the evaluation indicated that the success of year 1 was continued, and in most cases improved upon, in year 2. In addition to the obvious experience gained during the first year, two significant changes occurred in year 2 that contributed to continued improvement in overall program quality. The first was the addition of six VISTA members, and the second was the hiring of a cadre of reading specialists by the school system, which added another layer of support.

Close to 6,000 children have received individualized tutoring in reading from South Florida America Reads tutors since 1996. Children who didn't know the alphabet or any of the sounds of their letters are now reading at or above grade level. When tutors walk into a classroom, children shout out, "Can I go read now? I want to read!" Children have improved self-esteem and confidence, and want to read out loud to the entire class. Calls come in weekly from other schools and other community programs that want to be part of our program and want us to assign tutors so their children can also reap these benefits.

In addition, an unanticipated benefit of America Reads has been the transformational impact it has had on the tutors. Many of the college students in South Florida's program were recently in remedial courses themselves and are struggling simply to stay in school. Many had never had a job or worked with children. But the experience of being an America Reads tutor—seeing those smiles, hearing the children shout your name, realizing that every child in the room wants to read with you, and knowing that you are giving another human being a tremendous gift—has transformed many of our tutors. Many have changed their majors to education or the human services field. They are more focused on their own studies and career goals, and they feel better about themselves. America Reads is giving them an experience that will help them be better parents, better students, and better citizens.

BEYOND FEDERAL WORK–STUDY INVOLVEMENT: THE BLOSSOMING SUCCESS OF AMERICA READS

Although South Florida's America Reads program began with an emphasis on placing FW-S students as tutors, it has continued to blossom into new directions and new areas.

What about Parents?

Tutors in year 1 of the program were very satisfied with their one-on-one sessions, but repeatedly noted that to build on the gains made in the America Reads sessions, the children needed more support from their parents. In response to this feedback, the coalition developed a parental involvement guide titled *America Reads! At Home.* This guide assists parents in helping their children become better independent readers. It includes activities, reading tips, and ways to make reading part of their children's everyday lives. In addition, an accompanying workshop kit was developed to introduce the manual and provide parents with hands-on experiences using several activities in the manual. Ninety-five parental involvement kits were created and are being distributed to elementary schools and parental involvement specialists across Miami–Dade County. More than 25 parental involvement workshops have been held so far at America Reads schools, and this important part of the project is just beginning to take off.

America Reads tutor Jacqueline Caldwell, a FW-S student from M-DCC, with Phillis Wheatley Elementary first-grade student Jeromeka Terry.

Improving Training Materials and Creating an Intermediate Model

To improve the usability and effectiveness of the primary tutorial model, and to make it easier to disseminate, we developed a tutorial training video and an accompanying video workbook. The 18-minute training video is a demonstration of the primary tutorial model. The steps and strategies demonstrated provide intervention strategies to assist tutors in becoming more effective in the delivery of the tutorial plan. The workbook serves as a reinforcement of the concepts presented in the tutorial video. Copies are sent to each school's reading coordinator for on-site training and review with tutors and teachers.

In addition, the M-DCPS Division of Language Arts/Reading has developed an America Reads intermediate tutorial model, based on the procedures and frameworks established in the primary model. This intermediate curriculum is successfully being used in several middle schools serving struggling readers in grades 6–8.

Involving Community Volunteers with Limited Time

Our 220 FW-S tutors are doing a terrific job, but the literacy needs of South Florida's children are overwhelming schools and community sites that desperately need more tutors. Although the structure of the primary tutorial model is its strength (the extensive training, the specialized curriculum and materials, the limited number of sites, multiple weekly tutoring sessions, etc.), this also makes it difficult for prospective volunteers with limited time to fit easily into this model. Unfortunately, other than the America Reads primary tutorial model, there was until recently no countywide infrastructure to train and place reading tutors.

It became evident, therefore, that we needed an easy-to-implement, materials-minimal program—one that high school students, service–learning students, and community volunteers who only have an hour or so a week can use. We also knew we needed a means to continue providing support to children who had received tutoring in first grade, but had graduated to second grade and were no longer receiving the individualized tutoring. A writing team of teachers, reading coordinators, reading specialists, adult education professionals, and VISTA members developed a Buddy Reading program based on the work of Keith Topping (1987, 1988, 1989). Buddy Reading was designed to build the fluency of developing readers. The procedure can be used with a wide range of readers from elementary to high school. Volunteers attend a 2-hour training workshop, after which they are asked to tutor at least once a week for

America Reads tutor Latasha Scales, a FW-S student from M-DCC, with a first-grade student at Phillis Wheatley Elementary.

1 hour. In addition to the community volunteers, Buddy Reading has a fifth-grade/second-grade module, whereby fifth graders are trained as peer tutors to work with younger children.

To disseminate the program, the writing team prepared four handbooks to provide clearly outlined procedures and all necessary support documents. The Buddy Reading modules include a school handbook, school training handbook, volunteer handbook, and volunteer training handbook. Table 3.1 lists and describes these and all other South Florida America Reads materials. For details about securing copies of these materials, contact Jodi Bolla at the M-DCPS Division of Language Arts/ Reading, 1500 Biscayne Blvd., Room 326L, Miami, FL 33132; phone (305) 995-1918; fax (305) 995-2910.

PROS AND CONS OF AMERICA READS IN SOUTH FLORIDA

Like any project of this magnitude, the South Florida America Reads program continues to be a work in progress that has had its share of challenges and successes. A summary of these is given below, to provide a realistic sense of the project's strengths and weaknesses.

Pros

- *Outstanding, effective, structured curriculum.* The success of any tutoring program is dependent on having a sound curriculum. South Florida's primary tutorial curriculum is research-based, has been field-tested, and has been proven effective. Teachers love it, tutors find it easy to use, and parents notice marked improvements in their children's reading and self-confidence. Kids love it too!
- *Tutoring curriculum connected to classroom.* The South Florida curriculum is an in-class tutoring model that relies on the input, supervision, and guidance of the first-grade teacher, and is connected to the classroom by having tutors work with a class "chunk" (several sentences taken from that week's class) as an integral part of the lesson plan.
- *User-friendly curriculum.* Both tutors and teachers have found the primary tutorial curriculum easy to understand and use.
- *Commitment to ongoing support and training.* Because the majority of our tutors are not education majors and have no experience in tutoring, training and ongoing support are essential. M-DCPS, especially the Division of Language Arts/Reading, is the key to this critical aspect. In addition to the initial training, regular in-service

TABLE 3.1. Description of South Florida America Reads Materials

Materials	Materials description
Primary tutorial guide	This tutorial guide provides intervention strategies for first-grade readers who are experiencing difficulty in learning to read. Also, it includes an Intensive Care Unit (ICU) component that provides intervention strategies for second through fifth grades.
Tutorial training video and workbook	This video is a demonstration of the America Reads primary tutorial model. It provides intervention strategies to assist tutors to be more effective in the delivery of the tutorial plan. The workbook serves as a reinforcement of the concepts presented in the tutorial video.
Buddy Reading handbooks	This program is designed to build the reading fluency of developing readers. It can be used with a wide range of readers from elementary to high school, and it contains a fifth-grade/second-grade in-school module. This strategy consists of four handbooks: • Buddy Reading school handbook • Buddy Reading school training handbook • Buddy Reading volunteer handbook (fifth/second grade) • Buddy Reading volunteer training handbook
America Reads! At Home parental involvement guide	This guide assists parents in helping their children become better independent readers. It includes reading activities, reading tips, and ways to make reading a part of their children's everyday lives. An annotated parental involvement workshop agenda and tips on how to use these materials to conduct a parental workshop are included.
America Reads evaluation instruments	This set of evaluation instruments can be used to tap stakeholders' perceptions of America Reads. The instruments included are as follows: • Student Survey • Student Individual Interview • Tutor Survey • Tutor Individual Interview • Reading Coordinator/Teacher Survey • Reading Coordinator Individual Interview • Principal Telephone Interview • Session Observation Protocol

TABLE 3.1. (*continued*)

Materials	Materials description
America Reads program support materials	This set of materials is designed to assist sites in maintaining and supporting the implementation of the tutorial model. The materials included are as follows: • Reading coordinator handbook • Tutor handbook • Biweekly Tutor Check-In Form • Tutor timesheets • Tutor Placement Confirmation Form

training sessions are conducted every 6 weeks to allow tutors to refine their skills, ask questions, and share their experiences.

• *Strong operational infrastructure.* While the South Florida America Reads Coalition relies on a number of partners that each perform their roles excellently, M-DCC is the key to this, as it provides the day-to-day management and decision making necessary for high-quality tutoring to take place.

• *Clearly defined roles and responsibilities.* All partners contribute, based on their resources and areas of expertise, to help the project run smoothly and effectively.

• *Ease of replication.* The primary tutorial model is easily understood and easily replicated.

• *Children's benefits from one-on-one intervention.* Many of the children who receive tutoring get little or no individualized instruction outside of their time with their America Reads tutors. Teachers, tutors, and parents report that this individualized attention makes a profound difference.

• *Stakeholder satisfaction.* Every stakeholder has indicated a high level of satisfaction with the program.

• *Effectiveness.* Children are learning to read.

• *Reciprocal effect in learning reading strategies.* Tutors report that their training in America Reads is making them better parents, grandparents, and students, due to their increased understanding of reading and their skills in helping children learn to read. In addition, many tutors, in the course of their work in the program, change their career direction to something related to teaching and education, thus providing our community with much-needed teachers who are committed to children and a love of learning.

Cons

- *Complex logistics for managing the efforts of multiple partners.* The sheer number of partners involved is inherently challenging.
- *Labor intensive nature.* Because we require a comprehensive infrastructure to assure high-quality tutoring (orientation/training, ongoing support, recognition, evaluation, etc.), and because of the number of tutors, tutoring sites, and partners involved, day-to-day management operations are very labor-intensive.
- *Tutor quality and retention.* Overall, the quality and commitment of our America Reads tutors have been very good. However, even though the percentage is small, we still have too many tutors who begin tutoring but fail to complete the semester (approximately 15%). We also have had several incidents where tutors were caught falsifying their timesheets. Properly screening tutors is an ongoing challenge.
- *Inadequately trained classroom teachers.* Some of the first-grade teachers do not have time to coach tutors and may not have been trained in the tutoring curriculum. This is an ongoing challenge, and even though the reading coordinator is responsible for overall administration of the program, a classroom teacher has the most contact and the most opportunity to supervise and mentor a tutor. Helping almost 200 already overloaded first-grade teachers fully understand their role in supervising and communicating tutors is challenging.
- *Required investment in materials* ($500–$1,000 in leveled texts for emergent readers). Because of the structure of the curriculum and the 30-minute lesson plan, the program requires leveled texts for tutors to use with the lesson plan. This complicates implementing the program, especially in many after-school programs that have few resources and materials.
- *Required supervision by someone with reading expertise.* Again, this is mainly a problem in after-school programs, which usually do not have a trained reading specialist on site.
- *Required monitoring and regular communication.* Reading coordinators, classroom teachers, and after-school program supervisors are generally overworked and overextended, thereby easily compromising the amount of time available to support and communicate with tutors.

LESSONS LEARNED/SUGGESTIONS FOR SUCCESS

- Do not reinvent the wheel—almost every community has myriad resources that can be tapped to build a successful America Reads program.

- Investigate the power of partnerships, so that you can use different expertise to develop the program.
- Emphasize the critical importance of training and in-service sessions.
- Be sure to use a sound curriculum, drawing if possible on successful models already in existence.
- FW-S monies are a tremendous resource—7% of a college's FW-S funds must be used in "community service" projects such as America Reads. College students receiving FW-S can easily serve as the cornerstone for an America Reads program. If there is a college or university in the area, find out whether it is willing to assign some work–study slots to America Reads.
- Overestimate the need for on-site support.
- Build layers of support for a solid infrastructure—at schools, colleges, and universities, and within the community. Corporations, TV and radio stations, and community agencies can all contribute to a solid America Reads program.
- Secure the backing of college/university presidents. This will be vital when accessing FW-S monies.
- Meet with the directors of financial aid and the coordinators of FW-S programs at local colleges and universities to request that they assign FW-S students to America Reads. Education faculty members are also often a great resource.

Members of the America Reads team at Silver Bluff Elementary. Left to right: University of Miami FW-S tutor Julie Delfina; Silver Bluff Elementary's reading coordinator, Ana Monnar; and Silver Bluff first-grade teacher Cora Bynum. In front are two America Reads children from Bynum's class.

SUMMARY

At first reading made me feel bad, but now reading makes me feel good!
—First-Grade Student at Linda Lentin
Elementary School in North Miami

America Reads in South Florida has pulled together the resources of colleges, universities, schools, community programs, and local school system administrators to work together to help children learn to read, one child at a time. We are very proud of what we have accomplished and are indebted to President Clinton, the U.S. Department of Education, and the leaders in our community who recognized the importance and potential of this initiative and made America Reads a reality. We are confident that the vast majority of the almost 6,000 children tutored to date are now more likely to experience school success, that they have increased self-esteem, and that they are better equipped for success in life. Their teachers and parents attest to this success every day. The approximately 500 college students who have worked as tutors have also benefited greatly. Our tutors are using the tutoring techniques learned in America Reads with their own family members and children; they have a new sense of their own ability to make a difference; and they are being given the opportunity to make an important contribution to their community.

Our message to others is that although building a high-quality program takes hard work, it is very much an achievable goal, especially if developers work collaboratively and utilize the resources that exist in most communities. These resources include school system reading specialists, college and university faculty members, service–learning and volunteer center coordinators, local literacy coalitions, and college/university FW-S students. We are pleased to have the opportunity to share what we have learned and the materials we developed. We are committed to helping others build vibrant America Reads programs so that even more children, tutors, families, and communities can reap the rewards of this inspiring initiative.

ACKNOWLEDGMENT

We would like to acknowledge Karla Gottlieb of Miami–Dade Community College for her writing and editing assistance.

REFERENCES

Clay, M. M. (1993a). *An observation survey of early literacy achievement.* Portsmouth, NH: Heinemann.

Clay, M. M. (1993b). *Reading Recovery: A guidebook for teachers in training*. Portsmouth, NH: Heinemann.

Invernizzi, M., Juel, C., & Rosemary, C. (1996–1997). A community volunteer tutorial that works. *The Reading Teacher, 50*, 304–311.

Johnston, F., Invernizzi, M., & Juel, C. (1998). *Book Buddies: Guidelines for volunteer tutors of emergent and early readers*. New York: Guilford Press.

Johnston, F., Juel, C., & Invernizzi, M. (1995). *Guidelines for volunteer tutors of emergent and early readers*. Charlottesville: University of Virginia.

Topping, K. (1987). Peer reading makes a comeback. *Special Children, 9*, 14–15.

Topping, K. (1988). *Peer tutoring handbook promoting cooperative learning*. Cambridge, MA: Brookline Books.

Topping, K. (1989). Peer tutoring and paired reading: Combining two powerful techniques. *The Reading Teacher, 42*(7), 488–494.

Chapter 4

AMERICA READS AND COMPREHENSIVE NEIGHBORHOOD REVITALIZATION: THE YALE-NEW HAVEN EXPERIENCE

Michael J. Morand

> America Reads is the first community service that I've done in New Haven that I feel has brought me into the community and made me feel like a real member of it.
>
> —YALE TUTOR

The America Reads Challenge, launched by President Clinton in 1996, provides an opportunity both to expand opportunities for college students to help younger children learn to read, and at the same time for colleges and universities to expand institutional partnerships with communities for comprehensive neighborhood revitalization.

UNIVERSITIES AND COMMUNITIES

American higher education has, from its earliest days, held that community service beyond the walls of the campus is an integral part of its mission. Yale's founding charter of 1701, for example, described the college's role as educating young people so that they "may be fitted for Publick employment both in Church and Civil State." This community service ethos has flourished across the centuries. It was evident in the work of Yale students and faculty who tutored enslaved Africans in 1839 and helped galvanize public support for their freedom in the legendary

Amistad incident. It could be seen at the end of the 19th century, when students taught English-language skills to immigrants newly arrived in the industrialized city of New Haven, Connecticut. It remains vibrant today, with more than half of all undergraduates engaged in community service while at Yale.

This long-standing mission has been joined by a newer phenomenon: Institutions of higher education are occupying a prominent place as primary economic actors in urban America. According to research by Harmon Zuckerman (1997) at the University of Pennsylvania, 40% of the 20 largest cities in the United States have universities and their affiliated health care centers as at least three of the top five private employers. This trend is equally pronounced in smaller and midsized cities, with places as diverse as Birmingham, Alabama; Bethlehem, Pennsylvania; Galveston, Texas; New Haven, Connecticut; Provo, Utah; and Winston-Salem, North Carolina counting a university as their largest employer.

The combination of historic mission and new socioeconomic reality compels American colleges and universities to consider more ambitious approaches to working with their home communities. The need for a comprehensive approach to university–community partnerships is particularly true for institutions in older urban areas. Former U.S. Secretary of Housing and Urban Development Henry Cisneros (1995) has pointed out:

> Our nation's institutions of higher education are crucial to the fight to save our cities. Colleges and universities must join the effort to rebuild their communities, not just for moral reasons but also out of enlightened self-interest. The long-term futures of both the city and the university in this country are so intertwined that one cannot—or perhaps will not—survive without the other. (p. 2)

Yale recognizes its responsibility for community development, rooted in its three-centuries-old tradition of service and the current challenges and opportunities of its hometown. In the 1990s, Yale has launched a comprehensive initiative to promote economic development, strengthen neighborhoods through increased homeownership and improved public schools, and revitalize downtown. President Richard C. Levin signaled Yale's institutional urban citizenship on his inauguration in 1993:

> As we seek to educate leaders and citizens for the world, as our discoveries spread enlightenment and material benefits far beyond our walls, we must remember that we have important responsibilities here at home. We contribute much to the cultural life of New Haven, to the health of its citizens and to the education of its children. But we must do more. Pragmatism alone compels this conclusion. If we are to continue to recruit students and

faculty of the highest quality, New Haven must remain an attractive place in which to study, to live, and to work.

But our responsibility to our city transcends pragmatism. The conditions of America's cities threaten the health of our republic. Our democracy depends on widespread literacy, and literacy is declining. Freedom for all requires that those without privilege have both access to opportunity and the knowledge to make use of it. We must help our society become what we aspire to be inside our walls—a place where human potential can be fully realized.

This aspiration finds concrete expression in Yale's partnerships with New Haven neighborhoods, where it has pursued integrated initiatives to support new economic activity, revitalize housing and increase home-ownership, and strengthen public education. This effort is evident in the Dwight neighborhood, just west of the main campus, where Yale has developed its America Reads program in the context of a comprehensive neighborhood partnership.

THE DWIGHT NEIGHBORHOOD, YALE, AND THE DWIGHT ELEMENTARY SCHOOL: PARTNERS FOR COMPREHENSIVE NEIGHBORHOOD REVITALIZATION

The Dwight neighborhood is similar to many other older urban areas in the nation. Encompassing about 0.81 square miles, it was home to approximately 6,800 persons as of the 1990 census. The overall population is approximately 50% African American, 40% white, and 9% of Hispanic origin, though 86% of the 1,312 children under 18 years old are African American or Hispanic. The 1989 household median income was $18,235, with nearly 30% of all persons living below the poverty level, including 502 children (or 38% of children) living below this level. The poverty rate in the neighborhood increased by almost 50% from 1980 to 1990. Of persons 25 years or older, 22% have less than a high school diploma, though 42% have an associate's or higher degree, reflecting the neighborhood's socioeconomic diversity. Nearly 200 households are classified as linguistically isolated, and more than 400 of the households with children under 18 have only one parent present. A large portion of the neighborhood children of school age attend the Timothy Dwight Elementary School from kindergarten through fourth grade, and the Troup Magnet Academy from fifth through eighth grades.

Although Dwight has the challenges common to all too many urban neighborhoods, it maintains a healthy mixed-race diversity, along with desirable proximity to New Haven's downtown and major institutions, providing a competitive advantage for community development. With a few exceptions, the neighborhood remains physically intact and continuous in its residential fabric. Most importantly, Dwight enjoys a vibrant core of citizen leaders who have taken neighborhood revitalization from a hope to a reality in progress.

In the late 1980s and early 1990s, serious violence, often associated with organized drug dealing, plagued the area and frustrated community organizing. However, at the beginning of the 1990s, committed residents came together to support New Haven's newly implemented community policing program through the Dwight Central Management Team (DCMT). Although its initial focus was on specific crime issues, the DCMT's vision grew early to include long-term, comprehensive neighborhood renewal, since it recognized that real public safety required economic and human development along with effective law enforcement.

Yale joined with the DCMT, offering human and other resources to neighborhood residents to assist them in charting their priorities and developing strategies to achieve their goals. The university took initial steps to strengthen the neighborhood by helping to stabilize properties in the area. In 1993, Yale and a local developer purchased a blighted 84-unit apartment building that had been a locus of criminal activity and was identified as a high priority by area residents. The building was improved and is now an asset that contributes to neighborhood stability.

In 1994, the university created the Yale Homebuyer Program, which offers a financial incentive of $25,000 to Yale employees who purchase homes in city neighborhoods like Dwight. Since 1994, it has helped 384 employees purchase homes, including a number in Dwight. Nearly half have been minority group members, and a significant number have been first-time homebuyers, including many service, maintenance, clerical, and technical employees who had previously been renters.

The neighborhood's drive for broad-based renewal received a major boost in 1995, when Yale was one of six universities selected by the U.S. Department of Housing and Urban Development (HUD) to receive a multiyear Joint Community Development Program (JCDP) grant for university–community partnerships. Yale secured $2.4 million from HUD, and these outside funds leveraged matching funds and in-kind contributions of $2.8 million from Yale and $3.2 million from other sources. The aims of the proposal included the creation of a community development corporation to implement the neighborhood's redevelopment plans. The comprehensive nature of neighborhood revitalization is evident in the focus on a set of interrelated strategies, including the following:

- Renovating blighted and abandoned buildings, and developing attractive and secure open space.
- Promoting homeownership.

- Promoting responsible behavior by landlords and tenants.
- Improving security.
- Mobilizing citizen engagement.
- Increasing employment through job training, recruiting, and placement.
- Developing small businesses.
- Promoting optimal development of children and youth, in and out of school.

Yale's JCDP grant funds have gone directly to neighborhood renewal, including seed funding to create the Greater Dwight Development Corporation (GDDC). The university has dedicated student, staff, and faculty teams to help the neighborhood refine goals and plans. With the assistance of the Yale Urban Design Workshop, the neighborhood developed a dynamic community action plan, formally endorsed on October 1, 1996. Among its priorities are these:

- Developing the Timothy Dwight Elementary School as a neighborhood campus, providing community resources that support school and neighborhood initiatives.
- Promoting regional and local economic development.
- Promoting homeownership.
- Creating attractive streetscaping.

This community action plan provides the framework within which Yale focuses its resources. The university recognizes that its efforts can only succeed if it works to achieve the stated goals of the community and assists with ongoing planning, assessment, and implementation of these goals.

The results of this partnership are strong and growing. In 1998, the neighborhood celebrated the opening of a major supermarket anchoring a new retail development. The supermarket is the first major urban grocery store to open in Connecticut in generations, offering residents high-quality food at reasonable prices. The Yale Law School has served as neighborhood counsel, providing more than $300,000 worth of in-kind legal services to the GDDC, which owns 51% of the development. The GDDC's codeveloper role gives it voice and control in employment, ensuring access to jobs for neighborhood residents.

Yale has also helped the community define and achieve its goals for the Timothy Dwight Elementary School, at the heart of the neighborhood. The school's physical campus is limited, with a multipurpose room that does triple duty as cafeteria, gymnasium, and assembly hall, and that is too small to accommodate all students at one time. The Yale School of

Architecture has worked with the school administration and with faculty and neighborhood residents to design an addition with another, larger multipurpose room where the entire school can gather; additional meeting rooms; and space that will promote parent and community involvement in the school. The collaborative design process has resulted in plans for a 9,300-square-foot addition to be funded by resources provided through Yale's JCDP grant and by city and state funds, with groundbreaking in June 2000.

THE AMERICA READS PROGRAM AT DWIGHT: DESIGN AND IMPLEMENTATION

It was in the context of this multifaceted community action plan and the growing success of neighborhood revitalization in Dwight that President Levin and Yale decided to respond to President Clinton's 1996 call to university and college presidents to mobilize their universities to support literacy through the America Reads Challenge. Rather than merely spread the resources available across the city in a multitude of sites, Yale focused its energies on a large-scale program in Dwight to achieve deep, sustained results and complement the other elements of neighborhood renewal underway, including housing and economic development. Given the neighborhood plan's emphasis on youth development, Yale saw America Reads as another way to support the community's defined objectives.

The Dwight Elementary School, like its neighborhood, has both strengths and significant challenges. As of the 1997–1998 school year, it had an enrollment of 443 children from prekindergarten through fourth grade, according to statistics compiled by the State of Connecticut Department of Education. Of these students, 77% were eligible for free or reduced-price meals, 26% came from non-English-language homes, 67% are African American, 29% Hispanic, 2% white, and 2% Asian American. Reflecting the New Haven Public Schools' commitment to preschool education, an increasing number of students have attended preschool, nursery school, or Head Start prior to kindergarten, with 67% in the entering kindergarten class of 1997–1998 having some preschool experience. The school has an average class size of 23 students. In recent years, it has improved library services, and its students' Connecticut Mastery Test scores have improved from 1993–1994 to 1997–1998 in all three tested areas of reading, writing, and mathematics.

With the focus on adding to its comprehensive partnership with the Dwight neighborhood in mind, Yale approached the school system and Dwight Elementary School with a proposal to initiate an America Reads program in the 1997–1998 school year. The superintendent of schools and the school principal responded enthusiastically, and staff representatives from Yale, the school, and the New Haven Free Public Library spent the summer of 1997 designing the program. As suggested by Yale President Levin, it was decided that the partners would seek to recruit and train students from Yale College (the undergraduate division of Yale University) to serve as individual tutors for every student across a single grade level, with Yale committing itself to maintain the program on an ongoing basis over multiple years.

The focus on one-on-one tutoring has proven to be one of the program's strongest attributes. One Yale junior commented, "What I enjoy about America Reads is that I have one child to work with all the time, and that means so much to me. I really like the fact that we have a personal relationship and that she considers me the big sister she's never had. Not only am I tutoring—I am mentoring as well." Indeed, many tutors have found that the one-on-one emphasis allows them to develop personal relationships that are critical for learning. As a sophomore noted, "America Reads has been the best. The one-on-one tutoring allows for the creation of wonderful friendships and promotes a great deal of progress."

The inclusion of all students in the third grade has also proven to be a successful decision. Because all children are involved, the America Reads program at Dwight is not stigmatized as one only for students with reading challenges. The third grade was chosen as an appropriate age for tutoring, as the additional support would build on the literacy foundation already built by the school in earlier grades. Moreover, the partners chose to design a program based on reading for pleasure, in order to cultivate a love for reading by the children and to extend learning beyond the classroom, while avoiding the reality or perception that the purpose of the tutoring was merely homework help.

The partners recognized the constraints posed by the already large demands for classroom instruction and learning during the school day, and by the relatively limited availability of a large group of college students on a regular basis during the morning and early afternoon. The school and the university designed the program to run immediately after the school day, with 90-minute sessions held from 2:30 to 4:00 P.M., Mondays through Thursdays. At the Dwight School, Yale's America Reads program serves as the official after-school program for third-grade students, and the school system uses already available resources to provide a late bus for students, so that parents do not need to arrange alternative transportation on their own. In order to extend learning and promote a mentoring relationship between college tutors and elementary school students, the program was designed to encourage them to schedule a weekly session at the public library outside of regular hours, especially on Saturdays.

With the basic program outline in place, Yale and the Dwight School began the 1997–1998 academic year by respectively recruiting college student and elementary school student participation. Neither was sure what the response would be to this new program. Both were more than satisfied. At Yale, President Levin sent a letter to all undergraduates who qualified for federal work–study funds, encouraging them to consider the America Reads Challenge. His communication highlighted America Reads as a way that students could join with an important national initiative, make a real difference in their local community, and earn the funds required as part of their financial aid packages. The response was tremendous, with more than 300 Yale College students applying to serve as tutors.

Likewise, the Dwight School achieved great results in its recruitment outreach to third-grade students and their parents. Information was sent home with children from school, and a parent information session was held at the school on an early September evening. Many motivated parents responded at that point. The school's principal and parent liaison followed up with home visits, including on weekends, to families whose children had not yet responded. Although America Reads at Dwight is a voluntary after-school program, the efforts of the school leadership resulted in a remarkable 100% sign-up rate among third-grade students.

In total, 69 Yale students were selected to serve, and were matched as individual tutors for each of the third graders during the fall semester in 1997. Of these Yale students, 20 were male and 49 female. The tutors included 61 freshmen, sophomores, and juniors, ensuring a large pool of potential returning tutors for the subsequent school year. In consultation with the school staff, Yale worked to match its students carefully with Dwight students who might most benefit from their particular skill and experience. For example, Latino Yale students were often matched with Dwight students who came from primary Spanish-language homes.

All the partners agreed that it was essential for the program to include extensive training for the college tutors before they began their work. At Yale and elsewhere, some community outreach programs have at times done a disservice to the student participants and the community's children alike by sending the college students out armed merely with their enthusiasm and energy. Students have responded very positively to the training and structure of the program. One student reported, "This program has been great. The organization and care with which everything is done is impressive. It feels more efficient than other community service programs at Yale."

To ensure that the college students are effective and able tutors, Yale has devoted its own resources to funding training sessions with school officials and other skilled experts. Training topics include questioning strategies, story mapping, retells, choosing appropriate books, lesson planning, behavior management, and characteristics of a typical third-grade student. All Yale students participate in 12 to 16 hours of organized training before tutoring sessions begin, as well as being given bibliographies for self-directed training on their own time.

Just as training is essential, so too the partners knew that structure and ongoing supervision and support are necessary for the Yale tutors to succeed. This aspect of the program has been identified by tutors as an important strength: "I have found America Reads to be much more helpful, due to the constant support system and overall organized plan of action." Two Yale College students were hired to serve as coordinators during the 1997–1998 school year. They oversaw scheduling, including informing Yale tutors if their elementary school students were absent on any given day, and likewise organizing substitute tutors if any Yale students were ill. For security and administrative purposes, all tutors signed in at the school and displayed name-tag identification. For the beginning weeks, an adult staff member from Yale was also on site to observe and troubleshoot, joining with members of the Dwight School administration, who are present after school at all times. Outside of the tutorial sessions, Yale tutors received daily e-mails with administrative information and reminders and tips for their tutoring sessions.

With strong training and supervision in place, the 69 tutors and elementary school children started the program well and kept up a high level of commitment throughout the first year. Each pair of students met three afternoons a week from Monday through Thursday, with about 75% thus present on any one day. Tutoring sessions were held in the library, the multipurpose room, available classrooms, and the hallways. Crowding was an issue, given the school's physical limits and its use for after-school programs for other grade levels. Attendance for the after-school sessions was strong, with Yale tutors missing on average only 1 day of tutoring each semester, and Dwight students absent on average fewer than 2 days per semester. A total of 3,201 individual after-school tutoring sessions were held in 1997–1998.

Weekend tutoring sessions were encouraged to be held at the New Haven Free Public Library, to promote further reading for pleasure and reading outside of school. The library provided Yale tutors with an orientation to its children's collections, and a lunch for parents, children, and tutors was held at the beginning of the school year to introduce them to each other and the program. Parents were responsible for transportation during the school year for the weekend sessions, which posed a barrier to some. Other children had conflicting obligations or limited motivation for the weekend session. Thus only 47% of tutors and their children met for any weekend sessions in the fall of 1997. The school and the university sought to encourage both families and tutors to give higher priority to the weekend sessions in the spring, resulting in a participation rate of 71% of the pairs, with an average number of 4.4 sessions each.

At the end of the 1997–1998 school year, Timothy Dwight Elementary School and Yale staff members reviewed the progress of the America Reads Challenge program, considering feedback from Yale students, Dwight School teachers, and parents. All constituencies reported enthusiasm for the program in its first year and recommended that it be continued. The comments of Yale tutors are illustrative of the overall response and match the typical responses of classroom teachers:

"When [my student] started reading with me, she read short picture books. By the end of the semester, we ended up reading two books—real books. The first one was 150 pages. The second was 180 pages."

"I think [my student's] vocabulary has increased, and he has started to use higher-level vocabulary in his everyday speech."

"[My student] is awesome! He has a great attitude and a good nature. He has begun challenging himself with difficult reading material. He is more willing to ask questions about things he doesn't understand, and his enjoyment of reading as an avocation is steadily increasing."

"[My student] has moved from Special Ed to a 'regular' class, and his reading has improved amazingly."

"[My student's] writing is gaining sophistication, and her oral reading ability has improved vastly."

"What is very encouraging about [my student] is that his self-esteem about reading has improved dramatically. I think America Reads has motivated him to improve his reading and to develop a better appreciation of reading."

Responses about the structure of the program and its benefits for the college students were likewise positive, with consistent comments such as "My experience has been very rewarding," "It's one of the best programs I've been involved with," and even "I have actually found America Reads to be my most rewarding experience at Yale."

Based on the positive feedback from students, teachers, parents, and administrators, Yale reaffirmed its commitment to be a sustained partner in literacy with the Timothy Dwight Elementary School. In the two subsequent academic years, 1998–1999 and 1999–2000, the program has continued to offer a trained and supervised Yale College student to serve as an individual tutor for every third-grade student, with a participation rate of more than 95% each year from the elementary school. The program has expanded to include individual tutoring for some fourth-grade students who might benefit from additional reading support as identified by their teachers and parents, so that Yale has recruited and trained a total of 90 tutors in 1998–1999 and 89 in 1999–2000.

Yale and the Dwight School have also sought to refine the program over these 3 years. One major area of focus has been scheduling, an always difficult area in programs that link two institutions with vastly different timetables. Elementary school days begin early, and all students are in school at the same time every day, 5 days a week. College students, on the other hand, have individual schedules that vary from day to day, and no two students have exactly similar schedules. This poses difficulty for aligning the schedules of college tutors with that of the elementary school, and it limits the potential pool of college students who might work in an after-school program with a fixed schedule. In 1998–1999, the partners experimented with Friday after-school sessions, as Friday is a day when virtually all Yale students have no structured afternoon classes. However, it became clear during the year that (as common sense might suggest) Friday afternoon, at the end of a long week of study for all involved, is not an optimal time for tutoring, and so the experiment was not continued beyond 1998–1999.

Perhaps the most important development in the 3 years is that the Dwight Elementary School principal and staff have provided increasing leadership and direction to the program. For the first 2 years, training was organized with an array of skilled experts, often drawn from outside the school. Elementary school faculty members have taken on primary responsibility for training beginning in the fall of 1999. This has been a positive development, as it provides the Yale tutors with the best information on the strengths and challenges of the elementary school and its students, and promotes a stronger link between what happens in the classroom and what occurs in after-school tutoring.

The elementary school also suggested that the program bring college and elementary school students together for their one-on-one tutoring sessions two, rather than three, afternoons a week at the school, along with the Saturday supplemental session at the public library. They had observed that while three afternoons a week offered more quantity than two, this quantity did not necessarily bring a commensurately higher level of quality. Requiring two sessions per week would also increase the size and diversity of the pool of potential college student applicants. The school has also assumed increased responsibility for the ongoing supervision and support of the Yale tutors, with the university funding a Dwight School faculty member who is on site after school every afternoon. This has replaced a previous, Yale-based drop-in center and is felt to be an important improvement by the Yale tutors, who are now able to get immediate assistance when they encounter problems or simply want to talk about the progress of their work. This leadership from the school, combined with the U.S. Department of Education's ongoing support through the federal work–study funds and Yale's continued commitment of additional resources, strongly indicates that America Reads in New Haven will remain strong for many years.

SUMMARY: RESULTS AND LESSONS LEARNED

To date, the America Reads program in the Dwight neighborhood has worked with more than 200 children in the neighborhood, touching the lives of a good proportion of the more than 600 families with children under the age of 18. As it continues into its next few years, and well beyond, its impact will increase in the neighborhood. Given the continued positive response from school administrators, classroom teachers, parents, and college students, it is hoped that the program will play a role over time in meeting the neighborhood's objective of providing community resources to promote school initiatives and promote the optimal development of children and youth, both in and out of the school setting. In doing this, it will complement other steps taken by the elementary school and the neighborhood to strengthen literacy and other learning.

Although the program's success will be measured over many years, initial signs suggest that improvement is being made. These include modest increases in Connecticut Mastery Test scores, and a dramatic decline in the number of third graders identified for retention because of their reading level. It is clear that the partnerships among neighborhood residents, the elementary school, Yale, and other partners must continue if more progress is to be achieved. As the university and the school maintain the America Reads program over time, they will be guided by some lessons learned during its first 3 years—lessons that may also be of interest to other university–community collaborations for literacy and neighborhood revitalization. These lessons learned include the following:

1. *Presidential leadership matters.* The federal government was right to recruit college and university presidents to champion America Reads on their campuses and in their communities. At Yale, the involvement of the president from the beginning gave the program immediate credibility, and it united staff members responsible for community outreach with those responsible for financial aid in a common purpose. Presidential

involvement in recruitment has led to higher visibility and response among students.

2. *Community- and school-based leadership matters just as much.* Universities can be catalysts and help assemble the necessary resources, but a program will take root and grow only to the extent that it addresses community priorities and has leadership and direction "on the ground" every step of the way.

3. *A healthy respect for different organizational cultures is essential.* Both the university and the elementary school have been open to each other's needs and constraints, especially around issues of scheduling. They have adapted the program each year to try to work out the optimal match between the two.

4. *A long-term commitment matters.* America Reads brings the best aspects of institutional strength and staying power together with undergraduate enthusiasm and talent. Over the years, new students bring renewed energy to the program. At the same time, the elementary school knows it can count on Yale as an institution to be there for the foreseeable future, even as individual students graduate and move on.

5. *A schoolwide program works well.* Having America Reads be a program for all third graders removes any potential stigma and helps integrate it into the school culture.

6. *Nothing good happens without strong training and supervision.* Even the most talented undergraduates benefit from ongoing training and a good structure, and universities and schools must be willing to dedicate the necessary resources to complement the federal government's commitment of work–study funds and technical assistance.

A final, and perhaps overarching, lesson from the experience of New Haven and Yale in the America Reads Challenge is that the program works best when it exists in the context of an overall initiative for community revitalization. Certainly America Reads as a program can thrive in isolation, but the maximum benefit occurs when it is part of a inclusive strategy that includes economic development, housing, and other school improvements. Working with the leadership of Dwight, Yale has helped in various and complementary ways—some large and some small—to strengthen the prospects for human development. Through the development of a neighborhood retail center with a supermarket, the partnership has increased the quality of life and the employment opportunities for neighborhood families, including parents of children at the Dwight School. Through the design of an addition to be built at the elementary school, the partnership has helped address crowding at the school while providing space for community activities after school, on the weekends, and in the summer. Through homeownership incentives, the partnership has helped strengthen the housing market and increase the number of residents with a stake in the neighborhood's future. And through America Reads, the partnership has helped the neighborhood's children learn and develop.

In many ways, Yale, the Dwight neighborhood, and the Dwight School, like Yale and New Haven overall, have only just begun. There are solid reasons for optimism, including the strong support and leadership of the federal government through the America Reads Challenge and other initiatives. The neighborhood, the elementary school, and the university all share a long-term commitment to comprehensive community renewal. Just as the neighborhood's children learn more and develop better, so too will the partnership among Yale, Dwight, and New Haven learn and develop, to the mutual benefit of all.

ACKNOWLEDGMENTS AND NOTES

Yale University would like to acknowledge and thank Howard A. Gray, Jr., Yale College Class of 1943, for his generous support that has provided financial resources to cover the training, material, and other costs of the America Reads program in New Haven beyond the resources provided by the U.S. Department of Education for student stipends through the federal work–study program. In addition to the efforts described above, Yale University supports other literacy initiatives, through America Reads and its own funds. These include the work of Jumpstart, a national initiative founded in New Haven by two Yale students, and the work of the Fair Haven Community Health Clinic's Reach Out and Read program. There are more than 100 Yale students serving as America Reads tutors throughout New Haven.

REFERENCES

Cisneros, H. C. (1995). *The university and the urban challenge.* Washington, DC: U.S. Department of Housing and Urban Development.

Levin, R. C. (1993). *Beyond the ivy walls: Our university in the wider world.* Inauguration address, Yale University, New Haven, CT.

Zuckerman, H. (1997). *Eds and meds and employment in America's major cities.* Unpublished report, University of Pennsylvania, Philadelphia, PA.

Chapter 5

A TUTORING PROGRAM
FOR STRUGGLING READERS
IN ARGENTINA

María Celia A. de Córsico

María Rosa Carbajo

La Plata, Argentina, is an important administrative center with a bustling economy and many attractions, including the prestigious National University of La Plata, the Cathedral, the Museum of Natural Sciences, the Argentinean Theater, and the Children's Republic. Unfortunately, many people living in La Plata have neither the opportunity to visit these places in person nor the skills to read about them.

A strong correspondence exists among school failure, school dropout, and poverty (See Córsico & Rosetti, 1994). Like many other Latin American countries, Argentina recognizes that better primary education programs could serve as building blocks for economic development and growth.

We believe one way to start improving this situation is to improve reading and writing skills among primary school children. Our initial efforts in this regard were greatly aided by our establishment of an America Reads-style tutoring program in Argentina. We modeled our program on one introduced to us by Dean Louise C. Wilkinson of the Graduate School of Education, Rutgers—The State University of New Jersey. The tutoring program was designed and directed by Lesley Mandel Morrow, a professor in the Department of Learning and Teaching, Rutgers Graduate School of Education. We have implemented an adapted version of America Reads since 1998.

Our program was a success, according to information gathered from third-grade students, tutors, teachers, and principals. At least 60% of the students improved their performance in reading and writing, as well as their attitude toward themselves and their schoolwork.

PURPOSE

In Latin America (including Argentina), no significant, systematic research has been carried out on the contribution of school, politics, and family to the educational achievement of children. We do know, however, that failure to learn is an important factor contributing to school dropout.

Children should be independent readers by the end of primary school, but national statistics and teacher evaluations show that a significant percentage of children are not independent readers and are at risk of failure. Since reading facilitates nearly all school activities, the effects of poor reading skills are dangerously cumulative. In addition, research demonstrates that most poor readers have low self-esteem.

When Argentinean children do poorly in school, they must repeat a grade level. A substantial number of students who repeat subsequently drop out of school, which lessens their ability to positively affect their own or their community's prosperity.

We felt that the tutoring program would help break the cycle by increasing literacy and decreasing school failure and dropout rates.

THE PROGRAM

Changing children's attitudes about themselves and learning is an important part of teaching reading, and we were attracted to the Volunteer Tutors in Reading and Writing project because it provides one-on-one education with the potential to improve children's literacy skills, self-esteem, and attitude toward school.

This type of tutoring can be offered to a single student or to a small group of students with learning difficulties for which additional help is needed. The cornerstone of the program is a very positive relationship between the tutor and the child, backed by good organization that makes the most of the tutoring sessions.

Our goal was to implement a program with the following characteristics:

1. The tutors would have a positive attitude toward the children; that is, they would encourage, accept, and give support to the children, and would promote enthusiasm for the learning tasks.

2. The tutors would be familiar with basic instructional techniques and materials.
3. Administrative support, continuity, and appropriate evaluation would be provided.

While establishing our program, we took into consideration available linguistic and psychopedagogical support, as well as external factors (e.g., the children's cultural and socioeconomic levels). We then imitated the Rutgers University model as we did the following:

1. Identified a sample of third-grade students with reading difficulties who were at risk of grade repetition, according to a survey administered to school principals and teachers.
2. Obtained a group of volunteer students from the educational psychology course at our university who were qualified to be tutors.
3. Supervised the volunteers during tutoring sessions.
4. Provided technical support by means of tutor assistants who transcribed tape recordings of the children's reading and evaluated their writing.
5. Trained and supervised the tutor assistants.
6. Adapted the Volunteer Tutors in Reading and Writing project created by Rutgers University to suit local characteristics, and carried it out with the students of La Plata University.

For the purposes of this chapter, we explain the activities connected to the above-mentioned procedures, for which we adapted the Volunteer Tutors in Reading and Writing project developed at Rutgers University. We worked with three different types of materials:

- Tutor training (i.e., translated and adapted handbooks and local texts).
- Tutoring (i.e., guides, writing books, cards, reading materials, narrative texts).
- Evaluation materials (i.e., tests used to measure reading and writing achievement, abilities, motivation, and attitude).

One of us (María Celia A. de Córsico), a full professor of educational psychology at La Plata University, planned and directed the project. She began in 1998 by inviting the other chapter author (María Rosa Carbajo, an associate professor in her department) and three assistant professors (Ana M. Machado, Teresa Queirel, and Alicia Riera) to participate. We were joined by Sandra Basualdo, Marta González, and Alejandra Mosca of the Institute for Educational Research, and by Celina Olocco, a professor of applied linguistics.

As a team, we established and maintained connections with the schools and teachers and also supervised tutors and tutor assistants during the training course. The team was an essential part of the project.

We translated and adapted to Spanish (Río de la Plata versions) two books for internal use: Morrow and Walker's (1997) *The Reading Team* (translation by María Rosa Carbajo), and Herrmann's (1994) *The Volunteer Tutor's Toolbox* (partial translation by María Celia A. de Córsico). We also made use of the original (English) version of Walker and Morrow's (1998) *Tips for the Reading Team.*

We introduced other protocols to be used as answer sheets for tests and questionnaires, and we distributed a chapter of an unpublished book written by Córsico on reading comprehension. Olocco elaborated upon several documents and recommended a bibliography for the university staff and students involved in the project.

The third edition of Morrow's *Literacy Development in the Early Years: Helping Children Read and Write* (1997) was a fundamental source of information for the whole project.

TUTOR AND ASSISTANT TUTOR SELECTION

Every year we offer a course on educational psychology for 60 undergraduate students studying education and physical education at the School of Education, National University of La Plata. As a part of their studies, students must complete special activities without a final exam. In 1998, we invited them to participate in this project to fulfill their special activities requirement.

We explained the new program to all the students and asked those interested in volunteering to complete the questionnaire shown in Figure 5.1.

Based on their responses, selected students were invited for in-person interviews, during which we posed the following questions:

1. Why do you want to take part in this project?
2. What is the basic philosophy or premise of this project?
3. What is your opinion of this project?
4. Have you ever worked with children? If so, please explain.
5. How would you define "reading competency"?
6. What do you like to read?
7. Has your appreciation for reading been influenced by school or by your family?

Please indicate your feelings about each statement, using the following scale:

1. Strongly agree
2. Agree
3. Neutral
4. Disagree
5. Strongly disagree

	1	2	3	4	5	Not applicable
I devote most of my free time to reading.						
Children should be encouraged to read anything they wish.						
I cannot handle another activity in addition to my studies.						
I work with children.						
I am a coach.						
Children with difficulties in reading experience failure.						
I frequently read for pleasure.						
I am an elementary school teacher.						
I have not worked with children.						
If individuals read and write well, they do well in school.						
I work, so I have limited time for other activities.						
I am a teacher.						
Most books bore me.						
Strong reading and writing skills usually enhance student performance.						
My handwriting is legible.						
I don't have any free time.						
My family and I read newspapers and magazines.						

Statement				
Children might find me boring.				
I am the liveliest person at children's parties.				
I only have time to read material related to my schoolwork.				
If unsure of a word's meaning while reading, I skip over it.				
I enjoy telling stories to children.				
I divide my time between work and studying.				
Literacy is fundamental to a satisfying life.				
I try to understand what I read.				
I have worked with groups of people.				
I have always been a top student in reading classes.				
I sometimes help children with their homework.				
Reading is the most important learning tool.				
I am only concerned about my studies.				
I am able to communicate my ideas through writing.				
Children who read poorly need personal support.				
Children like to spend time with me.				
Responsibilities at home occupy all my free time.				
I am a poor speller.				
I have a lot of patience with children.				
Difficult reading materials are a challenge for me.				
I don't like to read the newspaper.				
It takes constant practice to become fluent and have good intonation and comprehension in another language.				
I read all kinds of magazines carefully.				
Children who read and write poorly don't perform well in school.				

FIGURE 5.1. Questionnaire for prospective tutors.

8. How would you rate your skills and/or knowledge of language arts?

We selected 20 tutors and 20 tutor assistants; all the tutors signed the contract shown in Figure 5.2 before taking the training course.

TUTOR TRAINING

After selecting 40 students for the team, we began a training course that met for 1 hour each week. The main topics covered in the course are described in the books by Walker, Morrow, and Herrmann cited earlier. In addition, we used the following materials developed by Olocco for us:

1. Short stories: Structure models for wonderful short stories, including main features and narrative sequence.

Acceptance of this contract indicates that the tutor will:

- Respect the children in the project.
- Respect the teacher's work, taking into account his/her teaching style.
- Respect the spirit of the project.
- Discuss any concerns or questions that arise during tutoring with the co-ordinator.
- Try to complete the entire tutorial plan while taking into account individual students' circumstances.
- Maintain an attendance record.
- Attend all training sessions.
- Be prepared for tutoring sessions by having materials on hand (pens, pencils, notebooks, books, a watch, a tape recorder, etc.).
- Be on time for tutoring sessions.
- Maintain an orderly file of tutoring activities (i.e., samples of the students' work, a list of readings, etc.).
- Read, follow, and keep the instructional materials provided to you by the project coordinator and trainer(s).
- Read the materials on the project reading list.

Signature _____

Date _____

FIGURE 5.2. Tutor contract.

2. Vocabulary: Classification, meaning, and relationships with the selected short stories.
3. Spelling: Problems, relationships between phonemes and graphemes in the Spanish system, characteristics of the written language, didactic strategies for teaching.
4. Written text and its composition or production: Analysis of words, sentences, paragraphs, spelling, spatial orientation, strategies for text production, and strategies for summaries.

The tutors learned about the project's main goals, which were to create a space in which children could obtain pleasurable and successful experiences in reading and writing, and to support teachers by coordinating activities with them. They were also trained in the goals, activities, and expected results of each part of the sessions. Training sessions continued after tutoring began, and the sessions included discussions about the children's work.

In the course of this project, we learned that while the volunteers' desire to tutor is important, other qualifications must be considered during the tutor selection process. Candidates must be able to understand that their role is to deal specifically with children's attitudes toward reading; they are not to consider themselves reading teachers.

After their first contact with the children, some of the tutors became worried that they did not know enough about the reading process and/or the children's cognitive processes. The tutors requested a more academic training course, but we were faced with the problem of how to balance the tutors' development of socioemotional skills with appropriate level of knowledge about the reading process and reading's interrelationship with writing. (See Rayner & Polletsek, 1989).

THE SCHOOLS

Once our tutors were ready, we needed to obtain permission to work in the schools. This could have been difficult due to the complexities of Argentina's educational reform process, but we have a good relationship with many schools in our district and have conducted many successful educational research projects. We were very grateful to them for opening their doors to us for this project.

Our tutors were unpaid, so they wanted assignments that were geographically convenient. We chose three schools near the university and a fourth school in a distant suburban area that could be served by tutors living nearby.

We appointed one coordinator per school whose responsibilities included making contact with the principal, explaining the project, and giving a brief written presentation with the tutors' signed contracts. All the schools we approached accepted the tutoring plan, and the principals selected teachers who expressed interest in the project. The coordinators made contact again and gave a complete presentation. We eventually had 12 teachers involved.

STUDENT SELECTION

We asked third-grade teachers to make a list of children with reading difficulties, and then to rank them according to the severity of their reading deficits. In accordance with the project's philosophy, our intent was to exclude children with severe difficulties. Initially, for the most part, the teachers recommended students with normal difficulties for tutoring.

A total of 40 children were intially included in the project; 38 remained by the end of the study. Two students were assigned to each tutor.

As part of our work with the students, we measured two aspects of third-grade children (8 and 9 years of age, primarily) with reading difficulties: initial reading performance and self-esteem.

Initial Reading Performance

Tutors recorded each session on audiotape cassettes, which the tutor assistants transcribed. One of the initial sessions representing typical reading performance at the beginning stages was selected for each child. The analysis of utterances consisted of a sample of 2 minutes of reading. (See Crowder, 1982). The categories of the rough analysis and the averaged results for the group (38 children) are shown in Table 5.1.

The first row of Table 5.1 shows that on average, children within this struggling group were very slow readers initially. The next four rows show that the children made many mistakes while reading. The last two rows show that on average, children requested help in decoding some words, but that no silences lasting more than 10 seconds were found in the recorded utterances.

Self-Esteem

Reading is the central learning activity of the early primary school years, because it is basic to success in school. Some authors consider self-esteem to be a significant factor in the development of reading skills. The motivational influence of the self-system is said to determine whether children seek or avoid opportunities to read and the amount of effort they expend during reading.

TABLE 5.1. Characteristics of the Children's Initial Reading Performance per Minute

Reading performance characteristic	Number per minute
Total number of words	38
Number of mispronounced words	5.4
Number of omitted words	1
Number of repeated words	1.3
Number of substituted words	2
Number of requests for help	0.3
Silence of more than 10 seconds	0

Studies of factors associated with school achievement have found significant correlations between children's school achievement and self-esteem. For this reason, we considered it very important to evaluate self-esteem in the children included in our project. The tutors administered the Self-Esteem Scale shown in Figure 5.3 to their students during the third or fourth week of tutoring.

The average score we expected, based on our previous work with a nonselected group of third-grade children, was about 40, with a standard deviation near 10. Data from the Self-Esteem Scale produced scores with a mean of 32 with a standard deviation of 9. The sample was relatively small, and the administrative conditions were not under our complete control; therefore, we can only conclude that a significant difference probably existed between these third graders with reading difficulties and the general third-grade population.

Toward the end of the 1998 project, we administered the Self-Esteem Scale again. It showed an increase of about 5 points in the average score. It is interesting to note that this numerical result coincided

My name is Graciana Perez Lus. I am finishing my studies in education at the National University of La Plata. The tutoring program is one of the best learning experiences I have ever had. My participation in the program has changed my life and heightened my sense of responsibility as a teacher.

I am Elina. I am in third grade. My tutor is Noelia. She is very nice. She helps me when I'm stuck on a word. I've learned a lot. I enjoy playing reading games with her.

with teachers' and tutors' reports about the general improvement in the children's self-confidence.

TUTORING SESSIONS

The tutors conducted 16 tutoring sessions with each child. One or two sessions were devoted to gathering basic information about the students and establishing rapport. The tutors administered adapted versions of the Information about the Child You Tutor form and the Motivation Interview (Morrow & Walker, 1997) to the children.

The tutoring sessions followed the format described in the book *The Reading Team* (Morrow & Walker, 1997). Flexibility was permitted, depending on individual students' circumstances.

1. Reading old favorites (5 minutes)
2. Reading together (5 minutes)
3. Writing together (5–10 minutes)
4. Reading for enjoyment (5–10 minutes)
5. Talking about words (5–10 minutes)
6. Summarizing success (3–5 minutes)

Last Name: _____   First Name: _____

School: _____   Level: _____

	Yes	I don't know	No
My classmates ask me to help them during exams.			
Teachers always tell me to improve my homework.			
I have to be forced to study.			
Most of my classmates think I am a good student.			
I am intelligent, so I am a good student.			
I cannot improve my grades.			
My teachers say I am smart.			
I've always had good grades.			
My teachers use me as an example for my classmates.			
My parents do not think I put enough effort into my studies.			
My grades do not reflect my real abilities.			
My classmates think I should be on the honor roll.			
I think I am not going to pass.			
Most schoolwork is difficult for me.			
My marks are so low my classmates tease me.			
My parents reward me for good grades.			
My classmates think I am helpful.			
Everyone tells me I am a bad student.			
My teachers like me because I earn good grades.			
My classmates always check their homework with me.			
My classmates always ask me about homework.			

FIGURE 5.3. Self-Esteem Scale.

Traditional fairy tales were used during the sessions, and the tutors were encouraged by the children's enthusiasm about the stories. Some sessions were devoted in part to the administration of various tests and instruments, including Raven's Progressive Matrices, the Self-Esteem Scale (Figure 5.3), and tutors' materials.

The tutor assistants compiled the materials produced during the tutoring session by children and tutors. They transcribed the tape-recorded reading utterances and evaluated the children's writing. We obtained a great deal of valuable data in this manner and have completed a partial analysis of them. A full analysis is forthcoming.

IMPLEMENTATION DIFFICULTIES

Difficulties we experienced during the implementation of the project included the following:

1. We lacked adequate financial support for research, educational practices, and materials.
2. Some children did not attend school regularly, which wasted the tutors' time.
3. The university students' academic schedules made coordination with the schools difficult.
4. Some children referred to the program were not properly selected (e.g., 10% had severe difficulties, and one child was an advanced reader).
5. Most of the schools could not provide a private area for the tutorial sessions. Some tutor–student pairs had to share space with another person, which was inconvenient for all concerned.
6. The 1-hour weekly tutor training was insufficient, because we needed more time to address tutors' doubts, questions, and comments. The problem was compounded when classes were interrupted for teacher salary strikes and other circumstances linked with the Argentinean government's educational policy.
7. The public schools limited the children's availability for tutoring to once per week, which was insufficient.

RESULTS

The first attempt at this tutoring program was rewarding. At least 60% of the students improved their performance in reading and writing, as well as their attitude toward themselves and their schoolwork.

We have a great deal to refine in terms of tutor and student selection and data collection techniques. However, we have been encouraged to continue our work based on the success we experienced and the overall enthusiasm for our efforts expressed by everyone involved.

REFERENCES

Córsico, C. A. de, & Rosetti, M. M. de (1994). *Interacción lingüística entre maestros y alumnos y su influencia sobre el rendimiento escolar.* Buenos Aires: AZ.

Crowder, R.G. (1982). *The psychology of reading: An introduction.* New York: Oxford University Press.

Herrmann, B. A. (Ed.). (1994). *The volunteer tutor's toolbox.* Newark, DE: International Reading Association.

Morrow, L. M. (1997). *Literacy development in the early years: Helping children read and write* (3rd ed.). Needham Heights, MA: Allyn & Bacon.

Morrow, L. M., & Walker, B. (1997). *The reading team: A handbook for volunteer tutors K–3.* Newark, DE: International Reading Association.

Rayner, K., & Polletsek, A. (1989). *The psychology of reading.* Englewood Cliffs, NJ: Prentice-Hall.

Walker, B., & Morrow, L. M. (1998). *Tips for the reading team: Strategies for tutors.* Newark, DE: International Reading Association.

Part II

EVALUATION STUDIES OF AMERICA READS TUTORING PROGRAMS

Chapter 6

THE EFFECTS OF AN AMERICA READS TUTORING PROGRAM ON LITERACY ACHIEVEMENT AND ATTITUDES OF TEACHERS, TUTORS, AND CHILDREN

Lesley Mandel Morrow
Deborah Gee Woo

One ever-present issue in the debate on educational reform is the plight of the struggling reader, particularly in the urban setting. Children who cannot read early and well are hampered at the very start of their education and for the rest of their lives (Lloyd, 1978). To participate in America's highly skilled workplaces or effectively use the vast quantity of information available on the Internet, all children need to read better than ever before.

President Clinton proposed, and Congress endorsed, the America Reads Challenge Act of 1997 as a national, bipartisan strategy for improving literacy performance for children prior to entering the fourth grade. Families, schools, and the community are forming the foundation of this effort. One of the major components of the America Reads intervention is the utilization of volunteer tutors to supplement classroom instruction for at-risk students to increase their engagement in reading and writing. Many students do not read, in school or at home, because they lack the personal support when difficulty arises. In these situations, they often give up and disengage themselves from literacy tasks. Tutors can provide the personal support that will keep students working toward independence in reading.

However, the frameworks for implementation of tutoring schemes vary according to the underlying learning theories and methods of assessment upon which the schemes are grounded. The tutoring program designed, implemented, and evaluated by the Rutgers University Graduate School of Education and described in this chapter is based on research in reading instruction outcomes and assessments. The reading competencies that were determined to be the most readily improved through the efforts of volunteer tutors formed the basis for the framework of the tutoring sessions and the tutor training.

Once a tutoring model based on the research data available on best practices for reading instruction was created, the research reported by others on the topic of volunteer tutoring that most closely matched that model became pertinent for refinement.

There are many tutoring programs that utilize community volunteers in addition to college students, or are working with volunteers from AmeriCorps or Volunteers in Service to America (VISTA). One such program—the Howard Street Tutoring Program, a small after-school volunteer tutoring project in Chicago—was developed and evaluated by Darrell Morris, Beverly Shaw, and Jan Perney as a joint venture of the National Reading Center (at the National College of Education, Evanston, Illinois) and the Good News Educational Workshop (a community group) (Morris, Shaw, & Perney, 1990). The volunteers are a mix of community members and college students who are trained on the job and then closely supervised by a reading specialist. In addition, the reading specialist carefully plans the tutoring lessons for maximal benefit to each child. The results of the 2-year quantitative evaluation of the gains made by tutored second and third graders compared to a control group indicated that the tutored students outperformed the nontutored students on a number of literacy measures, including general word recognition, basal word recognition, spelling, and oral reading of basal passages (Morris et al., 1990).

Reading Together, a community-supported intergenerational tutoring program in Philadelphia developed by Susan Neuman, involves VISTA (Neuman, 1995). The VISTA volunteers help parents learn how to assist their children with reading through the use of themed prop boxes that are used with the children during two 1-hour sessions per week. Formal evaluations of the program have not been reported; however, the responses from the schools involved were positive.

Juel in (1996) reported on a project she developed and evaluated at the University of Texas at Austin. In this program, at-risk university students were trained to tutor at-risk first graders at a Title I school in Austin. The tutors met weekly for a 2½-hour class devoted to tutoring activities, the components of the tutoring process, literacy development, and questions regarding the children with whom they were working. In the evaluation, it was reported that there were statistically significant and substantial gains on the reading composite of the Metropolitan Readiness Test for the tutored students, compared to students who received mentoring but not tutoring. Upon further analysis of the data, it became apparent that some dyads were more successful than others. In the more successful dyads, more attention was given to scaffolding reading and writing processes; more explicit modeling of these processes was demonstrated by the tutors; and more time was spent on specific decoding strategies and direct letter–sound instruction.

PURPOSE OF THE EVALUATION STUDY

The primary purpose of the study described here was to determine whether students' achievement in reading and writing was enhanced as a result of being tutored by college students in an America Reads work–study program initiated by Rutgers, The State University of New Jersey. In addition, we hoped to determine the attitudes of teachers, tutors, and children toward the tutoring program. Finally, as a result of observing tutoring sessions and recording them via audiotape and videotape, we hoped to determine the literacy strategies employed by tutors to help with literacy development.

METHODS

Subjects

The study took place in a professional development school that has an ongoing partnership with Rutgers. Thirty-five undergraduates and 12 graduate students in the work–study program participated. The demographics of the elementary school were as follows: 55% Hispanic, 35% African American, and 10% European American. At least 75% of the students at the school were identified as eligible for Title I.

Teachers identified children in kindergarten through third grade for tutoring, and we randomly selected from each grade level equal numbers of boys and girls for the treatment group (those who would receive tutoring) and the control group (those who would not). There were a total of 80 children in the study, 40 in the experimental group and 40 in the control group, distributed equally among the four grades.

Procedures

Assessment Measures

Graduate assistants were trained to administer pretests in September and posttests in April. The children were assessed individually. Tests included an oral story-retelling test, a probed comprehension test, an assessment of writing development for kindergarten and first grade, an assessment of a written retelling for second and third grades, an inventory of concepts about print, and interviews to determine attitude toward and interest in reading. In addition, four dyads of tutors and tutees were observed via audiotapes (five sessions each) and videotapes (two sessions each) over a 6-month period to determine types of literacy strategies used. There was one dyad for each of the grades tutored: kindergarten, first, second, and third.

Quantitative Tests for Literacy Achievement

Tests to determine literacy achievement gains included a comprehension test in the form of an oral story-retelling test and a probed comprehension test at all grade levels. The second- and third-grade children were also given a written retelling test. An inventory of concepts about print was administered to emergent readers in kindergarten and first grade, as well as a test to determine stage of writing development. All of the pretests were administered again, at the end of the tutoring intervention, to both treatment and control group students.

Story-retelling and story-rewriting tests were used, since they are holistic measures of comprehension that demonstrate retention of facts, as well as the ability to construct meaning by retelling text. For both the story-retelling and story-rewriting tests, two different storybooks were used for the pretest and posttest. These were chosen for quality of plot structure, including strongly delineated characters, delineated setting, clear theme, obvious plot episodes, and definite resolution. The stories were similar in number of pages and words. Testing books were selected with attention to research on children's preferences in books (Monson & Sebesta, 1991). A research assistant administered the story-retelling tests on an individual basis, using the same script for each child. Classroom teachers administered story-rewriting tests to whole groups. When taking the story-retelling and story-rewriting tests, children listened to a story that was read to them. They were asked to retell it or rewrite it as if they were doing it for a friend who had never heard the story before. No prompts were given with the rewriting test. In the oral retelling, which was tape-recorded, prompts were limited to "Then what happened?" or "What comes next?" Both the written and oral story retellings were evaluated for the inclusion of story structure elements: setting, theme, plot episodes, and resolution. A child received credit for partial recall or for understanding the gist of a story event (Pellegrini & Galda, 1982; Thorndyke, 1977). Comparing the order of events in the child's retelling with that in the original text determined the child's ability to sequence. The interrater reliability of the scoring scheme (roughly 90%) and the overall validity of the measures were established in previous investigations with children from diverse backgrounds (Morrow, 1992; Morrow, Pressley, Smith, & Smith, 1997). For this study, six coders scored five protocols, with 92% agreement for story retelling and 95% for story rewriting.

Probed comprehension tests (Morrow, 1992) were administered by research assistants individually after reading a story to each child. The test included traditional comprehension questions focusing on detail, cause and effect, inference, and making critical judgments, plus eight questions focusing on story structure (setting, theme, plot episodes, and resolution). Research assistants read the questions and recorded children's answers. This instrument was found to be reliable in the range of 91% and above in previous research with children from similar diverse backgrounds (Morrow, 1992; Morrow et al., 1997). In this study, six coders scored the five pre- and posttests, with 93% agreement. The inventory of concepts about print was adapted from work by Marie Clay (1985) and tested children's knowledge about print, such as identification of letters, words, and concepts about books (including being able to identify the front and back of a book, the title, and the author).

In the assessment of writing development for kindergarten and first grade, children were asked to draw a picture depicting their family, a television show they liked, or something special to them. The research assistant helped the children decide what they would draw if they could not decide alone, telling the children that they would be asked to write something about their picture. If children said they couldn't write, they were told that they could "pretend write," and were shown samples of children's scribble writing, letter-like forms, letter strings, and invented spelling. After the children drew the pictures, they wrote about them. Using Sulzby's (1986) broad categories of writing development, we rated children's samples from 1 to 6. Our ratings were based on the following categories: writing via drawing, writing via scribbling, writing via letter-like forms, writing via letter strings, writing via invented spelling, and writing via conventional spelling. In this study, six coders scored the five pretests and posttests, with 97% agreement.

Qualitative Data

Teachers, tutors, and children were interviewed to determine their attitudes toward the tutoring program.

As noted above, four dyads (one each from kindergarten and from first, second, and third grades) were followed through the tutoring year. For each dyad, five sessions were audiotaped and two sessions were videotaped. Sessions were then transcribed to observe literacy strategies used by tutors, the affective rapport built between tutors and children, and other interactions that suggested emerging trends to help in training tutors to improve the progress of the students being tutored.

The qualitative data were analyzed to compare progress in literacy development for the children in the treatment and control groups. Categories were identified and the data were coded accordingly, with new codes added to the coding list as they were needed. We also assessed frequency of occurrence of these categories for the total sample and by grade. The approach to data analysis was not strictly inductive, because we began with previous knowledge about what literacy activities we might expect to see. It also was not strictly deductive, because we wanted to discover activities that might be happening that where not anticipated. Adapting the constant comparative research procedure used by Miles and Huberman (1984), we reviewed the data and reduced them into categories, from which trends emerged concerning literacy activities initiated by tutors. To check for coding reliability, five research assistants recorded data, coded data into literacy activity categories, and recorded the number of appearances of these activities by grade. There was 95% agreement concerning types of literacy activities recorded and 90% agreement concerning how often they occurred. We felt that this information should shed light on what occurred during tutoring sessions and should help support the findings in the quantitative analysis.

Materials

During the training sessions, the work–study students were introduced to the book *The Reading Team* (Morrow & Walker, 1997), which outlines a program for tutoring. In addition, the book *Tips for the Reading Team* (Walker & Morrow, 1998) was used. The following materials were also made available for the tutors: books to read with children; notebooks to be used as journals for writing by students and tutors; 3 × 5 cards for building sight and writing vocabularies; and folders for creating portfolios that would include student work samples for the purposes of assessing progress.

The Training Program for Tutors

Prior to tutoring, the tutors received four 3-hour sessions to review tutoring techniques and materials for tutoring. In addition to instructional strategies, the training included strategies for building rapport with the tutored children and with the children's teachers. Also discussed were appropriate professional dress and behavior while working with tutees, as well as advice on interacting with parents and teachers. The tutors were trained by a certified teacher who has taught reading to children in kindergarten through third grades.

Monitoring Tutors

After the first week of tutoring sessions, the instructor for tutors met with the group to discuss questions and concerns, offer guidance, and continue training. Whole-group meetings with the tutor trainer took place the fourth week of tutoring and then once a month thereafter. The instructor observed each tutor early in the tutoring period, to observe the quality of the interaction between tutor and child. In addition to group meetings, the instructor was available for office hours twice a week, for individual appointments with tutors who had questions, and for telephone conferences.

Tutors also met weekly with graduate assistants in small groups to talk about successes and concerns. They were observed by the graduate assistants to determine the quality of the rapport that was developing with their tutees, and they met with classroom teachers to coordinate their tutoring with classroom instruction.

The Tutoring Program

Tutoring sessions occurred three times a week for 30 minutes each session. The tutoring took place during school hours, but never during regular reading instruction. Tutors were instructed to prepare lesson plans before working with children and to keep records after each session. Tutors supported the work of the teachers. The tutoring occurred for most of the school year, beginning in mid-October and continuing through April, to allow for about 60 sessions of tutoring per child.

The Framework for Each Tutoring Session

There are six elements in the tutoring framework developed at the Rutgers Graduate School of Education and used in this study, and each element has a specific purpose for developing fluent reading with understanding. One underlying goal is for children to read an abundance of easy material. Fluent understanding arises from reading material that is easy to read. When children read books over and over again, not only does fluency increase, but also enjoyment. That is why many young children read favorite books over and over again. Together, a tutor and a student read and discuss many selections. The strategies used are designed to enable students to meet with success. The following explains the elements within the framework.

- Reading something familiar (5 minutes)
- Reading something new together (12 minutes)
- Working with words (5 minutes)
- Supported writing and shared writing (10 minutes)
- Reading for enjoyment (5 minutes)
- Summarizing the success of the tutoring session (1 minute)

Reading Something Familiar. Books are like old friends. They support you, and they are fun to visit again and again. Like a visit with an old friend, reading something familiar is fun and supports the development of good, fluent reading. Reading familiar texts provides for successful reading experiences. Familiar stories are selections children have already read and know well, and such a story is the first thing to read in a tutoring session. Rereading familiar selections helps students practice reading skills and notice features about print.

Reading Something New Together. Everybody loves to learn from new challenges. Readers are not different. New selections stretch the learning of young children. In this phase of the session, the tutor and student

Ashlynne Milson reads a familiar story to Michelle Harp, an America Reads tutor.

select something new to read together. New material presents new challenges; therefore, the tutor guides the reader with some discussion before the book is read, in order to develop interest, elicit background knowledge that the student may already have about the topic, and set a purpose for reading. The tutor begins by reading the story aloud and then invites the child to follow. Tutor and child share their ideas during pauses while reading. They discuss various aspects of the text after the story is read. Eventually, the student reads the new selection alone.

Working with Words. It is important to discuss with the child's teacher the strategies he/she is working on and the reading material with which the student is working in the classroom. The teacher and child will find this particularly helpful, since it involves their daily schoolwork. When the tutor finds out the strategies that the student is working on (rhyming words, initial consonant sounds, compound words, word endings, etc.), the tutor can reinforce knowledge of these concepts.

Supported Writing and Shared Writing. Tutoring materials should include a notebook called a "journal" for writing stories and other entries throughout the tutoring period. Each time young students write, they have to think about the thoughts they want to get down on paper, and they

America Reads tutor Michelle Harp and James Sullen sort picture–word cards by initial consonant sounds.

have to think about letters and sounds in words. The tutor can help support all of these writing skills by helping the child brainstorm ideas about what he/she would like to write about. Writing encourages students to look at how words are put together and the consistent patterns that many words have. The tutor can take the opportunity to point out spelling patterns in our language. The knowledge the child gains about print when writing helps him/her to figure out words when reading. The tutor and student can jointly write a story, deciding on a topic and alternatively writing sentences. They can also write their own stories, sitting side by side. Sharing the writing with each other is an important part of the task.

Reading for Enjoyment. Good readers become good readers by reading. Often time is not set aside in school to read for pleasure. Therefore, children need time to read self-selected materials silently for their own enjoyment. At all sessions, both tutor and student set aside some time to read their own books, sitting side by side. After the designated time for reading, they share what they have read.

Summarizing the Success of the Tutoring Session. Students begin to take charge of their own literacy when they describe and evaluate what they are learning. Each session closes with a time for the tutor and student to

Kindergartner Claudia Pardilla and America Reads tutor Michelle Harp write about a favorite story.

review what was completed during that session. They discuss the activities that went well and what they will do at the next session. They end by discussing activities for the student to do before they meet again, including what the student can do at home with his/her family.

RESULTS

The study reported here was conducted as a randomized two-factor within-subjects design. The two factors of interest were group (tutored, control) and grade (K, 1, 2, 3). The within-subjects factor was the result reported for the two separate administrations of each test (pre and post). Initial independent sample *t*-tests conducted on each pretest variable to determine preexisting differences between the tutored and control groups revealed no such differences (all p's > .96). A repeated-measures analysis of variance technique was utilized.

Achievement Data

Literacy Achievement

Table 6.1 presents the pretest and posttest means and standard deviations for the literacy measures that were administered to all grades (kindergarten through third). In the analysis of covariance for the total score on the oral story-retelling measure, there was a statistically significant mean difference between the two groups, with the tutored group ($n = 40$) outscoring the control group ($n = 40$), $F(1, 79) = 6.31$, $p < .02$. For the total score on the probed comprehension test, the tutored group again scored significantly better than the control group, $F(1, 79) = 13.31$, $p < .001$.

TABLE 6.1. Means and Standard Deviations for Literacy Achievement Measures, K–3

| Measures | Tutored group ($n = 40$) | | | | Control group ($n = 40$) | | | |
| | Pretest | | Posttest | | Pretest | | Posttest | |
	M	SD	M	SD	M	SD	M	SD
Oral story retelling	5.75	4.22	8.97$_a$	2.94	4.94	3.64	6.78$_b$	2.97
Probed comprehension	15.50	7.49	23.90$_a$	4.38	12.95	5.97	19.28$_b$	4.96

Note. Posttest scores are significantly different ($p < .05$) if they do not share the same subscript.

Because the writing assessments were different for kindergarten and first grade versus second and third grades, and because the inventory of concepts about print was administered only to the lower two grades, the data are presented in separate tables. Table 6.2 presents the pretest and posttest means and standard deviations for the kindergarten and first-grade measures; Table 6.3 contains the pretest and posttest means and standard deviations for the second- and third-grade measures. The descriptive statistics revealed that the tutored groups achieved higher mean gains on these measures than the control group, but that the mean differences did not reach significance. For the repeated-measures analysis for writing 1 (K–1), the tutored group ($n = 20$; mean pretest score = 4.25, mean posttest score = 5.40) outscored the control group ($n = 20$; mean pretest score = 4.70, mean posttest score = 5.80), $F(1, 39) = 0.14$, $p < .71$. For the repeated measures analysis for writing 2 (2–3), the tutored group ($n = 20$; mean pretest score = 5.05, mean posttest score = 9.69) outscored the control group ($n = 20$; mean pretest score = 5.42, mean posttest score = 8.68), $F(1, 39) = 0.17$, $p < .68$). For the concepts about print measure, the tutored group ($n = 20$; mean pretest score = 21.75, mean posttest score = 32.65) outscored the control group ($n = 20$; mean pretest score = 20.70, mean posttest score = 29.25), $F(1, 39) = 1.89$, $p < .18$. From these data, it can be inferred that the decreased sample size (40 vs. 80) on these measures may have had a profound effect on statistical power.

A comparison of the improvement in test scores for the combined sample is presented in Figure 6.1. For each measure, the tutored group achieved higher average gains.

Comparison of the average improvement in all test scores by grade (Figure 6.2) indicates that students tutored in grades K–2 averaged more improvement than the students in the control groups. However, the scores of third-grade students did not follow this trend. When we looked at the oral story-retelling data by individual grade, the greatest differences in

TABLE 6.2. Means and Standard Deviations for Literacy Achievement Measures, K–1

| | Tutored group ($n = 20$) | | | | Control group ($n = 20$) | | | |
| | Pretest | | Posttest | | Pretest | | Posttest | |
Measures	M	SD	M	SD	M	SD	M	SD
Oral story retelling	3.66	4.03	7.29	2.58	4.57	3.84	6.82	3.00
Probed comprehension	11.50	6.76	24.45	4.66	11.15	5.75	20.55	4.17
Writing development	4.25	1.86	5.40	0.82	4.70	1.53	5.15	0.88
Concepts about print	21.75	9.60	32.65	4.68	20.70	9.63	29.25	4.82

TABLE 6.3. Means and Standard Deviations for Literacy Achievement Measures, 2–3

Measures	Tutored group ($n = 20$)				Control group ($n = 20$)			
	Pretest		Posttest		Pretest		Posttest	
	M	SD	M	SD	M	SD	M	SD
Oral story retelling	7.84	3.33	10.66	2.26	5.32	3.48	6.75	3.01
Probed comprehension	19.50	5.99	23.35	4.12	14.75	5.78	18.00	5.44
Written retelling	5.05	2.56	9.69	3.19	5.42	3.54	8.68	3.01

gains were in kindergarten and in first and second grades (Figure 6.3). Similar results were found on the probed comprehension measure, with the exception that the third-grade control group made a greater mean gain than the tutored group (Figure 6.4). In all measures, the third grade made the smallest gains of the four grades.

Figures 6.5 and 6.6 indicate that the tutored groups did make larger gains than the control groups in the writing assessment measures, although the differences between groups were small.

In the concepts about print test (Figure 6.7), given only to kindergarten and first-grade children, the experimental group scored better than the control group did. A closer look at the data suggests that the greatest gains were made in kindergarten. This might have been expected, since by first grade many of these children had learned the skills on this

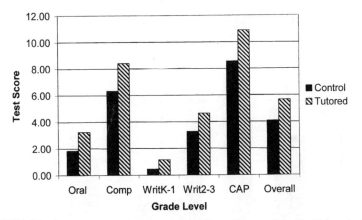

FIGURE 6.1. Improvement in test scores, all grades combined. Abbreviations: Oral, oral story retelling; Comp, probed comprehension; WritK–1, writing assessment for K–1; Writ2–3, writing assessment for 2–3; CAP, concepts about print (for K–1 only).

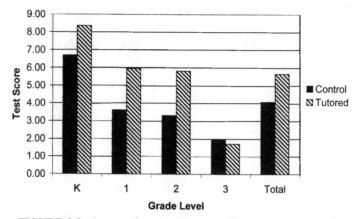

FIGURE 6.2. Average improvement in all test scores, by grade.

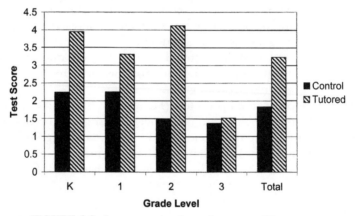

FIGURE 6.3. Improvement in oral story-retelling scores.

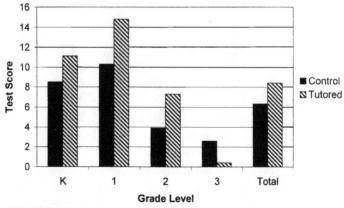

FIGURE 6.4. Improvement in probed comprehension scores.

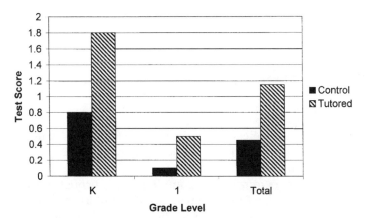

FIGURE 6.5. Improvement in writing development (K–1) scores.

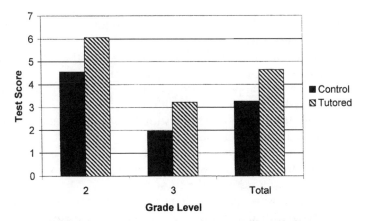

FIGURE 6.6. Improvement in written retelling (2–3) scores.

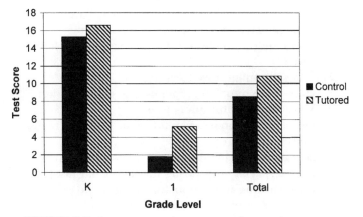

FIGURE 6.7. Improvement in concepts about print scores.

assessment measure; their pretest scores were thus much higher than those of the kindergarten students, with not as much room for improvement in the posttests.

Interview Data

Interview data were collected from teachers who had volunteer tutors, from tutors after their tutoring experience, and from children who had experienced being tutored.

Twelve teachers, representing kindergarten through third grade, were interviewed to determine the benefits of the tutoring program, what they liked about the program, and what they felt could be improved. Their comments were pooled and are listed below.

1. What did you think was the most important accomplishment of the Rutgers tutors?
   - "Children who are struggling benefited from the individualized help and improved in reading and writing."
   - "The warm rapport that tutors developed with their students seemed to help improve children's self-esteem."
   - "The children enjoyed being with the tutors; consequently, they worked hard for them."
   - "The tutors are good role models."
   - "Children seemed to develop a more positive attitude toward reading as a result of the tutoring."
   - "Meeting with college students was a treat for struggling readers, since they had a positive perception about meeting with these young adults."
   - "Remedial-type help is viewed by many of these students in a more negative fashion, with a stigma attached."
   - "Struggling readers felt special about meeting with tutors, since other children who weren't tutored wanted to have the tutors as well."
2. How would you improve the program?
   - "Have more tutors to accommodate more children."
   - "More materials for tutors to use."
   - "More interaction between tutors and teachers to discuss child needs and progress."
   - "Scheduling during the school day was difficult sometimes."
   - "Have a special time during the school day just for tutoring."
   - "Have tutoring after school for teachers who prefer not to have it during school."
   - "Have the tutors come more often, daily if possible."

3. What types of children do you feel can benefit most from the tutoring program?
   - "Children with short attention spans."
   - "Children who have trouble concentrating."
   - "Children with low self-esteem."
   - "Children who are reading below grade level."
   - "Students with limited ability in the English language."
   - "Children from homes where they receive little assistance with schoolwork."
   - "Children who are shy."
   - "Children with behavior problems in the classroom may work better in the one-on-one setting with a young college student."
4. What strategies did tutors use that you felt were useful for the children?
   - "Reviewing work learned in the classroom."
   - "Open discussions about families, pets, school, etc., to motivate drawing and writing."
   - "Skill games to motivate interest in learning skills."
   - "Read stories from classroom materials to provide reinforcement."
   - "Work with phonics."
   - "Oral and silent reading."
   - "Expanding vocabulary."
   - "Use of context clues to figure out words."
   - "Predicting outcomes in stories."
   - "Summarizing stories read."
   - "The use of leveled reading materials to provide students with books to read at their instructional level."
   - "Providing reading materials of interest to the child."
   - "Journal writing."
   - "Keeping very own words to enhance vocabulary development, sight vocabulary, and writing vocabulary."
   - "The use of humor in teaching, and extending friendship."
   - "Offering support and encouragement."

The 45 tutors involved in working with children in kindergarten through third grade were interviewed to determine their attitudes about tutoring in relation to the benefit to the children, their evaluation of their own tutoring, materials used and needed, what they liked about the program, and what they felt could be improved. The comments were pooled and are listed below.

1. Why did you become a tutor?
   - "Seemed like a good opportunity."
   - "I like the idea of helping children."

2. What is the most important thing you can do as a tutor?
   - "Give the student my full attention."
   - "Try to be positive and encouraging."
   - "Build a good rapport."
   - "Be patient."
   - "Make learning fun."
   - "Create a friendship and trust with the child."
   - "Help them understand what they are having difficulty with."
3. What kind of strategies, materials, and activities do you use in your tutoring sessions?
   - "Teaching the alphabet."
   - "Teaching how to sound out vowels and consonant sounds."
   - "Help children with the pronunciation of words."
   - "Play skill games."
   - "Use flash cards for word identification."
   - "Read to children."
   - "Have children read to me."
   - "Review things we learned."
   - "Journal writing."
4. What do you enjoy most about tutoring?
   - "Helping the children."
   - "Seeing the children succeed."
   - "Interactions and the experiences we have together."
5. What is the most difficult part of tutoring?
   - "Getting the child to pay attention."
   - "Motivating the children."
   - "Figuring out how to help kids with what they need."
   - "Having materials to work with."
   - "Earning the trust of the child."
   - "Trying not to get frustrated when it seems the child[ren] will never get what you are trying to teach them."
6. What do you see as the difference between what you do as a tutor and what a teacher does?
   - "Tutors can be less formal and have more fun with children."
   - "As a tutor I can meet individual needs, since I'm working one on one with the child."
   - "As a tutor I can reinforce what the teacher has taught."
   - "The tutor does not have the experience or knowledge of a classroom teacher and should be support for [the teacher]."

The children in kindergarten through third grade who had tutors from mid-October through April were interviewed to determine their attitudes about their tutors and the tutoring experience. Their comments were pooled and are listed below.

1. Would you like to continue having a tutor?
   - At all grade levels, when the children were asked whether they would like to go on having a tutor at school, 96% said "yes."
2. Why do you want a tutor?
   - "Because I can't read very good."
   - "Because I want to read better."
   - "To help me when I don't know stuff."
   - "I want to learn more."
   - "I want to get better grades."
   - "I like to get help when I need it."
   - "Because I need lots of help."
   - "The tutor makes me feel good."
   - "The tutor makes me feel happy."
   - "It is quiet with the tutor."
   - "The tutor makes me feel smart."
3. Describe your tutor, what your tutor was like, and what you think a tutor should be like.
   - "A nice person."
   - "A girl."
   - "A boy."
   - "A Rutgers student."
   - "A person who likes to read books."
   - "A person who is fun."
   - "A person who is happy."
   - "Someone who is friendly."
   - "Someone who treats me good."
   - "Someone who is helpful."
   - "Someone who is gentle."
   - "Someone who is smart."
   - "Someone who is pretty."
   - "Someone who listens to me."
4. What did your tutor help you with?
   - "I had help with figuring out words."
   - "She helped me to sound out words."
   - "She helped me with reading rules."
   - "He helped me with letters."
   - "He helped me with spelling."
   - "He helped me with my work pages."

- "He helped me read, so I don't have to make up the words."
- "She helped me with writing."
- "He helped me to read by myself."
- "She helped me with my homework."
- "She read to me, and that helped me."

Literacy Strategies Used by Tutors

The literacy strategies observed were coded into four major categories: "reading," "word analysis," "comprehension," and "writing." Within these major headings, there were subcategories.

Several types of reading took place. Tutors read to children; children read to tutors; and tutors engaged children in shared reading, where they took turns reading the same material, and they also read text together in unison. In addition, there was independent reading, with the child and tutor sitting side by side and reading independently for pleasure.

Word analysis was used a great deal during the sessions. The most common type of assistance was a tutor's simply telling a child a word when the child was having trouble. Tutors often encouraged students to look at the pictures in the text to help them get the words. Tutors encouraged children to sound out words often, and also asked them to read the rest of the sentence to figure out from its meaning or context what a word was. Tutors would repeat words that children had difficulty with after it was figured out. Tutors discussed word meaning, within the context of stories read.

Comprehension strategies used most often were questions. These questions were mainly within the literal level of thinking. Prereading discussion centered on pointing out the title, author, and illustrator in the book. Children were often asked to retell stories for sequence and inclusion of story structure elements after reading a story. Inferential and critical questions were asked infrequently. Those that were asked focused on what students liked about particular stories and predicting what they thought would happen next in the story. Some questions asked students to relate stories read to real-life experiences.

Writing was not as much a part of the tutoring as reading. Decoding strategies and spelling were used most often by the tutors to help their students with writing. The tutors helped the students to spell individual words. Questions about letter names or their sounds were posed to encourage students to spell words more independently. Tutors also asked questions to structure their tutees' writing, and they verbally modeled written language by dictating phrases.

DISCUSSION

It is apparent from the quantitative data that the children in the experimental group benefited from being tutored. On two of the four literacy measures, they scored significantly better than the children who did not receive tutoring. On the two measures that were given to all grade levels, more of the improvement occurred in kindergarten and first grade, and less in second and third. There could have been several reasons for this. It may have been easier to show gains with younger children than with those who had been struggling longer. It was also apparent from interview data that the kindergarten and first-grade teachers liked having the tutors more than the second- and third-grade teachers did. The K–1 teachers discussed with the tutors the help the children needed; they gave tutors materials; and they set aside time for the tutoring to take place in their regular school day. Tutors worked with children when these teachers took reading groups. Then the teachers took the children for their guided reading instruction as well.

None of the grades made significant gains in the tests of writing given to them. In the observational data of the dyads during tutoring sessions that were audiotaped and videotaped, it was apparent that tutors spent little or no time on writing activities during the entire 30 weeks with the children they tutored.

The affective qualities described by teachers, tutors, and children related to tutoring in the qualitative interviews suggest that the program had a very positive influence in this regard, and that there was a desire to continue by all. In reviewing the responses of the children, we perceived that the affective domain was of paramount importance to them.

LIMITATIONS OF THE STUDY

Teachers in second and third grades found the tutoring during school hours to be intrusive and often didn't let the tutors take the children. They tended to give the tutors the basic texts to work with, as well as workbook-type materials. The tutors had been trained to use a variety of strategies to motivate the children to read and write, but they were able to use these strategies less frequently with the older students than was observed in the sessions of the kindergarten and first-grade tutors. In addition, although they knew that this was an experimental group, some of the teachers in second and third grades were able to get tutors for children in the control group, which certainly could have had an effect on the study's outcome. Their doing this was understandable, because they felt students in need were being deprived of extra help, since we had randomly assigned experimental and control groups in the same classrooms. Although for the purposes of conducting a high-quality study this was an appropriate research design, it was not practical for the class-room. Children in the control group should have been drawn from an-other classroom or school that had similar students for the sample.

In spite of some of the problems that occurred, such as scheduling difficulties, teachers' feeling that tutors were interfering with the instruc-tion of children, and teachers' ignoring the experimental protocol by getting help for students in the control group, the interview data demon-strate that teachers, tutors, and children enjoyed the tutoring experience, and that all wanted the program to continue with some modifications. They felt that the tutoring was of great value for literacy improvement. These data are validated by the fact that the next academic year, when offered the opportunity for America Reads tutors, all teachers who had participated previously asked for tutors again. There were some stipula-tions made by the teachers, such as no control groups in their classrooms and more teacher input into scheduling. In response to the teachers' requests, the second and third grades received tutoring in the after-school program, and the kindergarten and first-grade students continued to receive tutoring during school hours.

In this preliminary study of the effects of a volunteer tutoring pro-gram on literacy achievement and attitudes, there are indications of modest, and in some cases statistically significant, gains. Further research with larger sample sizes is needed to confirm the impact tutors can have on student achievement, and to determine the best way to prepare and supervise nonprofessional tutors.

A very important word of caution is necessary, however. As Barbara Wasik (1998) has noted, effective tutors must be involved in a training program and must have materials to refer to as guides for tutoring. They also need one or more individuals to discuss concerns with them and to guide them through the tutoring experience. This type of careful mentoring will enable tutors to provide the one-to-one assistance that can be invaluable as children practice what they have learned in the classroom. Reading is a complex process that must be taught by indi-viduals who have had formal training, such as classroom teachers and reading specialists. However, we envision tutors as mentors who share personal thoughts and offer support for reading. Regardless of the tu-tors' age or experience, they have the ability to help students. The per-sonal support creates a sparkle in the students' eyes as they experience success. We hope the tutors will also have a sparkle in their eyes as they experience the excitement of sharing literacy. Federal work–study stu-dents and other interested members of the community can be valuable contributors in this ambitious and important effort to assist struggling readers.

REFERENCES

Clay, M. M. (1985). *The early detection of reading difficulties* (3rd ed.). Portsmouth, NH: Heinemann.

Juel, C. (1996). What makes literacy tutoring effective? *Reading Research Quarterly, 31,* 268–289.

Lloyd, D. N. (1978). Predictions of school failure from third grade data. *Educational and Psychological Measurement, 38,* 1193–1200.

Miles, M. B., & Huberman, A. M. (1984). Drawing meaning from qualitative data: Towards a shared craft. *Educational Researcher, 13*(4), 20–30.

Monson, D., & Sebesta, S. (1991). Reading preferences. In J. Flood, J. Jensen, & J. Squire (Eds.), *Handbook of research on teaching the English language arts I* (pp. 664–673). New York: Macmillan.

Morris, D., Shaw, B., & Perney, J. (1990). Helping low readers in grades 2 and 3: An after-school volunteer tutoring program. *Elementary School Journal, 91,* 133–147.

Morrow, L. M. (1992). The impact of a literature-based program on literacy achievement, use of literature, and attitudes of children from minority backgrounds. *Reading Research Quarterly, 27,* 250–275.

Morrow, L. M., Pressley, M., Smith, J., & Smith, M. (1997). The effects of a literature-based program integrated into literacy and science instruction with children from diverse backgrounds. *Reading Research Quarterly, 32*(1), 54–76.

Morrow, L. M., & Walker, B. J. (1997). *The reading team: A handbook for volunteer tutors K–3.* Newark, DE: International Reading Association.

Neuman, S. B. (1995). Reading together: A community-supported parent tutoring program. *The Reading Teacher, 49,* 120–129.

Pellegrini, A., & Galda, L. (1982). The effects of thematic fantasy play training on the development of children's story comprehension. *American Educational Research Journal, 19,* 443–452.

Sulzby, E. (1986). Kindergarteners as writers and readers. In M. Farr (Ed.), *Advances in writing research: Vol. 1. Children's early writing* (pp. 127–200). Norwood, NJ: Ablex.

Thorndyke, P. (1977). Cognitive structures in comprehension and memory of narrative discourse. *Cognitive Psychology, 9,* 77–110.

Walker, B. J., & Morrow, L. M. (1998). *Tips for the reading team: Strategies for tutors.* Newark, DE: International Reading Association.

Wasik, B. A. (1998). Volunteer tutoring programs in reading: A review. *Reading Research Quarterly, 33,* 266–292.

Chapter 7

AMERICA READS: A CLOSE-UP LOOK AT WHAT TWO TUTORS LEARNED ABOUT TEACHING READING

Jill Fitzgerald

The advent of the America Reads initiative in 1996 immediately engendered controversy in academic and practitioner literacy communities. The majority of prior literacy efforts to provide extra support for children in the early grades have been in-school programs that have involved one-on-one teaching by extensively trained professionals, with Reading Recovery as the prototype of such interventions (see Hiebert, 1994). At center stage in the controversy is the question of whether undergraduate work–study students with no or very little training in teaching reading can have a significant impact on young children's reading abilities (see Wasik, 1998). Unfortunately, few prior studies have directly examined tutor training for reading instruction. At least two recent studies do suggest that either *long-term training* of college students as tutors (Juel, 1996) or *intense and directed supervision* of community volunteers by graduates in reading education (Invernizzi, Rosemary, Juel, & Richards, 1997) can have an impact on children's reading progress. Still, little is known about the effectiveness of minimally trained tutors for children's reading achievement, and virtually nothing is known about what such tutors learn about teaching reading and/or how they conduct tutoring sessions.

The University of North Carolina at Chapel Hill was one of the original participants in the America Reads initiative. At our university, we collected data during the first year of tutoring (1997–1998) in an effort to address the central controversial issues surrounding the America Reads initiative. First, to examine the question of whether work–study students with minimal training could enhance children's reading abilities, I focused on the children's reading abilities and achievement across the year. Second, to explore the question of how minimally trained tutors work with children, I also closely followed two tutors to investigate what they learned about teaching reading as well as how they learned.

In this chapter, I focus mainly on the latter investigation. To provide some context, I first briefly describe selected features of the full evaluation of the program's effectiveness. Numbers of participants are given, the tutoring session format is described in detail, and broad results of the evaluation are provided. Next I discuss the case study of the two tutors, reporting details of the tutoring program and the tutor training, as well as the findings about what and how the two tutors learned about teaching reading. Finally, I explicate implications of the findings of the two-tutor case study.

BRIEF SYNOPSIS OF KEY FEATURES OF OUR AMERICA READS PROGRAM AND ITS OVERALL EFFECTIVENESS

As a preface to explicating the case study, here is a brief synopsis of the overall tutoring program and its effectiveness on our campus. Thirty-nine undergraduate college work–study students participated in our America Reads initiative during its first year (1997–1998). In all, 144 children in first through third grades received some amount of tutoring. The college students were trained over approximately 20 hours in various aspects of tutoring. Six work–study graduate students supervised the tutors.

The School of Education Literacy Studies faculty (James W. Cunningham, Dixie Lee Spiegel, and myself) at the University of North Carolina at Chapel Hill designed the tutoring sessions format based on assumptions gleaned from previous theory and research. The same faculty also conducted most of the training. Key assumptions about children's learning were as follows: (1) Children learn to read by reading in meaningful contexts; (2) the ultimate goal of reading is gaining and making meaning with text; (3) the major work of beginning reading is "getting words"; (4) "phonological awareness," or the ability to hear separate words, chunks in words, and separate sounds in words, is an important corollary to early literacy learning; (5) reading and writing develop simultaneously, and learning in one informs learning in the other; and (6) learning to read is facilitated through interaction with a more knowledgeable other.

The tutoring sessions format was modeled after aspects of Reading Recovery lessons and a format used by Invernizzi et al. (1997). This format was designed to incorporate sound techniques that have been documented in research studies to be effective. There were four parts: repeated reading of familiar text, word study, writing for sounds, and reading a new book. The first part of the session, rereading, has been shown to facilitate fluency (Samuels, Schermer, & Reinking, 1992), to aid automaticity in word recognition (Samuels, 1979), and to help in comprehension (Dowhower, 1987; Rasinski, 1990).

The word study portion consisted of various activities and games designed to (1) explicitly teach sight words; (2) explicitly teach several word-getting strategies (using context to get words, structural analysis, and/or phonics); and (3) provide practice in learning sight words and word-getting strategies. Prior research suggests that *explicitly* helping children to analyze words and learn strategies may be especially beneficial to at-risk readers (e.g., Lysynchuk, Pressley, d'Ailly, Smith, & Cake, 1989; Pearson, 1984, 1985).

In the writing-for-sounds component, children were asked to write a sentence of their choosing. During this writing, a tutor could use various prompting activities designed to assist a child in developing phonological awareness and knowledge of letters associated with sounds. Prior research suggests that segmenting speech and matching letters to sounds, which are required of young children as they begin to write short sentences, are excellent activities for developing phonemic awareness (Clay, 1985; see Invernizzi et al., 1997).

Last, a new book was presented to each child through guided reading. This part of the format was designed as a way for children to progress through increasingly difficult books via "scaffolded" instruction. Scaffolding provided by a knowledgeable other in material that has a few, but not too many, unknown words is a good way to increase children's learning (see Vygotsky, 1978).

Each child received two 40-minute tutoring sessions per week. These sessions were intended to supplement (not replace) classroom reading instruction. Tutors were required to maintain brief lesson plans. Tutors selected books for the tutoring sessions from a set of "leveled" books often used in Reading Recovery (e.g., Wright Group books). Supervisors visited tutoring sessions at least once a week, and also held 1-hour group meetings to address questions with their tutors once a month.

The main conclusions of the evaluation of program effects on first- and second-grade children's reading abilities (Fitzgerald, in press) were as follows:

1. Comparisons using a within-program control group showed that, on average, children made significant gains in instructional reading level that could be attributed to the tutoring. The average gain for children

receiving the full term of tutoring was 1.19 grade levels during 6 months of tutoring.

2. The greatest impact of tutoring was on children's ability to read words.

3. Among the children who received the full term of tutoring, most of their growth in instructional reading level occurred during the second half of the program.

4. Patterns of growth in instructional reading level were different for low- and high-gains groups of children. Whereas low-gains children made minimal progress and showed no marked differences between the first and second half of tutoring, high-gains children made reasonably good progress during the first half of tutoring and exceptional progress during the second half.

WHAT AND HOW CAN INEXPERIENCED TUTORS LEARN ABOUT TEACHING READING?

In the remainder of this chapter, I describe in detail the study of two focal tutors' learning about teaching reading.

The Two Focal Tutor Triads

For the case study of tutors' learning about teaching reading, two focal tutors were chosen and followed throughout the academic year of tutoring. One child tutored by each college student was also selected, so that the tutor was seen with the same child each time an observation was done. Although the main focus of the case study was on the tutors, the tutors, the selected children, and the tutors' supervisors formed two triads for the study.

One tutor was Naomi, a black sophomore majoring in psychology who was planning to go to graduate school. (Pseudonyms are used throughout this chapter.) Naomi had no prior tutoring experience. She wanted to be an America Reads tutor, she said, "to help children." She tutored Rob, a 6-year-old white child whose mother was a teacher assistant in his school. Her supervisor was Eva, a black woman in her late 20s who was a doctoral student in reading. Eva had a master's degree in reading education and had taught kindergarten and first grade for 4 years.

The other focal tutor was Reba, a white sophomore majoring in English who was considering becoming a teacher. When in high school, Reba had tutored a few elementary-age children in math for half a year. Reba wanted to be an America Reads tutor because she was interested in teaching and reading development. She tutored Ricardo, also a 6-year-old white child. Her supervisor was Jay, a white male who was in the School of Information and Library Sciences master's program. Jay had no prior tutoring experience and no prior work in education.

The two children had remarkably similar reading profiles at the beginning of the year. For example, they started in books at levels 2 and 3 (Reading Recovery levels), and neither could successfully pass a pre-primer passage on an informal reading inventory.

Data Collection and Analyses

Data were collected from six sources:

1. The tutors and supervisors completed entry and exit question-naires that emphasized demographic information, views on tutoring and supervising, self-ratings and ratings of each other, views on what was most and least important in making a good tutor or supervisor, and their sources for tutoring ideas.

2. Structured interviews were conducted with the two tutors and their supervisors at the beginning and the end of the year. These inter-views probed various issues, such as how things were going, where they were getting ideas for helping the children, ability to interpret diagnostic instruments, knowledge of appropriate instructional levels of materi-als, how to treat various kinds of miscues, their own thinking about gen-erating comprehension questions, and how to support vocabulary mean-ing development.

3. We also interviewed the children at the beginning and end of the year, and the classroom teachers at the end of the year.

4. Tutors were observed by either myself or a research associate once a month, and follow-up interviews were conducted with the tutor after each observation.

5. Also, each supervisor was interviewed after at least three observed sessions at the beginning, middle, and end of the year.

6. Tutors also tape-recorded at least one tutoring session every 2 weeks. All tape recordings were later transcribed.

We did four main kinds of analyses:

1. Interpretive analyses were done to locate patterns and themes, using case procedures outlined by Merriam (1988).

2. A microanalysis was done of randomly selected beginning, middle, and ending tutoring sessions, which involved detailed coding of the func-tion, form, and content of talk in the sessions. Reliabilities for coding ranged from .71 to 1.00.

3. From the beginning, middle, and ending tutoring session transcripts, randomly selected passages were analyzed in which a tutor responded to a child's word-reading errors.

4. Finally, we analyzed sections of the entry and exit structured interviews for the tutors' and supervisors' abilities to diagnose the following: appropriate instructional-level reading materials, ability to respond to reading errors during instruction, ability to formulate higher-level comprehension questions, and ability to facilitate students' derivation of word meanings.

Results

In the following sections, I first give the three main conclusions of the study. Then I explicate the three conclusions by providing examples of evidence from the beginning of the tutoring; by showing how each supervisor worked with the respective tutors; and, finally, by explicating and comparing the two tutors' growth by year's end in learning about teaching reading.

Conclusions: The Big Picture

Three main conclusions were drawn:

1. First, both Naomi's and Reba's tutoring changed in two main ways during the tutoring year. By the end of the year, both were more able to place their students in appropriate instructional-level reading materials, and both shifted the types of word recognition strategies they prompted their children to use, though Naomi made far more shifts than Reba.

2. Second, however, it is clear that learning about teaching reading is a complex and time-consuming process. Even by the end of the year, neither tutor's sessions contained a large number of essential features that most reading specialists would consider desirable characteristics of high-quality reading lessons.

3. Third, Naomi (the tutor who had a very knowledgeable supervisor) made substantially more changes, and more improvements, in her teaching than did Reba (the tutor who had a supervisor who was also learning about tutoring in reading).

Starting Out

The two tutors' initial tutoring sessions were highly similar in several respects. I illustrate here with one of Naomi's early sessions; however, similar conclusions were drawn about Reba's early sessions as well. For the part of the session given here, Naomi had chosen a new book that Rob had not seen before. This was the guided reading component of the lesson, though Naomi's interpretation of "guidance" was different from what a reading specialist might hold. That is, she did not actually "guide" or scaffold or structure the reading well.

Naomi spent several minutes asking questions about the book, mainly trying to use words as they talked that she thought Rob might have trouble reading. Here are some of the prereading questions she asked along with Rob's answers:

NAOMI: What kind of animal is that he's holding?
ROB: A cat.
NAOMI: And what are he and his cat doing?
ROB: Sitting together.
NAOMI: What does he have in his hand?
ROB: A book.
NAOMI: What is he drinking then?
ROB: Coffee.
NAOMI: What is this building?
ROB: A castle.

This sort of prereading questioning went on for several minutes. Then Naomi asked Rob to read, and the following sequence ensued. The first two sentences in the book were these: "I like sitting in my castle high up in the sky. I like sitting in my cottage with the forest just nearby."

ROB: I like sitting in my castle high up in the sky. I like sitting in my carriage . . .
NAOMI: You don't know what that word is? Look at the word. You know what sound that "w" has, don't you? What sound does a "w" have?
ROB: "Wuh."
NAOMI: Right, and that's a short "i" sound. So what does that sound like?
ROB: "Wuh" "ih."
NAOMI: What does a "t" and an "h" together make?
ROB: "Th."
NAOMI: Good. So what is that word? Put all those sounds together. What do you think that word could be? I'll tell you what. Go back and read the beginning of the sentence and see what makes sense.
ROB: I like sitting in my carriage wi . . .
NAOMI: OK. I'll tell you what. Before we begin on this word, you said this word was "carriage." Does this look like "carriage"? Does that

word look like "carriage"? What do you think that word is? Where did we say she was sitting? What kind of house?

ROB: (*Inaudible.*)

Rob stopped to work out about one out of every six words. In nearly every case, Naomi used a similar sequence for error correction—urging Rob to "look at the word" and to use phonics—although she occasionally prompted him to use context. At the end, there was no discussion of the book.

What can we see here? First, the text level was too hard. Rob's word recognition error rate while reading during this session was 19%.

Second, prereading questions mainly focused on low-level labeling. Table 7.1 also gives summary information about a randomly selected early session that supports this conclusion. It shows that during guided reading, of Naomi's talk about meaning (which was informative, eliciting, or directing sorts of talk), a full 52% was low-level labeling. (See the column

TABLE 7.1. Percentages of Tutors' Meaning Talk during Guided Reading That Involved Different Kinds of Content

Type of meaning talk	Naomi		Reba	
	Beginning (42 turns)	End (36 turns)	Beginning (38 turns)	End (11 turns)
Low-level	59	20	18	63
Demonstrating	0	0	0	0
Labeling	52	0	8	27
Describing	5	17	5	27
Observing	2	3	5	9
Medium-level	26	81	64	27
Declaring	0	0	3	0
Clarifying	7	11	5	0
Events	17	67	32	9
Goals	2	0	0	9
Reproducing	0	0	13	0
Word meaning	0	0	11	18
High-level	14	0	19	9
Evaluating	7	0	11	0
Real world	7	0	8	9

Note. Types of meaning talk are based on meaning talk that was already classified as informative, eliciting, or directing in function, because other function categories (such as reading or giving feedback) could not be subclassified. Also, percentages do not always sum precisely to 100% due to rounding.

marked "Beginning.") In this regard, Reba's talk was somewhat different from Naomi's in the beginning, in that she did use more medium-level (64%) and high-level (19%) meaning talk than Naomi. For example, Table 7.1 shows that 32% of her talk in a beginning session was about events, versus only 8% for labeling.

Third, an inordinate amount of time in this book reading focused on talk about words. Table 7.2 shows that 43% of Naomi's talk in a beginning session was about words. Similarly, Table 7.2 shows that 59% of Reba's talk in a beginning session was about words.

Fourth, Naomi displayed little knowledge about how to help Rob "get the words." She prompted him almost exclusively to "look at the word" and to use phonics. Table 7.3 again shows summary information for a beginning session that supports this conclusion for both Naomi and Reba. Thirty-one percent of Naomi's word-focused talk during guided reading (which was informative, eliciting, or directing talk), and 52% of Reba's, was directed toward calling the child's attention to a word—for example, by simply saying something like "Look at it," or by telling the word. Thirty-one percent of Naomi's word-focused talk, and 24% of Reba's, was about phonics. (Notably, Naomi did also encourage monitoring approximately one-fourth [28%] of the time.)

Supervisors at Work

The two supervisors worked with the tutors in significantly different ways. In this section, I illustrate these different work styles. I start with Eva, Naomi's supervisor.

From the start, Eva arrived at Naomi's tutoring sessions about halfway through a session at least once a week. She sat at the table with Naomi and Rob, and often she chimed in and helped with the lesson; she modeled how to work with Rob to encourage higher-level thinking, develop-

TABLE 7.2. Percentages of Tutors' Talk during Guided Reading That Involved Different Kinds of Content

Type of content	Naomi		Reba	
	Beginning	End	Beginning	End
	(115 turns)	(77 turns)	(87 turns)	(121 turns)
Meaning	53	66	39	31
Word-focused	43	31	59	58
Other	3	3	2	12

Note. Percentages do not always sum precisely to 100% due to rounding.

TABLE 7.3. Percentages of Tutors' Word-Focused Talk during Guided Reading That Involved Different Types of Content

Type of word-focused talk	Naomi		Reba	
	Beginning	End	Beginning	End
	(36 turns)	(22 turns)	(54 turns)	(45 turns)
"Just say the word"	31	9	52	36
Encouraging monitoring	28	36	2	13
Eliciting a general strategy	3	0	0	2
Asking to use context	6	18	13	4
Asking to use structural analysis	3	23	9	31
Asking to use graphophonics	31	14	24	13

Note. Types of word-focused talk are based on word-focused talk that was already classified as informative, eliciting, or directing in function, because other function categories (such as reading or giving feedback) could not be subclassified. Also, percentages do not always sum precisely to 100% due to rounding.

ment of a wide array of word-getting strategies, greater reliance on self-monitoring, cross-checking, use of context, and use of analogous words. Indeed, her considerable presence in the sessions is signaled in Table 7.4, which shows that 17% and 25% of all the talk turns in a beginning and ending session, respectively, were Eva's.

Here are a couple of examples. In the first illustration, from a lesson in January, Eva modeled how to ask questions. Naomi began with a prereading questioning sequence identical in nature to the one I have given above, showing Naomi at the start. After Naomi asked four low-level labeling questions, Eva jumped in and raised the stakes with a couple of higher-level questions.

TABLE 7.4. Percentages of All Talk Turns during Guided Reading That Were Tutor, Child, or Supervisor Talk

Person talking	Naomi		Reba	
	Beginning	End	Beginning	End
	(202 total turns)	(227 total turns)	(262 total turns)	(234 total turns)
Tutor	57	38	61	52
Child	26	38	38	38
Supervisor	17	25	1	11

Note. Percentages do not always sum precisely to 100% due to rounding.

Rob: A turtle.

Naomi: Yeah, the turtle is coming out of the water, isn't he?

Eva: I wonder why? Why do you suppose that's happening?

Naomi: (*As if on cue, echoing some of Eva's words*) I wonder what the turtle is going to do when he gets out of the water?

In the next example, Eva modeled how to prompt Rob to develop word-getting strategies. This segment was from the same January lesson, but it illustrates the writing-for-sounds component. Naomi had a small "white board" (similar to a blackboard, but with a white background; washable markers are used to write on it) and asked Rob to read the sentence she had written: "This is my ball." He read it successfully. She asked him to make the sentence say, "This is my fast ball," and Rob replied, "It's too hard," and he didn't want to do it. After considerable cajoling and sounding out of the word, Rob finished. Then Naomi asked him to change it to "His ball is fast." She struggled to help him with the word "his."

Rob: OK. His. How do you write "his," anyway?

Naomi: His.

Rob: H? S?

Naomi: . . . We went over it [before].

Then Eva jumped in and modeled a different kind of prompting that would help Rob to build the strategy of reading and writing words by using analogous words that he already knew.

Eva: What word do you know that kind of sounds like "his" that's already up here [on the white board]? There's one up there that kind of sounds like "his."

Rob: Oh.

Eva: Do you see one?

Rob: Yeah.

Eva: Which one is it? What is that word?

Rob: "Is."

Eva: How can you make "is" into "his?"

Rob: That's easy.

Eva: One letter that you have to add. Let's see if you can figure it out.

These excerpts show how Eva worked to model "good teaching." In effect, Eva performed mentoring work in which she demonstrated ways of showing, leading, coaching, and ways of talking that she felt would help Rob develop essential early reading strategies and habits. In interviews, Eva talked about how she consciously tried to do such modeling, believing that providing for Naomi the experience of seeing and hearing an "expert" do it was far better than "telling" Naomi what to do.

Jay's style of working with Reba was a stark contrast to Eva's. In interviews, Jay said that he thought his main job was to be a sort of "boss." He considered his primary responsibilities to make sure that Reba was on time; that she completed the four lesson parts; that she completed "paperwork" required by the America Reads coordinator; and, in general, that "things ran smoothly."

Though he sat in on tutoring sessions at least once a week, Jay rarely spoke during the lessons, and when he did, his presence tended to be a negative influence. For example, Table 7.4 shows that only 1% of the talk turns in a beginning session were Jay's, and only 11% were in an ending session. This latter percentage was an unusually high amount of talk for Jay.

His few comments during lessons tended to take Ricardo out of the lessons and to focus on nonrelated topics. Here is an example, from one of Reba's last tutoring sessions. She was beginning the guided reading component of the lesson, introducing Ricardo to a new book about T-shirts. Notice how Jay intruded upon the lesson and led Ricardo away from the topic to a discussion about his previous writing about his cruise trip.

REBA: OK. Let's talk about T-shirts. Do you like T-shirts?

RICARDO: Well, I'm wearing one.

REBA: I like that T-shirt.

JAY: There are many colors on that T-shirt. Did you make it yourself?

RICARDO: My brother made this one.

REBA: [Prepping for the story, in which the sizes and types of T-shirts give clues to the persons they belong to.] The neat thing about T-shirts is that you can tell a lot about the person that is wearing them. You got that on the cruise, didn't you? [Ricardo had gone on a cruise with his family and had been writing about it during the writing-for-sounds segment of the tutoring sessions.]

RICARDO: Uh-huh.

REBA: That is really neat.

JAY: That's the cruise that you have been writing about all this time, right?

RICARDO: Uh-huh.

JAY: "Royal Caribbean." That's a hard word. "Caribbean" is a hard word.

RICARDO: Well, I write it in the book.

JAY: Oh yeah. You were able to write "Caribbean," weren't you? Wasn't he?

REBA: I don't think he . . .

RICARDO: No. I never write it.

JAY: Oh. You didn't. You had written another word that was really difficult.

RICARDO: Hold on. Did I? Hold on. Let me see. Let me see my book. (*Shuffling*)

REBA: Ricardo, let's save your writing to the end.

JAY: Yeah. I'm sorry we have to read.

Notice also that in his last words, Jay negatively implied that reading and sticking with the tutor's direction were less enjoyable than general conversing.

Tutors' Growth and Plateaus

Both Naomi and Reba grew in learning about tutoring, although Naomi made far more growth. They both made progress in two ways. First, both grew in the ability to place their students in appropriate instructional-level materials. The importance of having students read at their instructional, and not frustrational, level was emphasized by the School of Education Literacy Studies faculty during large-group training sessions. Also, the faculty showed tutors how to determine appropriate levels of reading texts, and the America Reads coordinator visited tutoring sessions to provide advice on "best" levels. The tutors' increased ability to locate their children's instructional reading levels was reflected in the data in at least two ways. One indication was that during our observations of tutoring sessions, we noted that children's error rates were noticeably lower as time passed.

Other evidence came from the structured interviews that were done with tutors and supervisors. During the interview, each tutor was shown three versions of a child's reading of a primer-level passage. One version represented an independent reading level, in which the child's reading was 99% accurate. A second version represented instructional-level reading of 95% accuracy. A third showed frustrational-level reading, with less than 90% accuracy. During the pretutoring interview, both Naomi and Reba picked the frustrational-level passages as the ones they thought best represented the level of difficulty that should be used with the child reader. Naomi said, ". . . I think he [the child reader] did pretty good. If he was helped, this would be about the right level. If he read it this way, I would stay in this level." Reba said, "It's workable. There are things there he can work on." In the posttutoring interview, both picked the instructional-level passage.

Second, both Naomi and Reba shifted their ways of prompting children to use word recognition strategies, although Naomi changed far more in this regard than did Reba. Table 7.3 shows that by the end of the year they each decreased the amount of emphasis on their two earlier mainstay prompts to "just say the word" and use phonics, although Reba continued to rely considerably on "just say the word."

However, whereas Reba's tutoring did not change dramatically in other ways, the nature of Naomi's tutoring shifted in some additional areas. First, her questioning that was related to meaning became more sophisticated, moving away from the initial emphasis on lower-level labeling to a later emphasis on medium- and higher-level thinking. For example, the following is an extension of the January session in which Rob was reading about turtles. In the earlier excerpt we saw Eva's modeling. Notice in this segment how, following Eva's lead, Naomi's questions now more frequently tapped higher-level thinking.

NAOMI: . . . What is he doing? You see the dirt flying? What do you think that turtle could be doing?

ROB: He's digging.

NAOMI: He's digging a hole, huh? I wonder why he's digging a hole? Do you know why turtles dig holes?

ROB: For his eggs.

NAOMI: Yes, she's laying her eggs. Do you know why turtles dig holes to bury their eggs?

ROB: I don't know.

NAOMI: So all the other animals don't eat their eggs. . . . What do you think they're doing while she's watching, while she's laying her eggs?

Such movement toward higher-level discussion is also reflected in the figures in Table 7.1, which show a progression from early emphasis on low-level talk related to meaning (59%) to an ending emphasis on medium-level talk (81%). Also note in this table that Reba did not show a similar shift. Rather, her low-level talk increased (from 18% to 63%), and her middle- and high-level talk actually decreased over time (from 64% to 27% and from 19% to 9%, respectively).

Next, as time went on, meaning-related talk increased during Naomi's tutoring sessions, and word-related talk decreased. For example, Table 7.2 shows that her meaning-related talk during the guided reading portion of the session moved from 53% to 66% from the beginning to the end. Also note again that Reba did not show a parallel shift, with her meaning-related talk remaining relatively constant at 39% and 31% from the beginning to the end.

Finally, over time, Naomi emphasized a much wider variety of word-getting strategies. Table 7.3 shows that in contrast to her earlier reliance on "just saying the word" and using phonics, at the end of the year Naomi placed greater emphasis on encouraging Rob to monitor his errors (her main prompt at 36%), and also prompted him far more often to use context (18%) and structural analysis (23%). This wider range of prompting may be seen in the following example from a February lesson. Rob read, "She said, 'No more monkeys jumping on the bed.' So five little monkeys fell fast asleep." He then stopped and looked at Naomi. The next words in the book were "'Thank goodness,' said the Mama."

> NAOMI: You want to skip that word and go on to this one?
> ROB: I don't know that one.
> NAOMI: Do you know this word, if I cover that up [covering up "ness" in "goodness" to prompt for analysis of the structure of the word]?
> ROB: "Good."
> NAOMI: Yeah, and if I add this to it, what does that say? What sound does that "n" have [prompting for phonics]?
> ROB: Nn-nn.
> NAOMI: What could she possibly be saying that says "blank good . . ." [prompting to use context]? You had the "good" part right. Let's see if you can get your mouth ready to say this ending part [prompting to use phonics plus context], and see if you can figure out the word [prompting to be strategic].

Rob resisted all of Naomi's efforts and refused to attempt the word. Finally, she told him that the word was "goodness." Naomi then prompted him to use context to get "Thank," and he did.

> NAOMI: OK. Why did you think that was "Thank" [prompting to monitor his word recognition]?

Table 7.3 shows some similar shift in the variety of Reba's word recognition prompts, especially for using structural analysis, but the overall shift was not nearly as striking; most notably, her heavy reliance on prompting to "just say the word," an essential nonstrategic prompt, continued to the end.

Finally, it is important to point to some general impressions that I gleaned from reading and rereading the transcripts of tutoring sessions, as well as from observing some of the sessions. Even by the end of the year, neither tutor's sessions contained a large number of essential features that most reading specialists would consider desirable characteristics of high-quality reading lessons. For example, neither tutor provided much scaffolded or guided reading; neither engaged her child in extended postreading discussion; both tutors had difficulty keeping their children motivated and involved in the lessons, and, as a corollary, neither pace nor student energy expended in reading was optimal; and even

Naomi, who by the end was more adept than Reba at responding to word recognition errors, continued to struggle with fitting her responses to the particular errors.

The Children's Growth

How well did the two children read at the end of the year? Interestingly, the two children's reading profiles over the year remained remarkably similar! For example, at the end of tutoring in March, they were reading books at Reading Recovery levels 9 and 10, and both successfully passed the primer passage on an informal reading inventory. So it appears—at least with regard to achievement levels—that the distinctive differences between Naomi and Reba in learning about teaching reading, as well as their supervisors' different techniques for helping them, may not have been related to these two children's progress in reading.

CONCLUSION AND DISCUSSION

In sum, I reiterate three basic conclusions

1. Inexperienced tutors can make growth in learning about tutoring in reading. For instance, Naomi and Reba grew in the ability to place their students in appropriate instructional-level materials, and although Naomi made more growth than Reba, both learned at least some ways to prompt children to use word recognition strategies.

2. Learning to tutor in reading is tough. It is difficult to start with little or no knowledge about the reading process or about teaching reading and, in the span of just a few months, to produce high-quality reading lessons.

3. Although campus training can influence tutors' growth, an experienced coach/mentor may be a more powerful influence than distanced, albeit knowledgeable, university professors.

The conclusions of my study of two tutors' learning lead to questions about what factors enabled the tutors' growth, and especially about why one tutor made so much more growth than the other. These questions are not entirely answerable from the available data; however, the data do suggest possibilities that should be explored in future research. For example, evidence suggests that many factors probably contributed to Naomi's and Reba's learning. Both were open and absorbing tutors. During interviews, both mentioned that training sessions given at the university influenced some of their learning, and there were occasions when noticeable changes occurred in a tutoring session (e.g., in language and activities) immediately following a training session. The tutors' own intuitions about how to tutor may also have helped them to grow. Both indicated that they often relied upon their own beliefs about and past experiences in reading.

As for the differential growth between the two tutors, among all the possibilities, supervisor style stands out as the most central and powerful influence. The most obvious differences between the two tutor triads were in the supervisors' background, experience, and approaches to assisting the tutors. The data support the strong inference that a reading specialist who works as a coach/mentor alongside a tutor may more powerfully affect a tutor's learning about teaching reading than a directive, decontextualized "training" setting may. That is, a tutor may learn more about teaching reading in the collective moments of actual tutoring, through observing and working with a knowledgeable and experienced reading teacher who is working with the tutor's child, than from knowledgeable and experienced university professors telling about what and how to teach. This is not to say that distanced experts have no impact at all on tutors' growth. There was evidence in this study that in fact they can have an effect. However, situated coaches/mentors may have farther-reaching effects on tutors' understanding of central features of what they can do to nurture emergent readers' learning. Here we find fertile ground for future research on the roles of supervisors as potential mediators to children's learning about reading.

Perhaps one of the most significant findings of the study was that the children made nearly identical progress in learning to read. Yet one tutor, Naomi, seemed to be tutoring in ways that seemed more likely to lead to student instantiation of more beneficial reading habits; as well, she had an extremely knowledgeable and helpful supervisor. This is an extremely important finding to consider, because it suggests, albeit tentatively, that amount rather than quality of tutoring may be the most important factor in children's success in programs such as the America Reads tutoring program we implemented on our campus. This in turn leads to the question of what *is* important about tutoring in relation to children's growth in reading. Is quality of tutoring or amount of tutoring more important? Just what is the relationship between quantity and quality of tutoring? What are the key features of lessons that make a difference? Is simply reading to children all that matters? Do prompts for a variety of word-getting strategies matter? These are among the most important issues for future research. Within this exploration, it will be important to probe the children's meaning-making and word-analyzing *strategies* in relation to tutors' prompts for such strategies. That is, children's *thinking* about reading, as well as their reading levels or reading achievement, should be deeply explored, especially in relation to tutors' language and prompts.

Finally, results of the study of tutor triads suggest a future need for program designers to examine their own frameworks for assisting reading tutors. Research in teacher education has clearly shown that the positivist tradition of having experts tell about and talk about how to teach has generally had little impact on novice teachers' practices (Wideen, Mayer-Smith, & Moon, 1998). On the other hand, research in teacher education more clearly supports a coach/mentor model. In a limited way, the present study supports the contention that such results may also apply to tutor education. Consequently, it seems important that the philosophical and operational frameworks for assisting tutors be closely examined.

ACKNOWLEDGMENTS

Many thanks go to research associate Ruth Wolery and graduate assistant Paula Grove for their help in collecting and coding data; to America Reads coordinator Sandra Swenberg for her facilitation efforts; and to the tutors, their supervisors, and the children who participated in this study.

REFERENCES

Clay, M. M. (1985). *The early detection of reading difficulties.* Portsmouth, NH: Heinemann.

Dowhower, S. L. (1987). Effects of repeated reading on second grade transitional readers' fluency and comprehension. *Reading Research Quarterly, 22,* 389–406.

Fitzgerald, J. (in press). Can minimally trained college student volunteers help young at-risk children to read better? *Reading Research Quarterly.*

Hiebert, E. H. (1994). Reading recovery in the United States: What difference does it make to an age cohort? *Educational Researcher, 23,* 15–25.

Invernizzi, M., Rosemary, C., Juel, C., & Richards, H. C. (1997). At-risk readers and community volunteers: A 3-year perspective. *Scientific Studies of Reading, 1,* 277–300.

Juel, C. (1996). What makes literacy tutoring effective? *Reading Research Quarterly, 31,* 268–289.

Lysynchuk, L. M., Pressley, M., d'Ailly, H., Smith, M., & Cake, H. (1989). A methodological analysis of experimental studies of comprehension strategy instruction. *Reading Research Quarterly, 24,* 458–470.

Merriam, S. (1988). *Case study research in education.* San Francisco: Jossey-Bass.

Pearson, P. D. (1984). Direct explicit teaching of comprehension. In G. G. Duffy, L. R. Roehler, & J. Mason (Eds.), *Comprehension instruction: Perspectives and suggestions* (pp. 223–233). New York: Longman.

Pearson, P. D. (1985). Changing the face of reading comprehension instruction. *The Reading Teacher, 38,* 724–738.

Rasinski, T. (1990). Effects of repeated reading and listening-while-reading on reading fluency. *Journal of Educational Research, 83,* 147–150.

Samuels, S. J. (1979). The method of repeated readings. *The Reading Teacher, 32,* 403–408.

Samuels, S. J., Schermer, N., & Reinking, D. (1992). Reading fluency: Techniques for making decoding automatic. In S. J. Samuels & A. E. Farstrup (Eds.), *What research has to say about reading instruction* (pp. 124–144). Newark, DE: International Reading Association.

Vygotsky, L. (1978). *Mind in society* (M. Cole, V. John-Steiner, S. Scribner, & E. Souberman, Eds.). Cambridge, MA: Harvard University Press.

Wasik, B. A. (1998). Volunteer tutoring programs in reading: A review. *Reading Research Quarterly, 33,* 266–291.

Wideen, M., Mayer-Smith, J., & Moon, B. (1998). A critical analysis of the research on learning to teach: Making the case for an ecological perspective on inquiry. *Review of Educational Research, 68,* 130–178.

Chapter 8

AMERICA READS:
LITERACY LESSONS LEARNED

Ann J. Dromsky
Linda B. Gambrell

If hindsight is 20/20, then we have learned several critical lessons that continue to inform evaluation and reconceptualization of the America Reads tutoring program at the University of Maryland at College Park. Although research on America Reads is limited, the initial data from our evaluation efforts highlight many of the dynamic benefits of the program for students, schools, tutors, administrators, and the university.

This chapter examines the lessons we learned from implementation to evaluation of the America Reads program at the University of Maryland at College Park. Following a brief history of this program, we discuss current research on literacy tutoring and practices associated with successful literacy programs. In the next section, we describe the America Reads tutoring program at the University of Maryland in greater detail. In particular, we focus on the research-based principles that informed decisions about our program design in collaboration with the local school system. Then we present research on the literacy achievement of elementary students and the experiences of college mentors participating in the America Reads tutoring program. The chapter concludes with a discussion of the research findings and lessons for future research and program development.

PROGRAM HISTORY: AMERICA READS AT
THE UNIVERSITY OF MARYLAND

In December 1996, President Bill Clinton invited the University of Maryland at College Park to serve on the Presidential Steering Committee for the America Reads Challenge. In response, the university established the President's Task Force for America Reads, which currently includes members of the faculty and staff from the Commuter Affairs and Community Service Programs, the College of Education, the Office of Financial Aid, and University Cooperative Programs; it also includes the supervisor of reading and language arts for the local school system. Through the efforts of these individuals, the University of Maryland designed a tutoring program that currently places approximately 75 undergraduate mentors in eight local elementary schools each semester. These 75 mentors tutor approximately 400 elementary students. America Reads mentors must commit to working a minimum of 6 hours across 2 days per week. Mentors, as well as administrators, participate in regular evaluation and reflection. As America Reads expands to include more college and volunteer programs across the United States, an examination of the successful elements of tutoring programs becomes critical to maintaining high standards for literacy tutoring.

PRACTICES ASSOCIATED WITH EFFECTIVE LITERACY TUTORING

Results of the National Assessment of Educational Progress (1994) found that 40% of our nation's fourth graders were reading below expected levels. These data, coupled with increasing literacy demands in the workplace, prompted schools and politicians to develop tutoring and support programs for literacy instruction. The federal government likewise showed bipartisan support for tutoring with the America Reads Challenge Act of 1997 and the Reading Excellence Act of 1998. Although these initiatives provide literacy support for schools, few guidelines exist in the legislation for program development (Edmondson, 1998; Wasik, 1998a, 1998b). Institutions can therefore interpret and implement the America Reads Challenge Act without having to conform to the typical parameters of other educational programs. Wasik (1998a) has asserted, however, that the success of the America Reads Challenge depends on careful consideration of research on effective tutoring programs.

Wasik (1998) and Juel (1993) have reviewed literacy tutoring programs to identify the practices of various programs, as well as the existing knowledge base about volunteer literacy tutors. One-to-one tutoring is considered a powerful form of instruction; however, researchers have emphasized that several elements are necessary in order for individual tutoring sessions to be successful (Invernizzi, Juel, & Rosemary, 1996–1997; Juel, 1993; Wasik, 1998a, 1998b; Wasik & Slavin, 1993). Of primary importance is the lesson design (Juel, 1993; Wasik, 1998b; Wasik & Slavin,

1993). Research on early literacy acquisition favors a balanced approach to instruction that includes reading familiar texts for fluency, word/phonics study, writing, and reading a wide range of new materials to introduce and expand strategic reading behaviors (Bader, 1998; Morrow & Walker, 1997; Pressley, Rankin, & Yokoi, 1996).

In addition to the basic lesson followed by tutors, Wasik (1998a, 1998b) has identified eight components that have been documented as essential to the success of tutoring programs. According to Wasik (1998a, 1998b), successful tutoring programs include (1) a certified reading specialist to supervise tutors, (2) ongoing training and feedback for tutors, (3) structured tutoring sessions that incorporate basic literacy elements, (4) consistent and intensive tutoring, (5) access to high-quality materials, (6) ongoing assessment of students' progress, (7) school-based plans to monitor tutor attendance, and (8) coordination of tutoring with classroom instruction. These elements have been drawn from the research on early literacy tutoring models. First, Wasik (1998b) asserts that a certified reading specialist should supervise reading tutors. A reading specialist has the knowledge of literacy development that most tutors lack, and can offer the support necessary to execute lessons. Ideally the specialist, who plans lesson design and conducts ongoing observations and training of tutors, coordinates the program.

Training is an integral part of the University of Maryland's America Reads tutoring program. Wasik (1998b) suggests that literacy tutors receive training and feedback throughout program participation. Sufficient training of tutors requires more than a one-time in-service approach. The task of teaching individuals a basic understanding of the reading process is complex, and tutors require ongoing training to develop concepts (Invernizzi et al., 1996–1997; Juel, 1993; Wasik, 1998a). As tutors encounter new problems, they must have access to knowledgeable professionals who can provide the necessary interventions (Cox & Krueger, 1994; Wasik, 1998b).

Third, research shows that successful tutoring sessions are structured and contain basic elements (Wasik, 1998b). A balance among four common components of well-planned lessons—rereading of familiar text, word study, writing, and the introduction of new stories—is ideal (Invernizzi et al., 1996–1997; Morrow & Walker, 1997; Wasik, 1998a, 1998b). Students in the early stages of literacy development need explicit instruction in the reading of connected text at the same time that they are developing word analysis skills (Stahl, Duffy-Hester, & Stahl, 1998). A lesson composed of several elements demonstrates the nature of the reading process.

Wasik's fourth element emphasizes tutoring that is consistent and intensive. Struggling readers, in particular, need intensive practice with authentic reading tasks to develop the skills of independent readers (Allington, 1994; Wasik, 1998b). In addition to well-planned lessons and consistent tutoring, Wasik (1998b) suggests that tutors have access to high-quality materials that facilitate good literacy models. The availability of better reading materials enables tutors to select books that match planned objectives for students. Likewise, tutors should be equipped with materials such as paper, writing instruments, and sentence strips needed for word study or demonstration (Wasik, 1998b).

Sixth, Wasik (1998b) stresses the importance of assessing students' needs throughout the tutoring process. Informal assessments of areas such as concepts about print or high-frequency word recognition help educators make informed decisions about students' strengths and weaknesses (Sarracino, Herrmann, Batdorf, & Garfinkel, 1994; Wasik, 1998a, 1998b). Tutors who are trained to assess students' literacy learning can use information to plan future sessions that build upon students' strengths and develop new concepts.

Wasik's (1998b) last two elements of effective tutoring involve attendance and communication. Schools must first ensure that tutors attend sessions, and then seek ways to coordinate tutoring with classroom instruction. Far too often, students pulled for tutoring or after-school sessions do not read or connect lessons to classroom objectives (Allington, 1994). This practice leads to isolated instruction that further impedes progress for the struggling reader. Wasik (1998b) points out, however, that tutoring is not a "mirror image" of the classroom, but rather an extension and supplement to instruction.

Research on the effectiveness of tutoring provides a foundation for successful programs. The University of Maryland relied on current research when designing the literacy tutoring program. The eight elements described by Wasik (1998b) are evident in every aspect of the University of Maryland's America Reads tutoring program.

PROGRAM DESIGN: AMERICA READS AT THE UNIVERSITY OF MARYLAND

The America Reads tutoring program at the University of Maryland includes comprehensive training of tutors (called "mentors" in this program), ongoing observations of mentors, feedback/reflections from tutors, and assessment of the program at several levels. This reciprocal design of training, observation, feedback, and assessment allows for reconceptualizations of the program and contributes to initiatives that improve tutoring. This section outlines the basic design of the tutoring program.

At the core of our program is an intensive and consistent training schedule that prepares mentors for literacy tutoring (Wasik, 1998b). Mentors receive 12 hours of training prior to tutoring sessions, and 8 hours of training and development during the semester. Two reading specialists and Reading Recovery teachers from the local school system conduct initial training and two follow-up training and development sessions. America Reads staff members observe the mentors at least once, and school site supervisors evaluate each mentor over the course of the semester. These training sessions and evaluations help the America Reads staff identify areas of the program that need improvement.

Assessment is an important source of information before, during, and after any literacy instruction (Lipson & Wixson, 1997; Sarracino et al., 1994; Walker, 1996). Student performance should be monitored at several points over the course of the intervention program, to ensure that lessons are appropriate and effective (Lipson & Wixson, 1997; Walker, 1996). Careful observation and assessment also allow mentors to select the most practical techniques for individual students (Sarracino et al., 1994).

Prior to tutoring sessions, University of Maryland America Reads mentors learn to administer four simple literacy measures that help determine preliminary reading levels. The measurements include letter identification, high-frequency word recognition, writing, and dictation tasks. Mentors assess students' knowledge in these four areas at the beginning and end of each semester. The data are recorded on a final summary sheet for an uncontrolled statistical analysis of our program. Guidelines for administration of all assessments are covered in training and outlined in the America Reads training manual. This information, in addition to summary sheets of reading behaviors completed by the classroom teacher, aids each mentor in planning an effective lesson.

During training sessions, mentors learn to follow a four-part plan that incorporates key elements of a balanced literacy lesson (Bader, 1998; Morrow & Walker, 1997; Wasik, 1998b). A mentor records a student's performance during each lesson and uses the information to plan future sessions. Known as the Daily Log (see Figure 8.1), this record outlines the time allotment and instructional teaching points for each element of the lesson. Mentors begin by asking students to select and reread familiar books to practice fluency and automaticity in word recognition (Juel, 1993; Morrow & Walker, 1997). Familiar reading is one of the longer components of the lesson, as research shows that it is important to spend the majority of tutoring sessions engaged in real reading and writing tasks (Morrow & Walker, 1997; Pressley et al., 1996; Wasik, 1998a, 1998b).

The second part of the lesson incorporates word study, based on a student's familiar reading and/or basic sight words and word families. Word study helps develop phonemic awareness, orthographic knowledge, and vocabulary (Clay, 1993; Cunningham & Cunningham, 1992; Morrow & Walker, 1997; Stahl et al., 1998). Mentors use a variety of high-quality materials such as magnetic letters, dry-erase boards ("white boards"), and

Student's Name _____   Mentor's Signature _____

Lesson Number _____   Date _____

Time	Activities	Comments/Reactions
Suggested: 10 minutes Spent: _____	1. **Student Reading of Familiar Books:** Level: _____ Title: _____ Title: _____ Familiar or New Book: _____	Positives: Challenges:

Suggested:
5
minutes
Spent:
_____
	2. **Word Study:**
	
	Magnetic Letter Work
	High-Frequency
	  Words: _____
	Making Words: _____
	Word Families: _____
	
	White Board
	Fast Writing
	  Practice: _____
	Flashcard Practice
	  Needed? Yes No	

Suggested: 10 minutes Spent: _____	3. **Writing:** Negotiated Sentence: _____ _____ _____ Words Boxed: _____ Words to Fluency: _____ Letter Formation: _____ Cut-Up Sentence Needed? Yes No	
Suggested: 5 minutes Spent: _____	4. **Read-Aloud Selection:** Title: _____	

FIGURE 8.1. America Reads Daily Log. Reduced to fit page parameters.

sentence strips to help students in various contexts, as suggested by Wasik (1998b). Students "make words" that follow common patterns, and they quickly write new words until they achieve fluency. Word study helps students develop automatic recognition of sight words, build a bank of familiar words, and improve fluency (Clay, 1993; Cunningham & Cunningham, 1992; Morrow & Walker, 1997).

In the third part of the literacy lesson, students work on writing meaningful messages that express personal thoughts and feelings. This component of the lesson emphasizes the difference between written and spoken language and the need for clear communication in writing (Bader, 1998; Morrow & Walker, 1997; Wasik, 1998b). A mentor engages a child in a meaningful conversation and guides the student to negotiate a sentence. Using a two-page journal, the student uses a practice page and a final page to work out a clear sentence. On the practice page, the mentor uses "Elkonin boxes" (Elkonin, 1973), letter boxes, and analogies to help students figure out the orthography of new or challenging words. Students also move toward fluency by repeatedly writing high-frequency words that cause confusion. The final sentence is written on a clean page, and the mentor then makes a cut-up sentence for the child to take home in an envelope (Clay, 1993). This sentence can be reconstructed later, thereby reinforcing concepts covered during parts of the lesson (e.g., mentors can cut off the rime for a word, or the ending to highlight a pattern covered in word study).

During the fourth part of the lesson, the mentor reads aloud to the student. Reading aloud exposes students to rich language and texts above their oral reading level (Morrow & Walker, 1997). The mentors model fluent reading and engage the students in meaningful conversations about books. Reading aloud therefore supports concept development and motivation—characteristics of good readers.

The four-part lesson provides a balance of high-quality literacy events. Important skills, such as word study, are embedded in real, contextualized reading. Research supports early literacy instruction that focuses on the interactive process of reading (Lipson & Wixson, 1997; Pressley et al., 1996). The lesson design developed for America Reads at the University of Maryland gives mentors the training, structure, and guidance to deliver quality instruction to young learners.

RESEARCH AND EVALUATION

Since the start of the America Reads Challenge at the University of Maryland, research and evaluation have been important components of overall program development. As noted earlier, our program is relatively large, with approximately 75 mentors tutoring over 400 elementary students; therefore, we developed a three-pronged approach to research and evaluation. During the first year of the program, we conducted an initial evaluation of the tutoring program at three levels: documentation of student progress, school-based evaluations of the program from site supervisors and classroom teachers, and mentors' assessments of program effectiveness. Data from these sources suggest that the America Reads tutoring program at the University of Maryland has had a positive impact on schools, mentors, and elementary students. The following descriptions and examples from the above-mentioned measures highlight the successes and ongoing efforts of the program.

The Office of Research, Evaluation, and Accountability's Study

For the 1997–1998 academic year, the Prince George's County (Maryland) Public Schools' Office of Research, Evaluation, and Accountability (OREA) conducted a study in which second-grade students from one participating school were randomly assigned to the America Reads tutoring program or to a comparison group that did not receive tutoring. Students in both the America Reads tutoring program and the comparison group took the California Test of Basic Skills (CTBS) in the spring of 1998. Table 8.1 summarizes the performance of these two groups on the standardized reading and language tests of the CTBS.

One limitation of the design of the OREA study was that the sample was drawn from the school's total population at this grade level, as per OREA's requirements. Therefore, some second-grade students who re-

TABLE 8.1. Second-Grade Students' Mean Scores on the California Test of Basic Skills (CTBS)

	CTBS scores			
Group	Reading Comprehension	Language	Language Mechanics	Language Composite
15–45 sessions (n = 19)	590	577	588	583
1–14 sessions (n = 49)	580	578	585	582
Comparison group (n = 70)	579	582	590	586

Note. Data from Prince George's County (Maryland) Public School's Office of Research, Education, and Accountability.

TABLE 8.2. Students' Mean Scores on the Letter Identification Measure

Grade level	Pretest mean	Posttest mean	Mean difference
First grade ($n = 40$)	45.10	51.28	6.18 ($p < .05$)
Second grade ($n = 87$)	44.75	54.44	9.69 ($p < .05$)

Note. Highest possible score was 55. Overall $t = 4.385$, $p < .05$.

ceived tutoring and some who were in the comparison group were reading at or above grade level.

One important piece of information revealed in this study was that 49 out of 70 students received fewer than 10 tutoring sessions. On the CTBS Reading Comprehension measure, students who received 16–45 sessions scored higher than those students who received fewer sessions or no tutoring. This difference approached statistical significance. The results indicated the need to match students and mentors for regular, consistent sessions during the 1998–1999 academic year.

Student Literacy Measures

In the fall of 1998, mentors administered several informal literacy measures to students, including letter identification, word recognition, writing, and dictation tasks. These assessments served two purposes. First, the results helped mentors design instruction to meet students' individual needs. Second, the pre- and posttest scores demonstrated the progress of children identified as reading below grade level. Students participating in the America Reads tutoring program were assessed at the beginning and end of the fall 1998 semester. Table 8.2 shows the pre- and posttest means for first and second graders on the letter identification measure, and Table 8.3 shows results on the high-frequency word recognition assessment. Statistical analyses for these two measures included means and *t*-tests of paired samples.

Although pretest–posttest assessments have a number of recognized limitations, the results provided some tentative information about stu-

TABLE 8.3. Students' Mean Scores on the High-Frequency Word Recognition Assessment

Grade level	Pretest mean	Posttest mean	Mean difference
First grade ($n = 40$)	7.07	15.49	8.42 ($p < .05$)
Second grade ($n = 87$)	17.57	19.14	1.57 ($p < .05$)

Note. Highest possible score was 20. Overall $t = 8.746$, $p < .05$.

dents' progress. The *t*-test analysis revealed that means for the paired differences were significant on both assessments. Thus, on both the letter identification and high-frequency word recognition tasks, students who participated in America Reads made significant ($p < .05$) progress from September 1998 to December 1998.

School-Based Evaluations of America Reads: Fall 1997, Spring 1998, and Fall 1999

At the end of each semester, site supervisors (usually the reading specialist or school administrator) and the teachers at each school complete evaluations of mentors' performance. Table 8.4 summarizes results for the fall 1997 through fall 1998 semesters.

The data from all schools indicated that America Reads mentors were consistently rated as "very good" to "exceptional" in all categories, with averages closer to "exceptional." In addition to the numerical data, the site supervisors and teachers also included narrative comments on the positive aspects of the program for students and the schools. Teachers commonly noted changes in elementary students' attitudes toward literacy: "I've noticed a renewed interest in reading and writing for students [participating in America Reads] in my class especially." Other teachers commented on the program's instructional impact: "This program has become an essential part of our grade level!" and "The America Reads program has been the best tutoring program that we have developed with

TABLE 8.4. Site Supervisors' Ratings of Mentors' Performance

Criteria	Fall 1997 average ($n = 59$)	Spring 1998 average ($n = 79$)	Fall 1998 average ($n = 64$)
Dependability	4.32	4.34	4.80
Productivity	4.49	4.66	4.82
Attitude toward work	4.71	4.65	4.81
Communication skills	4.64	4.64	4.77
Initiative	4.76	4.69	4.90
Relationships with mentees	4.73	4.76	4.83
Relationships with colleagues	4.69	4.60	4.75
Contribution to school	4.59	4.65	4.83
Overall mean	4.62	4.62	4.81

Note. Scale: 1 = "unsatisfactory," 2 = "below average," 3 = "satisfactory," 4 = "very good," 5 = "exceptional." n = number of mentors evaluated by site supervisors.

any organization." In response to teachers' evaluations, site supervisors at three schools have requested additional mentors each semester.

Mentors' Reflections and Evaluations

At every phase of training and development, mentors in our program reflect on personal experiences during tutoring, as well as their perception of the overall program. The information gleaned from this feedback helps the America Reads staff tailor training and development sessions to meet the needs of the mentors. Comments listed in Table 8.5 represent new and returning mentors' reflections and evaluations at three points in the fall 1998, spring 1999, and fall 1999 semesters. In addition, it should be noted that mentors have the opportunity to reflect at monthly training sessions and on the America Reads Internet mailing list, where others can view comments about the program.

Analysis of the reflections of mentors gathered from small-group discussions, questionnaires, and journals revealed several common attitudes about the America Reads tutoring program. Of the 74 mentors from the spring 1998 semester, from the original 79, who completed postsemester evaluations, the most frequently mentioned reason for working for the program was the value of helping children (59 responses). Other responses included experience (14), money (8), and holding a job related to their college major (4).

TABLE 8.5. New and Returning Mentors' Reflections

New mentors	Returning mentors
Primary training: "This was a very productive training, and I feel that I have a wealth of knowledge to take to my school."	*Primary training:* "The whole program is better organized this year. You've given me all the info I need to know—Thanks!"
Training session 1: "One of my students came right up to me and hugged me after I walked him back to the classroom. He told me he had learned and felt good about it, and now all his friends call him 'smart guy.'"	*Training session 1:* "The training on identifying students' reading habits was helpful, in that it made me think critically about how to address different problems such as decoding and comprehension."
Training session 2: "My students are using the terms and techniques I've been trained to instill! One child looked up at me and said, 'Hey! I see the /ee/ chunk!'"	*Training session 2:* "After several weeks, two teachers approached me to tell me that they really see an improvement in the students I tutor."

The student reflections also revealed changes in perceptions of the program across the two semesters for fall 1997 and spring 1998. Perhaps the most significant shift was an increased awareness of children's literacy problems and barriers to learning (26). Also, students indicated an awareness of overall program improvement (14). The improvements the mentors noted included having team leaders in the schools, better-organized training procedures, and a tutoring handbook. There were 30 examples in the students' responses that reflected concerns or frustrations related to the tutoring program, including schedule and communication conflicts (14), behavioral and disciplinary concerns (11), and difficulty with lesson implementation (8).

DISCUSSION

The focus of our evaluation of the University of Maryland's America Reads tutoring program was three-pronged. We were interested in the effects of the program on children's reading development, the perceptions of the university tutors, and evaluation of the program by school-based personnel. Taken together, the findings of this evaluation suggest that the America Reads tutoring program at the University of Maryland is serving children well, that the training of tutors is effective, and that school-based evaluations of the program are very positive.

Although the OREA study found no statistically significant difference on CTBS Reading Comprehension scores for children participating in the America Reads tutoring program versus children in the comparison group, the means were in the expected direction in favor of the America Reads group (see Table 8.1). One limitation of the OREA assessment, as noted earlier, was that children were randomly selected from the school's entire second-grade population. Therefore, children who participated in the America Reads tutoring program, as well as the children in the control group, included children who were reading on or above grade level. The America Reads mentors in our program are specifically trained to work with struggling readers, and the program goal is to increase the reading performance of below-average readers. As a result of this design limitation, future research designs will specifically target those children most in need of tutoring.

The assessments of letter identification and high-frequency word recognition skills for below-average first and second graders who participated in the program revealed that statistically significant progress was made in these areas in only one semester. These findings are particularly interesting, in that these children were identified as struggling readers who had previously failed to show progress in reading. Several other studies have documented the positive effects of participation in America Reads programs at other sites. Woo and Morrow (1998) reported that first and second graders participating in America Reads outperformed a control group on measures of reading achievement (see also Morrow & Woo, Chapter 6, this volume). In a qualitative study of America Reads tutors, Fitzgerald and Wolery (1998) documented that tutors grew in their ability to place students in appropriate instructional materials and learned ways to prompt children to use word recognition strategies (see also Fitzgerald, Chapter 7, this volume). These studies suggest that America Reads affects students' reading progress and has a positive influence on tutors' knowledge of literacy learning.

Reflections from mentors in the University of Maryland's America Reads tutoring program, drawn from small-group discussions, questionnaires, and journal entries, revealed that the mentors are aware of the importance of literacy development in young children and derive great satisfaction from tutoring. Likewise, school-based personnel rated the performance of mentors very highly. Across three semesters, the ratings of school personnel indicated that mentors improved in dependability, productivity, and contributions to the school.

The results of this evaluation of the America Reads tutoring program at the University of Maryland also provided significant information for improving the program. For example, at the end of the first year, we were surprised to find that in the school where an America Reads group and a group receiving no tutoring were compared, the majority of America Reads students received very few (1–14) tutoring sessions across the school year. In the second year, procedures were put into place to assure consistent tutoring across the school year for all children in the program.

Clearly, additional quantitative and qualitative research is warranted to more fully explore the effects of America Reads programs on children, tutors, and school culture. We are currently conducting a quasi-experimental study in two schools, with random assignment of second-grade students to the University of Maryland's America Reads tutoring program and a comparison group. In addition, it appears that more attention should be devoted to how America Reads tutoring programs affect the culture of schooling, as well as to the perceptions of parents and guardians who have children involved in these programs. The America Reads Challenge is still in the initial stages of development, and there is much we need to learn. It is clear that future research should focus on describing and documenting the consistency and the quality of America Reads tutoring programs.

REFERENCES

Allington, R. L. (1994). The schools we have. The schools we need. *The Reading Teacher, 48*(1), 14–29.

Bader, L. A. (1998). *Read to succeed: Literacy tutor's manual.* Upper Saddle River, NJ: Prentice-Hall.

Clay, M. M. (1993). *Reading Recovery: A guidebook for teachers in training.* Portsmouth, NH: Heinemann.

Cox, B. G., & Krueger, J. G. (1994). Effective literacy instruction. In B. A. Herrmann (Ed.), *The volunteer tutor's toolbox* (pp. 15–26). Newark, DE: International Reading Association.

Cunningham, P. M., & Cunningham, J. W. (1992). Making words: Enhancing the invented spelling–decoding connection. *The Reading Teacher, 46,* 106–115.

Edmondson, J. (1998). America Reads: Doing battle. *Language Arts, 76*(2), 154–162.

Elkonin, D. B. (1973). USSR. In J. Downing (Ed.), *Comparative reading* (pp. 551–579). New York: Macmillan.

Fitzgerald, J., & Wolery, R. (1998, December) *What and how can volunteer tutors learn about teaching reading?* Paper presented at the National Reading Conference, Austin, TX.

Invernizzi, M., Juel, C., & Rosemary, C. A. (1996–1997). A community volunteer tutorial that works. *The Reading Teacher, 50*(4), 304–311.

Juel, C. (1993). What makes literacy tutoring effective? *Reading Research Quarterly, 31,* 268–289.

Lipson, M. Y., & Wixson, K. K. (1997). *Assessment and instruction of reading and writing disability: An interactive approach.* New York: HarperCollins.

Morrow, L. M., & Walker, B. J. (1997). *The reading team: A handbook for volunteer tutors K–3.* Newark, DE: International Reading Association.

National Assessment of Educational Progress. (1994). *America's report card.* Washington, DC: U.S. Government Printing Office.

Pressley, M., Rankin, J., & Yokoi, L. (1996). A survey of the instructional practices of outstanding primary-level literacy teachers. *Elementary School Journal, 96,* 363–384.

Sarracino, J., Herrmann, B. A., Batdorf, B. W., & Garfinkel, E. C. (1994). Effective literacy assessment. In B. A. Herrmann (Ed.), *The volunteer tutor's toolbox* (pp. 77–102). Newark, DE: International Reading Association.

Stahl, S. A., Duffy-Hester, A. M., & Stahl, K. A. D. (1998). Everything you wanted to know about phonics (but were afraid to ask). *Reading Research Quarterly, 33*(3), 338–355.

Walker, B. J. (1996). *Diagnostic teaching of reading: Techniques for instruction and assessment* (3rd ed.). New York: Merrill.

Wasik, B. A. (1998a). Volunteer tutoring programs in reading: A review. *Reading Research Quarterly, 33,* 266–292.

Wasik, B. A. (1998b). Using volunteers as reading tutors: Guidelines for successful practices. *The Reading Teacher, 51*(7), 562–570.

Wasik, B. A., & Slavin, R. E. (1993). Preventing early reading failure with one-to-one tutoring: A review of five programs. *Reading Research Quarterly, 28,* 178–200.

Woo, D. G., & Morrow, L. M. (1998, December). *The effect of a volunteer tutoring program on literacy achievement and attitudes toward the program of teachers, tutors, and children.* Paper presented at the National Reading Conference, Austin, TX.

Part III

EXEMPLARY MODELS OF EARLY LITERACY INTERVENTIONS

Chapter 9

THE HOWARD STREET TUTORING MODEL: USING VOLUNTEER TUTORS TO PREVENT READING FAILURE IN THE PRIMARY GRADES

Darrell Morris

It is an old, not a new problem. Our schools have historically had difficulty teaching a sizeable minority of children to read—from 15% to 40%, depending on socioeconomic circumstances (Allington, 1994; National Assessment of Educational Progress, 1995). Many children struggle with learning to read in first grade and, once they fall behind, have difficulty catching up with their peers (Clay, 1991; Juel, 1988; Stanovich, 1986). Moreover, those who finish third grade 1 or more years behind in basic reading skill are seriously at risk in an educational system that, from fourth grade on, demands grade-level reading ability.

The reasons for reading failure in the primary grades have been debated for over 100 years (see, e.g., Huey, 1908/1968). At various points, the teacher (poorly trained), the child (lack of "readiness"), or the English spelling system (hopelessly irregular) has borne the brunt of the blame. Overall, however, the debate has centered on what the "best" method is for teaching beginners to read (e.g., phonics, whole-word, sentence-based, etc.). The long-standing, spirited argument over method (see Adams, 1990; Chall, 1967) continues right up to the present, the most current trend, "balanced instruction," being no more than an undefined label that belies major methodological disagreements among both reading scholars and teachers.

Although issues of teaching method should continue to be addressed, there are other ways of thinking about the problem of reading failure in the primary grades. I suggest that the *opportunity* to learn to read is of critical importance. In a typical first- or second-grade classroom, with only 90 minutes of reading instruction and a 1:25 teacher–student ratio, there is surprisingly little time available for individual children to read aloud under the classroom teacher's direct supervision. This lack of supervised reading time—a long-standing, systemic problem in elementary schools— is particularly harmful to those low-achieving beginning readers who desperately need practice in a situation where feedback is available. Like most of us facing a difficult task, the struggling beginning reader requires help when trouble arises (e.g., an unknown word), and reassurance when things are going well.

One powerful way to provide low-achieving readers with needed practice and feedback is to tutor them. Recently, several first-grade intervention programs, including Reading Recovery (Pinnell, Lyons, DeFord, Bryk, & Seltzer, 1994), Success for All (Slavin et al., 1996), and Early Steps (Santa & Hoien, 1999), have demonstrated that one-to-one tutoring can significantly raise the achievement of at-risk beginning readers. The three programs differ in specific methods and materials used and mode of tutor training; however, each employs a carefully graded set of reading materials, and each provides instruction in the alphabetic code (Morris, 1999a). In truth, these tutoring programs have "opened the reading field's eyes," showing that at-risk children *can* learn to read—can catch up with their peers—if provided with sensible and intensive one-to-one instruction.

Unfortunately, using certified teachers to tutor children on a one-to-one basis is an expensive proposition. Shanahan and Barr (1995) estimated the cost of Reading Recovery to be $4,000 per child. Consider a poor urban or rural school with 24 at-risk readers spread across three first-grade classrooms. If we multiply 24 × $4,000, we find that it will cost $96,000 or the equivalent of three full-time teachers to provide pull-out tutoring to each child. Over the long run, this is an expense that most school districts in the United States will not be able to bear.

If one-to-one tutoring by carefully trained reading teachers is cost-prohibitive in schools serving large numbers of at-risk children, then what are the alternatives? First, we can develop and refine effective small-group interventions for low-achieving readers. Much attention should be given to this task, because small-group instructional routines can be used in both the regular classroom and supplementary pull-out programs (see Hiebert, 1994; Hoffman, 1987; Morris & Nelson, 1992). Note, however, that it is difficult for small-group instruction, no matter how well planned or skillfully implemented, to compete with a tutorial. As Wasik and Slavin (1990) have argued, a one-to-one setting ensures that a child is taught consistently at the appropriate level, and is provided with timely reinforcement and corrective feedback during reading. Such individually paced instruction is not possible in "even one-to-two or one-to-three instruction, where adaptation to individual needs becomes progressively more difficult" (Wasik & Slavin, 1990, p. 6).

A second alternative is to use paraprofessionals or community volunteers to tutor at-risk readers. The use of adult volunteers would greatly reduce the cost of tutoring and thus drastically increase the potential number of children who could be served. The question is this: Can volunteer tutoring work; can it produce results? A solid research base is lacking, but a few studies (Invernizzi, Rosemary, Juel, & Richards, 1996; Morris, Shaw, & Perney, 1990) suggest that volunteer tutors, if carefully supervised by a reading specialist, can significantly raise the achievement of at-risk primary-grade readers. In this chapter, I describe one of these volunteer tutoring models.

THE HOWARD STREET TUTORING MODEL[1]

A Brief History

The Howard Street Tutoring Program began in the fall of 1979 when an activist friend of mine, Megan Tschannen-Moran, decided to start up an after-school tutoring program in a poor neighborhood on the far north side of Chicago. Her idea was to have low-achieving public school students walk over to a small community center on Howard Street two afternoons per week, where they would receive tutoring in reading from adult volunteers. She asked me, a new reading professor in the area, whether I would help with the project.

I was very interested in Tschannen-Moran's concept of an after-school volunteer tutoring program for low-achieving readers. From my clinical training in reading education at the University of Virginia, I had become convinced that one-to-one tutoring, even only two or three times a week, could make a significant difference in poor children's literacy development. I was also curious about the potential effectiveness of adult volunteer tutors. I knew that I, a reading specialist, could teach children to read in a one-to-one situation, but could we train volunteers with little or no background in reading to become effective tutors? This was the challenge.

1. This description of the tutoring model is based on a more complete description found in Chapter 2 of *The Howard Street Tutoring Manual: Teaching At-Risk Readers in the Primary Grades* (Morris, 1999b). Copyright 1999 by The Guilford Press. Adapted by permission.

At Howard Street, we concentrated on serving low-achieving second- and third-grade readers. Over the first few years of the tutoring program, we learned some important lessons, mostly through trial and error (see Morris, Tschannen-Moran, & Weidemann, 1981; Morris, 1993):

1. *If volunteer reading tutors are to be successful, they require close, ongoing supervision by a reading specialist.* We learned this lesson the hard way when, in year 1, several of our college-educated volunteers became overwhelmed with the tutoring task and quit. Moreover, it became clear that although the other volunteers continued to show up for tutoring each time, they were often frustrated. They were uncomfortable with lesson planning and unsure about how much effort to demand of the children. We had to move in quickly and provide needed professional support.

2. *Volunteer tutoring programs should be kept small to ensure quality control.* In our second year, we succumbed to the universal temptation to "expand the program." With the best of intentions, we went from 8 tutor–child pairs in year 1 to 14 tutor–child pairs in year 2. Unfortunately, we discovered that one hard-working supervisor could keep up with, at most, 10 tutor–child pairs. Thus our well-intentioned expansion served to compromise the quality of the entire program.

3. *The interpersonal bond that develops between volunteer and child is a major factor in a tutoring program's success.* We recognized early that the bonding between tutor and child was what kept the volunteers coming back, week after week, month after month (a crucially important element in a volunteer tutoring program). Over the course of a year, the volunteers experienced good and bad tutoring days; however, their commitment to and affection for their students was unwavering.

4. *A volunteer tutoring program can significantly improve the reading ability of low-achieving primary-grade students.* From the start of the tutoring program, we documented the children's reading growth through careful record keeping and beginning-of-year/end-of-year testing. In the eighth and ninth years of the program, we conducted a more rigorous evaluation, comparing the achievement of the tutored children with that of a closely matched comparison group. Results showed that the tutored group consistently outperformed the comparison group on several measures of reading and spelling ability (Morris et al., 1990).

I moved away from the Chicago area in 1989, but the Howard Street Tutoring Program has continued to operate under the able leadership of Beverly Shaw, Betty Boyd, and Barbara Kaufman. At this writing, the program is in its 21st year of consecutive operation, serving 20+ children each year from the same inner-city public school.

Having established new academic roots at Appalachian State University in western North Carolina, in 1989 I began helping rural school systems set up in-school interventions for at-risk first-grade readers. The intervention model originally called First Steps and now known as Early Steps has had some success (see Morris, 1995; Santa & Hoien, 1999), but we have found that many low-achieving first-grade readers, even after a full year of one-to-one tutoring by a certified teacher, still require careful support as they move into second grade. For this reason, several North Carolina school districts have also instituted follow-up second-grade tutorial programs based on the original Howard Street model. It has been interesting to watch the volunteer tutoring concept, originally designed as a stopgap after-school program for inner-city children, evolve in a totally different setting. In rural North Carolina, low-achieving second-grade readers are tutored during the school day by volunteers who are supervised by the school-based Title I reading teacher.

Implementing the Tutoring Model

In the program description that follows, volunteer tutors, under the supervision of a reading specialist, work with low-achieving second-grade readers on Monday and Wednesday afternoons from 1:00 to 1:45 P.M.

Identifying Low-Achieving Readers and Recruiting Tutors

In September, the reading specialist asks the three second-grade teachers in her school to identify the five lowest-achieving readers in their respective classrooms. The reading teacher pretests these 15 children, using a set of graded word recognition lists, a set of graded reading passages, and a spelling inventory (see Morris, 1999b). The 10 students scoring lowest on the pretest measures are selected to participate in the tutoring program.

Because the program includes only low-achieving second-grade readers, the reading ability range of the students is appreciably narrowed (initially early- to mid-first-grade reading levels). This greatly simplifies the training and supervision of the volunteer tutors. It is one thing to provide volunteers with techniques they can use with children who read at first-grade level; it is quite another to provide them with the variety of techniques and knowledge required to work successfully with children whose reading levels range from early first grade to fourth grade.

One may ask why the volunteer tutoring is focused on second graders instead of first graders. My personal conviction is that intensive one-to-one reading help for at-risk children should be provided as early as possible. Nonetheless, experience has led me to believe that trained teachers and paraprofessionals are more effective with first graders than are volunteers (but see Invernizzi et al., 1997; Johnston, Invernizzi, & Juel, 1998). Ideally, a professionally staffed reading intervention in first grade (e.g., Reading Recovery, Early Steps) would be followed by volunteer tutoring in second and third grades. This ideal has become a reality in several school districts in western North Carolina, and the achievement results are encouraging.

In the recruitment of tutors, adult volunteers come from all walks of life: undergraduate education and liberal arts majors in local universities, graduate students in education or psychology looking for practicum experiences, parents whose children are in school, parents whose children are away at college, employees of businesses that grant release time for volunteer work in the schools, retirees looking for meaningful volunteer work, and so on. Because of population density, cities would seem to offer a more plentiful source of potential tutors. However, tutor recruitment is really a question of finding individuals with the necessary levels of commitment and energy. I have seen one reading teacher in an isolated rural community build up a solid volunteer tutoring corps by personally contacting her school's parent–teacher association (PTA), along with local church and civic groups.

In the start-up years, printed flyers and a few contacts at local universities, churches, and civic organizations can be used to attract potential tutors. After a few years of operation, a word-of-mouth recruitment network usually proves to be fairly reliable in securing the needed number of tutors. Most volunteers, particularly college students, tutor for only 1 year. However, a small group of community volunteers (parents, retirees) often returns year after year, finding the tutoring to be a collegial and rewarding experience.

The Tutoring Lesson

The volunteer tutors follow a set 45-minute lesson plan that includes the following activities:

1. *Guided reading at the child's instructional level (18 minutes)*. The tutor supports the child in reading and comprehending well-written stories. A true beginning reader will "echo-read" simple pattern books; a mid-first-grade reader will "partner-read," or alternately read with the tutor, pages of a basal story or trade book; and a late-first-grade (or higher-level) reader will read independently, requiring only incidental support from the tutor.

2. *Word study* (*10 minutes*). Word categorization activities and games are used to help children internalize basic spelling patterns. Depending on a child's developmental level of word knowledge, he/she may categorize or "sort" beginning consonant elements, short-vowel word families (rhyming words), or vowel patterns. Figure 9.1 provides an example of a word family sort and a vowel pattern sort.

3. *Easy reading* (*10 minutes*). This reading is done in trade books (e.g., Harper & Row's I Can Read series or Random House's Step into Reading series). The child may reread a favorite book or partner-read with the tutor a new but easy book. The purposes are to build sight vocabulary, to increase fluency, and to strengthen the child's confidence as a reader.

4. *Reading to the child* (*7 minutes*). At the end of each lesson, the tutor reads a high-quality selection to the child. This may be a fairy tale, a fable, a short picture book, or a chapter from a longer book.

Ninety minutes of focused reading practice per week may not seem like a lot, but it does make a difference. Given such practice in a supportive environment, low-achieving readers begin to progress, and as they do, the *pacing* of their instruction becomes an important concern (Barr, 1974). In reading acquisition, there is an optimal level of task difficulty that will produce the biggest gains in learning—a level at which the reader is sufficiently challenged but not overwhelmed. In the Howard Street model, we carefully monitor each child's current "instructional level," moving the student forward quickly when performance warrants such a move (e.g., to a higher contextual reading level or to a new or more complex set of word patterns). The supervisor of tutors plays a critical role in these instructional pacing decisions.

Word family sort			Vowel pattern sort			
hat	man	back	bag	lake	park	mail
cat	pan	sack	sat	name	hard	rain
mat	can	pack	fan	race	car	wait
	ran	black	clap	made	farm	paid
						tail
	flat			late		

FIGURE 9.1. Word sort activities. From Morris (1999b). Copyright 1999 by The Guilford Press. Reprinted by permission.

The Role of the Supervisor

A unique characteristic of the Howard Street model is the close monitoring of the tutoring lessons by a reading specialist "supervisor." During
the first 2 weeks of the school year, the supervisor pretests low-achieving
second-grade readers and actively recruits volunteer tutors for the children. However, this just sets the stage for his/her year-long supervisory
role.

    Getting the Tutoring Lessons Started. One of the most difficult parts of
the supervisor's job is getting the program started in September. Remember that most of the volunteers are neophytes when it comes to teaching
reading. Therefore, they require close supervision during the first month
if they are to master basic teaching techniques (e.g., monitoring oral
reading, conducting word sorts) and establish good "tutoring habits" (e.g.,
minimizing transition time between tasks, providing timely encouragement to the child for a job well done).

    Over the years, we have learned that on-the-job training for the vol-
unteer tutors is much more efficient than preservice lectures on "how to
tutor." Therefore, the supervisor begins the program each year by working with only two tutor–child pairs. On day 1, the supervisor teaches a
child (see "The Tutoring Lesson," above) while the volunteer tutors watch.
There is a debriefing after the lesson, with the supervisor carefully explaining the basic instructional routines the volunteers have just observed.
On day 2, the volunteers do the tutoring and the supervisor observes;
again, a careful debriefing afterward allows the new tutors to ask questions and receive constructive feedback on their performance. Once the
first couple of tutors have gained their "sea legs," usually after three or
four lessons, the supervisor starts another two or three tutor–child pairs.
In this way, the program stair-steps up to 8 to 10 children being served by
the end of October, with each beginning tutor having received special
attention from the supervisor in the early lessons.

    Ongoing Supervision. If they are to be successful, volunteer reading
tutors require ongoing support and supervision. We should not expect a
college music major or a retired accountant to be an instinctively good
teacher of beginning reading. Such volunteer tutors will invariably get
"stuck" from time to time, requiring the assistance of an experienced
reading teacher. By providing consultation and support throughout the
year, a knowledgeable supervisor can build up the competence and confidence of the volunteer tutors, and can help them (and the children they
work with) avoid damaging feelings of inadequacy and discouragement.

    The most important in-service support is provided to the tutors on
an individual basis. In the early years of the program, the supervisor ob-

served the tutoring lessons and then met with the individual tutors before, after, or even during the sessions to make suggestions or provide feedback. If a tutor was having difficulty, the supervisor was right there to model a specific teaching procedure with that tutor's child. Planning or sequencing of instruction across tutoring lessons was the responsibility of the volunteer in consultation with the supervisor. This proved to be a fairly workable system, but we discovered over the years that busy volunteers did not always have time, before or after the tutoring sessions, to consult with their supervisors regarding lesson planning; nor did some have the requisite knowledge or confidence to plan lessons by themselves at home (e.g., which story to read next or which word patterns to sort next).

Eventually we adopted a lesson-planning approach in which the supervisor, a trained reading specialist, assumes more responsibility. It works as follows. A lesson plan notebook (8½" × 11" spiral) is kept for each child. After a Monday tutoring session, the supervisor takes the 10 notebooks and plans the next tutoring lesson for *each* child in his/her group. (Note that the supervisor draws on his/her firsthand observations of the Monday tutoring lessons in making lesson plan suggestions for Wednesday.) When the tutor comes in on Wednesday afternoon, he/she picks up the lesson plan notebook for his/her student, notes the specific tutoring activities for the day, locates the needed materials, and proceeds to get to work. The volunteer is already familiar with the teaching routines (support reading, word sorting, reading to the child); what the notebook offers—free of charge, so to speak—is an appropriate plan for that specific lesson (e.g., *which* stories to read, *which* word patterns to sort). Following the lesson, the tutor quickly jots down in the notebook relevant comments on the child's performance that day, and these comments are then considered by the supervisor in planning the child's next lesson. In this way, the lesson plan notebook becomes an important secondary dialogue between supervisor and tutor regarding the child's reading development across the year (see sample lesson plan in Figure 9.2).

The supervisor's careful lesson planning ensures quality control in the program. Through the lesson plans, the supervisor is able to differentiate skill instruction (beginning consonants for one child, short-vowel word families for another) and to adjust the pace at which individual children progress through the graded reading materials (primer, late first grade, early second grade, and so on). Such instructional "fine-tuning" increases student achievement, but does come at a cost. That is, a supervisor of 10 tutor–child pairs must spend approximately 2 hours of planning per tutoring day during the fall and up to 1½ hours per tutoring day during the spring.

Preplanned lessons for the individual children are crucial, yet equally important is the supervisor's physical presence *during* the tutoring period.

LESSON PLAN	TUTOR'S COMMENTS
1. **Guided reading:** "A Pet in a Bowl" Laidlaw, 2-1	1. John did all the reading, so we stopped after 8 pages. He missed just a few words, and his comprehension was good. This level is just about right.
2. **Word sort:** *e* vowel patterns (e, ee, ea)	2. Some confusion on *ee* and *ea* at first, but he ended up doing a nice job. Should work on these patterns a few more times.
3. **Easy reading:** Partner-read the first half of the tradebook *Silly Sam*	3. We alternated pages and finished the book. John liked it.
4. **Read to John:** *Paul Bunyan* (deLeeuw)	4. No time today.

FIGURE 9.2. Sample lesson plan (with tutor's comments). From Morris (1999b). Copyright 1999 by The Guilford Press. Reprinted by permission.

As the supervisor walks among and observes the 10 tutor–child pairs, he/she sends an implicit message to children and tutors alike: "This tutoring is serious business." During a lesson, the supervisor can model a new teaching technique for a tutor or provide assistance when an old technique does not seem to be working. Moreover, the supervisor's firsthand observations of the tutoring enable him/her to make informed and necessary adjustments in upcoming lessons (e.g., to move a child up one reading level or one skill level).

Assessing the Program's Effectiveness

In May, the supervisor posttests the tutored students on the same reading/spelling tasks that were administered at the beginning of the school year (see Morris, 1999b):

1. *Word recognition:* Ability to read individual words on lists graded in difficulty (early-first-grade through third-grade lists).
2. *Passage reading:* Ability to read a set of passages graded in difficulty (early-first-grade through third-grade passages).
3. *Spelling:* Ability to spell a 20-word list of first- and second-grade words.

Table 9.1 shows the pretest–posttest scores of 10 second graders who were tutored in a rural North Carolina school during the 1995–1996 school year. Note in the table that on the September pretest, only 2 of the 10 second-grade students could read a primer or mid-first-grade-

TABLE 9.1. Pretest-Posttest Reading Performance of 10 Tutored Students

Student	September pretest		May posttest	
	Word recognition[a]	Passage reading[b]	Word recognition	Passage reading
Charlie	Below PP	Below PP	PP	Primer
T. J.	Below PP	PP	Primer	1-2
April	Below PP	PP	Primer	1-2
Marcus	PP	PP	1-2	2-1
Josh	PP	PP	Second	2-1
Christy	PP	PP	Second	2-2
Michael	PP	PP	Second	2-2
Stacey	PP	PP	Second	2-2
Bridgett	PP	Primer	Second	2-2
Victor	Primer	Primer	Third	Third

Note. From Morris (1999b). Copyright 1999 by The Guilford Press. Reprinted by permission.

[a]To attain a given word recognition level (e.g., preprimer [PP]), student had to score 50% or better on *flash* presentation of a 20-word list.

[b]To attain a given passage-reading level (e.g., 1-2 or late-first-grade), student had to read with 90% accuracy at a minimally acceptable rate.

level passage. After a year of tutoring, however, 7 of the 10 children could read a second-grade passage, and five were on grade level (2-2; i.e., late second grade) or better. This is a fairly typical finding in my experience. If low-achieving students enter second-grade reading near the primer (or 1-1) level, good classroom instruction supplemented by volunteer tutoring will enable these children to catch up with their peers (i.e., to become 2-1 to 2-2 level readers) by the end of second grade.

DISCUSSION

A volunteer tutoring program like the one described in this chapter can raise the reading achievement of at-risk primary-grade students. Moreover, such a program is cost-effective. If a reading specialist (salary = $40,000) spends 5½ hours per week supervising and planning lessons for 10 volunteer tutors, then 14% of his/her time (salary), or $5,500, can be assigned to the tutoring program. If we divide $5,500 by the 10 children served, the cost becomes $550 per child for 50 one-to-one reading lessons. Compare this with the $4,000-per-child cost of Reading Recovery tutoring (Shanahan & Barr, 1995). I am not trying to equate the quality of a volunteer tutoring program with that of a program like Reading Recovery; what I am trying to show is that, in terms of cost, volunteer tutoring is a practical means of providing one-to-one help to struggling beginning readers.

As mentioned previously, a volunteer tutoring program can be conducted during or after school hours. With a tutoring site, time slot, and sufficient materials secured, the next tasks are to identify the children to be tutored (no problem here) and to recruit a small group of committed adults who can volunteer 2 hours per week to tutor children in reading. Recruitment of tutors may be a problem at first, but this will become an easier task in succeeding years. Again, churches, community groups, local universities, retirees, and the school's PTA are logical starting points.

Training Supervisors of Tutors

In putting together a volunteer tutoring program, the most crucial piece of the puzzle is the supervisor of tutors. The supervisor is the hub around which the tutoring program revolves. In the beginning, the supervisor's greatest challenge is to convince both the neophyte tutors and the struggling beginning readers that they are going to be successful. Through model teaching, discussion, lesson planning, and consistent encouragement, the supervisor gradually educates the volunteers, who in turn teach the children to read. To accomplish these tasks, the effective supervisor must possess several characteristics: (1) theoretical knowledge of the beginning reading process; (2) experience in teaching beginners to read; (3) confidence (based on the first two characteristics) that almost all children can learn to read and write; and (4) an ability to work constructively with adults in a mentor–apprentice relationship.

Even if school-based reading specialists possess these characteristics, some may choose not to supervise volunteer tutors, preferring instead to work directly with their students in small groups (Broaddus & Bloodgood, 1999). Others (many, I hope) may be interested in the volunteer tutoring concept, but lack the knowledge and confidence to get a program underway. After all, working through adult volunteers to meet the learning needs of individual children is a new challenge for most reading teachers; experience in planning and implementing volunteer programs has not been part of their professional training.

I have come to believe that volunteer tutoring, however great its potential, will be a passing fad in the reading field *unless* we begin to develop effective programs for training school-based supervisors of tutors. It is one thing for a few college reading professors and their students (e.g., Invernizzi et al., 1997; Morris et al., 1990) to show that a group of closely supervised volunteers can significantly raise the achievement of at-risk readers. It is quite another to show that this phenomenon can be replicated by reading teachers in schools across the country.

Fortunately, there are several ways that reading teachers could be trained to supervise volunteer tutors. My preference would be a 3-week summer practicum. Twelve reading teachers and a trainer would come together from 9:00 A.M. to 12:30 P.M., Monday through Thursday. From 9:00 to 9:45 A.M., six of the teachers would each tutor a low-achieving second-grade reader while the trainer and the other six teachers would observe. Then from 9:45 to 10:30 A.M., six new second graders would come in, and the teachers would reverse roles (the original tutors becoming observers, and vice versa). After an hour of lesson planning and individual conferencing with the trainer, the teachers would attend a closing 1-hour seminar (11:30 A.M. to 12:30 P.M.). Here the trainer would lead discussions on teaching technique (guided reading and word study); would facilitate staffing of the tutored children; and, in the last few days of the practicum, would answer questions that the teachers might have about starting up their own volunteer tutoring programs in the fall.

In such a summer practicum, participating reading teachers would learn through direct experience how to organize and implement a volunteer tutoring program. They would learn about reading materials and specific teaching techniques by using them daily, and they would learn a method for supervising volunteer tutors through the experience of being supervised themselves. Such learning through doing, all the while receiving feedback from an experienced coach (Schon, 1987), is a powerful and efficient way to learn a complex set of skills.

The worth of such a summer training program could easily be evaluated. If, during the following school year, each of the 12 teachers in the summer practicum supervised 10 volunteer tutors in his/her school (and identified a matched control for each tutored student), then end-of-year testing would afford an achievement comparison between 120 tutored and 120 nontutored second graders. To my mind, such comparisons should have been an integral part of the federal government's America Reads Challenge volunteer tutoring initiative. The reading field, and the nation at large, will have wasted a huge opportunity if this large federal program is eventually discontinued, without there having been empirical tests of the efficacy of various volunteer tutoring models.

Is a Volunteer Tutoring Program Worth the Effort?

By this point, it should be clear that establishing an effective volunteer tutoring program is not an uncomplicated process. Knowledge, energy, and will are required of the program supervisor, along with specialized training in many cases. I would like to close this chapter by attempting to answer this question: Is it worth the effort?

Several years ago I decided to conduct a formal interview with three reading teachers in western North Carolina who had been supervising second-grade volunteer tutoring programs in their respective schools. I had originally trained the teachers and knew that they were still supervising volunteer tutors 3 years later, but I had had little contact with them during the intervening years. During the interview, I asked the teachers a number of questions, but here I want to focus on just one.

> INTERVIEWER: I know that supervision of volunteer tutors, especially planning their lessons two times per week, is time-consuming. Why do you keep doing it, year after year?
>
> TEACHER 1 [supervised 9 volunteer tutors on Monday/Wednesday and 7 more on Tuesday/Thursday]: The tutoring moves the children to a higher level faster. Even in a small [reading] group of three or four, the children will not all be on the same reading level. When we are reading as a group, it is difficult to get some children focused on the print when another child is reading. In tutoring this is not a problem; there is just more time on task.
>
> TEACHER 2 [supervised 10 volunteer tutors on Monday/Wednesday and 8 more on Tuesday/Thursday]: Tutoring allows you to get each child where he[/she] needs to be. When I pull them as a group of four, they are at different places. But [in our tutoring program] for 2 hours a week, they are reading at their instructional level and studying word patterns at the correct level. Fifty minutes of one-to-one reading is very rare in a public school. It makes a difference!
>
> TEACHER 3 [supervised 8 volunteer tutors on Tuesday/Thursday only]: There is no way time-wise for me to meet with my children one to one. And they are at different reading and skill levels. With the college students tutoring, we can zero in on a child's needs, and they love the one-to-one attention. The time I invest [in the program] is well worth it.

Although the interview question was posed to each teacher separately, the similarity of their respective answers is remarkable. Each teacher pointed out that her low-achieving second-grade readers were at different skill levels, making it difficult to meet their needs in small-group instruction. The teachers were willing to invest time in supervising the volunteers because they valued the power of one-to-one instruction. As one teacher said, "The tutoring moves the children to a higher level faster."

Is it worth the effort? Judging by their words and actions, the three reading teachers certainly seemed to think so, and I concur. Accelerating the progress of low-achieving readers—helping them catch up with their peers—should be a major goal of all primary-grade reading programs. If volunteer tutoring can help schools accomplish this goal, then the concept deserves serious consideration and study.

REFERENCES

Adams, M. J. (1990). *Beginning to read: Thinking and learning about print.* Cambridge, MA: MIT Press.

Allington, R. (1994). Critical issues: What's special about special programs for children who find learning to read difficult? *Journal of Reading Behavior, 26,* 95–115.

Barr, R. (1974). Instructional pace differences and their effect on reading acquisition. *Reading Research Quarterly, 9,* 526–554.

Broaddus, K., & Bloodgood, J. (1999). "We're already supposed to know how to teach reading": Teacher change to support struggling readers. *Reading Research Quarterly, 34,* 426–451.

Chall, J. (1967). *Learning to read: The great debate.* New York: McGraw-Hill.

Clay, M. (1991). *Becoming literate: The construction of inner control.* Auckland, New Zealand: Heinemann.

Hiebert, E. (1994). A small-group literacy intervention with Chapter 1 students. In E. Hiebert & B. Taylor (Eds.), *Getting reading right from the start: Effective early literacy interventions* (pp. 85–106). Needham Heights, MA: Allyn & Bacon.

Hoffman, J. (1987). Rethinking the role of oral reading in basal instruction. *Elementary School Journal, 87,* 367–374.

Huey, E. B. (1968). *The psychology and pedagogy of reading.* Cambridge, MA: MIT Press. (Original work published 1908)

Invernizzi, M., Rosemary, C., Juel, C., & Richards, H. C. (1997). At-risk readers and community volunteers: A 3-year perspective. *Scientific Studies of Reading, 1,* 277–300.

Johnston, F. R., Invernizzi, M., & Juel, C. (1998). *Book Buddies: Guidelines for volunteer tutors of emergent and early readers.* New York: Guilford Press.

Juel, C. (1988). Learning to read and write: A longitudinal study of 54 children from first through fourth grades. *Journal of Educational Psychology, 80,* 437–447.

Morris, D. (1993). *A selective history of the Howard Street Tutoring Program (1979–1989).* (ERIC Document Reproduction Service No. 355 473)

Morris, D. (1995). *First Steps: An early reading intervention program.* (ERIC Document Reproduction Service No. 388 956).

Morris, D. (1999a). Preventing reading failure in the primary grades. In T. Shanahan & F. Rodriquez-Brown (Eds.), *National Reading Conference yearbook* (Vol. 48, pp. 19–38). Chicago: National Reading Conference.

Morris, D. (1999b). *The Howard Street tutoring manual: Teaching at-risk readers in the primary grades.* New York: Guilford Press.

Morris, D., & Nelson, L. (1992). Supported oral reading with low-achieving second graders. *Reading Research and Instruction, 32,* 49–63.

Morris, D., Shaw, B., & Perney, J. (1990). Helping low readers in grades 2 and 3: An after-school volunteer tutoring program. *Elementary School Journal, 91,* 133–147.

Morris, D., Tschannen-Moran, M., & Weidemann, E. (1981). An inner-city LEA tutoring program. *Journal of Language Experience, 3,* 9–24.

National Assessment of Educational Progress. (1995). *NAEP 1994 reading: A first look—Findings from the National Assessment of Educational Progress* (rev. ed.). Washington, DC: U.S. Government Printing Office.

Pinnell, G. S., Lyons, C., DeFord, D., Bryk, A., & Seltzer, M. (1994). Comparing instructional models for the literacy education of high-risk first graders. *Reading Research Quarterly, 29,* 8–39.

Santa, C., & Hoien, T. (1999). An assessment of Early Steps: A program for early intervention of reading problems. *Reading Research Quarterly, 34,* 54–79.

Schon, D. (1987). *Educating the reflective practitioner.* San Francisco: Jossey-Bass.

Shanahan, T., & Barr, R. (1995). Reading Recovery: An independent evaluation of the effects of an early instructional intervention for at-risk learners. *Reading Research Quarterly, 30,* 958–996.

Slavin, R., Madden, N., Dolan, L., Wasik, B., Ross, S., Smith, L., & Dianda, M. (1996). Success for All: A summary of the research. *Journal of Education for Students Placed at Risk, 1,* 41–76.

Stanovich, K. (1986). Matthew effects in reading: Some consequences of individual differences in the acquisition of literacy. *Reading Research Quarterly, 21,* 360–406.

Wasik, B., & Slavin, R. (1990). *Preventing early reading failure with one-to-one tutoring: A best evidence synthesis.* Paper presented at the annual convention of the American Educational Research Association, Boston.

Chapter 10

BOOK BUDDIES: A COMMUNITY VOLUNTEER TUTORIAL PROGRAM

Marcia Invernizzi

My lesson plans are always completely individualized for my student, and everything is organized and ready to go by the time I get here. Susan (my coordinator) is looking right over my shoulder to steer me along. That's what makes Book Buddies so effective, and that's why I keep coming back.

> —HOLLY CONTI
> *Book Buddies Volunteer 1993–present*

Book Buddies is a volunteer reading tutorial program for first and second graders who are substantially behind their peers in literacy development. The parent program originated in Charlottesville, Virginia, a midsized city where one in three children live in poverty (Spar, 1997). The program was born of necessity, out of limited resources and seemingly unlimited need. Before the publication of reading results from the National Assessment of Educational Progress (1994), before the America Reads Challenge Act of 1997, and before the Reading Excellence Act of 1998, Charlottesville City Schools (CCS) administrators were searching for help: In 1993, 60% of their fourth graders scored below the 50th percentile on the Iowa Test of Basic Skills in reading achievement (CCS, 1994).

Conscientious CCS division administrators were looking for ways to provide one-on-one assistance for their struggling readers. They knew that one-on-one instruction yields better results than small-group instruction (Glass, Cahen, Smith, & Filby, 1982), and they worried about their use of Title I funds in the face of disheartening statistics. Although nationally, students receiving Title I services were showing larger increases in their standardized reading scores than were comparable non-Title I students, gains were minimal—increases of only 3 to 5 percentile rankings (Kennedy, Birman, & Demaline, 1986). CCS administrators knew that such small gains had no practical effect: Their Title I children remained among the lowest-achieving children for years (Dyer & Binkney, 1995).

To add to their worries about Title I, CCS administrators were aware of recent research underscoring the urgency of early reading achievement. The research of Juel (1988), Stanovich (1986), and others showed that children who did not learn to read well in first grade continued to do poorly in subsequent grades and even into adulthood (Bruck, 1992). Worse, this pattern of failure had a host of negative side effects: These children were found to experience persistent difficulty, frustration, and a loss of self-esteem because of their low reading achievement.

Happily, the research of Slavin, Madden, and Karweit (1989), Pinnell, DeFord, and Lyons (1988), and others has demonstrated the powerful effect of one-on-one instruction in curbing these disturbing statistics. Although exemplary classroom instruction is the first line of defense (Snow, Burns, & Griffin, 1998), some children need additional support beyond what even the most knowledgeable and talented teacher can provide in a room full of approximately 20 other children. According to Juel (1996), the key to teaching a struggling child to read is to provide "verbal interactions, instructions, and written materials that [are] on the right level and at the right time" (p. 288)—a task that may be difficult to accomplish in a whole-class situation. Torgesen and Hecht's (1997) research has also validated the power of one-on-one tutoring: "It may indeed be the case that the only way to provide opportunities for some children to acquire normal reading skills is to provide one-on-one instruction over a significant period of time" (p. 153). Considering the balance of information and reality, teachers, CCS administrators, researchers, and leaders from the community all agreed that early, one-on-one intervention was pivotal to the reading success of Charlottesville's at-risk children.

At the time, Reading Recovery (Clay, 1985) and Success for All (Slavin, Madden, Karweit, Dolan, & Wasik, 1994) were the only two large-scale reading interventions reporting significant effects. Both provide one-on-one tutoring in reading, but both are prohibitively expensive for a small, economically stressed school system—from $3,000 to $6,000 per child, by some estimates (Hiebert, 1994; Shanahan & Barr, 1995). Nevertheless, Charlottesville educators made the most of what research had to say about early intervention, and a creative alternative evolved: Book Buddies, a community volunteer, one-on-one reading tutorial program. In Book Buddies, volunteer tutors can provide the one-on-one instruction that is needed by, but would otherwise be unavailable to, struggling first-grade readers.

The idea was not original. The Howard Street Tutoring Program had already demonstrated the effectiveness of using volunteers to give supplemental, one-on-one instruction to struggling readers in the second grade. Posttests based on 17 matched pairs at the end of the program's first year showed significant differences for the tutored group over the control group on measures of spelling, general word recognition, and basal word recognition (from 0.5 to 1.5 grade levels). Data from the second year indicated similar findings (Morris, Shaw, & Perney, 1990). But unlike Reading Recovery and Success for All, the Howard Street format is affordable.

The key to Howard Street's success has been its model of on-site, ongoing supervision (see Morris, Chapter 9, this volume). In this program, reading specialist supervisors write individualized lesson plans and provide ongoing training, feedback, and direction to volunteer tutors who work under the supervisors' surveillance. Through the Howard Street plan, the expertise of one reading specialist is thus multiplied through a dozen volunteers. Though the program is small and serves only a dozen or two students per year, the Howard Street format has well-documented staying power, so CCS administrators knew the model was sound and could be trusted. What Book Buddies has added is a delivery system that substantially multiplies the number of children to be served, and a simplified lesson plan that can be mass-produced without compromising quality.

This chapter describes the history of Book Buddies from its inception as a pilot program with only 9 first-grade students in one school, to its present status as a permanent, divisionwide intervention program in six schools, serving approximately 130–140 first graders and 24 second-grade students per year. A detailed description of the Book Buddies program illustrates the lesson plans and management system that have contributed to its capacity to serve as a model for the America Reads Challenge. Since its inception, Book Buddies has served over 1,100 first and second graders in Charlottesville, and hundreds of additional students in other locations on the U.S. east coast. The chapter ends with some lessons learned through Book Buddies adaptations in other sites. Versions of Book Buddies have been transplanted to several other geographic localities—in some cases unexpectedly, through the natural transmigration of Book Buddies participants, and in other cases through intentional efforts to test the model in randomized, control-group settings. Each of these scenarios highlights important considerations for implementing volunteer tutorial programs.

BEGINNINGS

Book Buddies began in one school on a budget of approximately $3,000—a grant awarded from a local educational foundation. Early in the year, the principal selected nine of the neediest students from three first-grade classrooms. Although proficient in oral narration and other important language skills, these nine students could not name the letters of the alphabet, and they did not know that letters represent sounds. Although they could memorize a simple two- to four-line nursery rhyme, they could not accurately point to the corresponding words in print as they recited it. All nine had attended kindergarten, though their attendance records revealed more than the average number of absences.

The principal rounded up a group of committed volunteers. About half were mothers of high-achieving students in the same school who were not working outside their family households. Many of these women had advanced degrees, but had put their professional careers on hold until their children were older. Others were retirees in the school neighborhood (senior citizens who lived across the street). A few were men and women from local businesses seeking to establish partnerships with neighborhood schools. All committed themselves to one-on-one tutoring, two times a week—provided that the lesson plan was already prepared, materials were already gathered, and they were shown what to do and how.

The $3,000 went to a graduate student in reading education who was interested in adapting the Howard Street Tutoring model in an in-school context. She assessed each of the students for specific literacy needs, and wrote individualized lesson plans for each tutoring session. She gathered all necessary books and supplies for each lesson, and organized them in a separate basket for each child. She scheduled her tutors across the week so that she only had to supervise three at any given time. Once a week, directly following the tutorials, she met with her volunteers in small groups to reflect on their instructional efforts. At this time she modeled certain literacy routines, and answered questions about how children learn to read.

We began with the emergent-reader lesson plan outlined in *The Howard Street Tutoring Manual* (Morris, 1999), one of three lesson plans for emergent, beginning, and instructional-level readers detailed in that propitious volume. But because of logistical differences between the in-school format we had adopted, and the after-school, storefront prototype described by Morris (1999), we were forced to find ways to simplify. Our reading specialist/graduate student had to move back and forth between classrooms in order to direct the tutorials, and they were scheduled at different times throughout the week as opposed to simultaneously in one location. In addition, because children "took off" at different rates, volunteers had to switch from the emergent to the beginner plan at different times (often just as they were feeling competent in teaching from the emergent plan). In an effort to economize, we combined the essential components of Morris's emergent and beginner plans so that a volunteer could work with the same child using the same tutoring format for the majority of the school year. The new Book Buddies emergent-to-beginner plan consisted of rereading for fluency, alphabet and word study, writing for sounds, and learning a new book. Similar instructional components are common to other successful one-on-one interventions. Reading Recovery (Clay, 1985); Iverson and Tunmer's (1993) modified version of Reading Recovery, First Steps (Morris, 1995), now known as Early Steps (Santa & Hoien, 1999); and Success for All (Slavin et al., 1994) all include rereading of familiar material, phonics, writing, and supported reading of new material.

All nine children learned to read that year, and the volunteers were ecstatic about their success. A report summarizing student assessment data across the year prompted CCS division leaders to articulate a larger vision, to ensure the early reading achievement of all their at-risk students in all six elementary schools.

THE VISION

From the beginning, Book Buddies was only one piece of the CCS's long-range vision to ensure that all first- and second-grade children would learn to read "independently and well" by the third grade. Called the Charlottesville Reading Initiative, this long-range plan included several other components associated with effective schools: (1) a long-term commitment to staff development for all classroom teachers in kindergarten through second grade; (2) flexible use of Title I funds to increase the use of one-on-one tutorials; (3) the training and use of aides to provide instructional assistance in kindergarten and first-grade classrooms; and (4) proactive recruitment and retention of community volunteers to serve as tutors. Staff development, alternative configurations for the use of Title I teachers and instructional aides, and the community volunteer tutorial program known as Book Buddies would work conjointly to ensure that all children would learn to read independently and well by the end of third grade.

A partnership was subsequently formed among the CCS, the McGuffey Reading Center at the University of Virginia (UVA), and the community of Charlottesville. The CCS provided administrative support and a part-time volunteer recruiter who was well known in the community. Faculty and staff from the UVA's Curry School of Education provided the overall design, the instructional leadership, and data analyses. Citizens from the Charlottesville community provided the human resources necessary for a large-scale, one-on-one intervention. Working together with the other aspects of the Charlottesville Reading Initiative, Book Buddies set about (1) to improve the reading achievement of at-risk children, and (2) to establish and maintain the community's involvement in and responsibility for the education of all its children.

THE ORGANIZATION

By necessity, Book Buddies evolved a management system capable of delivering high-quality instruction to 140–160 students per year in six different schools using 140–150 volunteers. There were three critical groups of players: (1) the CCS and their volunteer recruiter, (2) professors from the UVA's Curry School of Education, and (3) reading specialist coordinators who worked on site with the community volunteers. Called the "envied triumvirate," these key players met twice a month to iron out the logistics of running a large-scale project, and to brainstorm solutions to problems as they arose.

Each partner in the Book Buddies organization took on a particular role and rendered a particular service. The CCS volunteer recruiter solicited interested community members through the local media, through public meetings with community service groups and business associations, and through personal contacts. She placed the volunteers in the school closest to their home or office, and introduced them to their on-site reading coordinator. Professors from UVA provided introductory large-group training sessions in the fall and spring, led biweekly discussions at the partnership meetings, organized the data collection for program evaluation, and fine-tuned the lesson plan from year to year. The reading coordinators (all trained reading specialists) provided ongoing training and support for the tutors by writing lesson plans; arranging materials for each lesson; and supplying routine feedback regarding specific activities, techniques, and pacing. They also acted as the intermediaries between tutors and teachers. Each coordinator supervised 15 volunteer tutors and their respective tutees. In schools where the numbers of at-risk children were high, two coordinators worked together to double their caseload. Nine coordinators organized the Book Buddies tutorial program in six elementary schools. Even now, the partners in the "envied triumvirate" still meet twice a month, at a different school each time.

Critical aspects of the Book Buddies organization emanated from the partnership meetings. At these biweekly meetings, details of each coordinator's set-up were shared and observed. The overall Book Buddies management system evolved from these regular meetings. Discussion topics included (1) the organization of the books; (2) the arrangement of the picture cards for phonics sorts; (3) the system for harvesting sight words; and (4) the organization of the tutoring boxes. These topics were picked over and tinkered with until the set-up in each school matured into a near-standardized format that supported the smooth and systematic implementation of the Book Buddies lesson plan.

Another critical part of the Book Buddies organization included the setting, and the setting changed after the very first year. In the beginning, the tutorials took place in the classrooms at tutoring stations set up in corners. The proximity of tutors to teachers spawned salutary interactions and a sharing of information, techniques, and materials. Many of the Book Buddies participants liked the in-class model, but many others just found it distracting. It was also difficult for the reading coordinator to move freely from tutorial to tutorial when they occurred in different classrooms. In effect, the in-class model prohibited efficient supervision of volunteers. As a result, in the second year, the Book Buddies tutorial format became a pull-out format that occurred in a separate classroom. Tutorials were scheduled during seatwork time or "special" activities (e.g., music, art, library visits), to avoid conflicts with academic instruction in the classroom. In some schools, second-grade tutorials were scheduled after school.

The move to separate classrooms did sacrifice beneficial interactions between tutors and teachers. The responsibility for communication between each tutor and teacher then fell to the coordinator, who now had to schedule time to coordinate reading homework and other instructional issues with each classroom teacher. Nevertheless, the move contributed greatly to the smoothness of the operation. Coordinators could more easily supervise four to five tutors at one time, and there was quiet space to reflect on their instructional efforts. Tutor-training seminars and discussions could be scheduled throughout the year in these rooms, and Book Buddies meetings provided opportunities to share the organizational systems at hand. Coordinators also now had all of the necessary materials at their fingertips; for example, books could be organized by reading level, and by phonics features within levels. The overall organization of the Book Buddies room and the coordinators' set-up are described in detail in Chapter 2, "The Role of the Coordinator," in the Book Buddies tutoring manual called *Book Buddies: Guidelines for Volunteer Tutors of Emergent and Early Readers* (Johnston, Invernizzi, & Juel, 1998).

As noted earlier, Book Buddies began as a local-grant-sponsored program in one pilot school. The first 3 years were jointly funded by CCS and private foundation grants awarded to the faculty at the UVA's Curry School of Education. Small grants were awarded by local foundations (mostly for the purchase of materials), and larger grants were awarded

Organization of books by level of difficulty and recurring phonics features.

by larger corporate foundations (mostly for coordinator salaries). By the third year, CCS assumed full responsibility for 100% of the salaries paid to all reading coordinators and the volunteer recruiter, as well as all expenses for books and materials. Significant in-kind contributions from the community, from UVA faculty and graduate students, and now from federal work–study (FW-S) students continue to support the program.

The cost per child has escalated over the years as the reading coordinators have moved from the periphery to the center of the CCS's intervention services. At first, reading coordinators were the linchpins of an experimental partnership, and their compensation reflected their ambiguous, grant-supported identity. After several years of research proving the program's effectiveness (see Invernizzi, Juel, & Rosemary, 1996–1997; Invernizzi, Rosemary, Juel, & Richards, 1997; Meier & Invernizzi, in press), the CCS assumed full financial responsibility for the program. No longer an experimental, volunteer tutorial, Book Buddies became the model for citywide intervention efforts. Today, working 20 hours per week, reading coordinators are paid as full-fledged, part-time reading specialists, and their salary equals that of any half-time faculty member with a master's degree, plus benefits. The volunteer recruiter is also a half-time employee of the school division. So, while the cost per child (including all salaries and all materials) was determined to be just $595 in 1996 (Invernizzi et al., 1996–1997), the per-student cost is now nearly $1,000.

Nevertheless, this per-pupil cost is still only one fourth to one eighth of the cost of other one-on-one tutorials using highly trained reading specialists (Hiebert, 1994; Shanahan & Barr, 1995).

THE LESSON PLANS

Although the Book Buddies program was originally designed primarily for at-risk first graders, the program has also served a small number of retained first graders by providing an additional year of one-on-one instruction. In addition to these retainees, Book Buddies serves second graders who are a year or more behind in reading. These students are often new to the school system or for some other reason have not benefited from previous intervention. A second lesson plan was fashioned specifically for these second graders—one that places more emphasis on reading comprehension and writing.

As a result, Book Buddies has two lesson plans: one for emergent-to-beginning readers who are, for the most part, in first grade; and the other for early readers in the second grade who have achieved at least a primer or mid-first-grade reading level. The instructional components of both plans have remained the same since their inception, though certain routines have been added and others refined by conscientious reading coordinators (e.g., Fowler & Lindemann, 2000; Lindemann & Fowler, in press). Although simple enough for volunteers to follow, these lesson plans can become more or less explicit, depending on an individual child's needs.

Tutors follow a sequence of core activities planned by the reading coordinators in a four-part lesson plan described in the Book Buddies tutoring manual (Johnston et al., 1998).

The Emergent-to-Beginner Plan

In the first-grade Book Buddies tutorial plan, the emergent-to-beginning reader completes a lesson that includes (1) independent, easy-level reading (rereading), (2) word study (alphabet and phonics), (3) writing for sounds, and (4) instructional-level reading (new reading). All activities are completed within a 45-minute session.

At the beginning of each lesson, the student rereads familiar books with the tutor, to develop fluency and confidence in reading. The student reads approximately four to six little books, and this activity lasts approximately 10–12 minutes.

In the second section of the lesson, word study, the student's attention is focused on individual sounds and words. Included in this part of

Rereading easy books to warm up. A Retired Senior Volunteer (RSV) AmeriCorps tutor rereads an easy book with her first-grade tutee.

the lesson are the word bank, "push and say it," and other word study activities. First, the student adds known words from one of his/her books to a personalized word bank. These words are then periodically reviewed (about every fourth session). Next, the student practices segmenting and blending sounds, using letter tiles that form words. The examples selected for "push and say it" correspond to the sounds and word patterns selected for that day's word study instruction. Finally, the student participates in several other word study activities. For instance, the student sorts picture and word cards, and writes the words from the sorts in his/her word study notebook. During all of these activities, the child compares and contrasts sounds and patterns in words (Bear, Invernizzi, Templeton, & Johnston, 1999). For the emergent-to-beginning reader, word study instruction begins with initial sound sorts, then word family and short vowel sorts, and finally consonant blend sorts. All of these activities last approximately 15–20 minutes.

During the third part of the lesson, writing for sounds, the child writes either a dictated sentence taken from one of his/her familiar books, or a dictated sentence composed of phonetic features previously taught. The child is responsible for using a capital letter at the beginning of each sentence and a period at the end of each sentence, as well as for correctly spelling any learned word patterns. The child is also encouraged to spell

Organization of picture cards by sequence of phonics instruction.

Recording a phonics sort in the word study notebook.

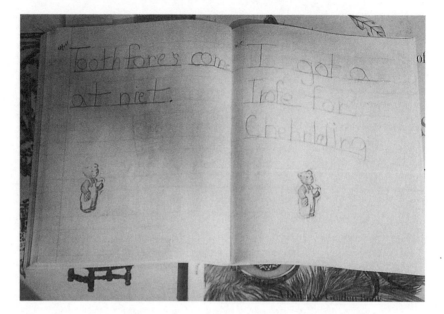

Writing for sounds: A Book Buddies writing sample.

high-frequency words correctly, and receives support with this task. As the student becomes a stronger writer, he/she is often required to write more than one sentence. This part of the lesson lasts approximately 8–10 minutes.

The lesson concludes with the child's reading from a new book. This activity allows the student to apply word knowledge and reading strategies to a new book. The tutor previews the book through informal conversation about the title and pictures, asks the child to make predictions, points out difficult words in the book, and talks about concepts or vocabulary that will be encountered in the story. After the preview, the child begins to read the book, and the tutor encourages the child and provides strategies for figuring out difficult words. This activity takes approximately 8–10 minutes to complete.

The Early Reader Plan

The early reader plan was designed primarily for second graders, though many first graders finish the year with this plan as well. The early reader is differentiated from the emergent-to-beginning reader by the student's level of achievement in reading, and by the ease of the student's writing. To work with the early reader plan, students must be able to read preprimer books independently, and their writing must include several sight words spelled correctly.

A balanced literacy diet for the early instructional reader includes (1) reading for fluency, (2) word study, and (3) reading and writing comprehension. As in the emergent-to-beginner plan, all activities are completed within a 45-minute period.

The early reader lesson begins with a brief warm-up in easy reading to build confidence, speed, and fluency. The easy-level reading selections are read orally in a variety of activities, including repeated readings of familiar books or favorite sections of books, timed repeated readings, poetry readings, or Reader's Theatre. These activities are completed within 5 to 10 minutes.

In the second part of the lesson, word study, the student's attention is focused on spelling patterns and decoding. The student sorts words into categories by spelling patterns. Usually two or three categories are compared. After sorting, the student checks to see that all the words are in the correct columns, and articulates what is similar and different about the categories. Next, the child writes examples of the words just sorted into his/her word study notebook. Additional activities that provide practice spelling or decoding words are incorporated as needed. These may include the use of letter tiles, onset-rime flip books, dice, or word games. In a 45-minute tutorial, the word study section of the early reader lesson lasts from 10 to 15 minutes.

The lesson concludes with an extended period of reading and writing. The student is encouraged to read silently when his/her reading level approaches the end of first grade. The purpose of the extended reading is to improve the student's comprehension of instructional-level material. The section is divided into before-reading, during-reading, and after-reading activities. Writing may be included in any one of these activities. Before reading, a student's prior knowledge is activated through a book or topic introduction. Students may be asked to predict what information might be contained in a book about animals, or they may be asked to list everything they know about the topic. During reading, the student is actively engaged through predicting and questioning techniques, summarizing, and/or note taking. Depending upon the student's level of prior knowledge, his/her interest in the topic, and his/her motivation to keep reading, the tutor may need to interact more or less frequently to ensure that the child comprehends what is read. After reading, the student revisits portions of the text as he/she writes or describes what he/she has learned from the new book. The lesson ends by summarizing what was learned that day.

The Book Buddies assessment determines whether a student will begin working with the emergent-to-beginner plan or the early reader plan. The assessment includes a thorough evaluation of a student's alphabet knowledge (alphabet recognition and letter sounds), knowledge of phoneme–grapheme correspondences (spelling and writing), and word recognition in and out of context. The Book Buddies assessment is described in detail in Chapter 3 of the Book Buddies tutoring manual, where necessary materials may also be found (Johnston et al., 1998).

THE TUTORING BOX

Once a child is assessed, the coordinator begins to plan the reading lessons. The lesson plan, and all books and materials necessary to conduct the lesson, are organized in a cardboard file box (such as those used to file magazines in libraries before the days of ERIC). These boxes are labeled with the names and pictures of the child and his/her tutor. Often the days and times of scheduled tutoring lessons are printed on the box as well. When the tutor arrives, he/she looks for the tutoring box, and then takes a few moments to go over the lesson plan and preview the materials. If the tutor has any questions, the coordinator is on hand to address them before the lesson starts.

In the Book Buddies tutoring box are the following: (1) the lesson plan; (2) familiar books to be reread for fluency; (3) word bank cards and a word bank folder; (4) a composition book for writing and recording word sorts; (5) picture and/or word cards for phonics sorts; (6) the new book to be read that day; and (7) record-keeping lists. It is the coordinator's job to prepare this box before every tutoring lesson. After each lesson, the coordinator checks the lesson plan for tutor comments, writes a new lesson plan based on those responses, then refreshes the box for the next lesson.

ADAPTATIONS

Book Buddies has been adapted in several other communities as a result of the natural transmigration of graduate students, teachers, and reading coordinators, who were touched in some way by the parent program in Charlottesville. In each case, the overall organization has been modified to meet the unique needs of a given school community. In Northumberland County, for example—a poor, rural fishing community—Book Buddies evolved into an after-school tutorial called Reading Partners. In this adaptation, Northumberland teachers who completed a graduate reading course on early intervention were paid to serve as reading coordinators after school. Each teacher wrote tutorial plans for three students and supervised three volunteers twice a week. With 15 teachers working

A Book Buddies tutoring box.

2 extra hours twice a week, 45 at-risk students were able to receive high-quality, one-on-one instruction throughout the year. The program is in its fourth year. Despite increased pressure to meet new state standards in literacy achievement, Northumberland's reading achievement scores are going up (Staples, 1998).

One noteworthy adaptation took the Book Buddies volunteer tutorial to Roosevelt Elementary School in a neighboring school division in central Virginia. Expectations for program implementation were initially similar to those of CCS; volunteer tutors were expected to take the major responsibility for providing one-on-one reading support. However, something quite different happened in this new context. Classroom teachers, administrators (including the principal), and other school staff members became tutors alongside of community volunteers, and by doing so became personally involved in the one-on-one intervention program. Classroom literacy practices began to mirror the content of the tutoring lesson plans, as teachers saw how children develop specific literacy skills within a focused, one-on-one setting. Schedules changed to accommodate extended periods of uninterrupted time for reading and to reduce class size for instruction. In an attempt to support classroom teachers and Title I teachers in accelerating the pace of literacy learning for their at-risk first graders, a school-based professional development program began.

Some parts of the adapted Book Buddies lesson plan, such as reread-ing familiar books and book introductions, were familiar to classroom teachers; others, such as "push and say it" and other word study activi-ties, were new. With the support of an on-site Book Buddies consultant—a reading specialist who continued to write lesson plans for teachers and volunteers alike—teachers felt less stress about taking on additional re-sponsibility and trying something new. The end result was more aggres-sive literacy instruction in the classroom with smaller groups of children.

Working together toward a common goal increased the academic communication among school personnel, parents, and community vol-unteers. Participating in an early intervention program encouraged the classroom teachers who were also tutors to reflect upon the individual literacy needs of children in the tutorial program and in the classroom. Tutoring also increased communication and collaboration among par-ticipating teachers, administrators, volunteers, parents, and university personnel. What began as a community volunteer tutorial program ended up serving as a catalyst for school reform (Broaddus & Bloodgood, 1999).

Book Buddies has also been transplanted into other geographical locations by design. One such effort took Book Buddies to a school in the South Bronx to test the model with tutors typically employed in America Reads and the Corporation for National Service: AmeriCorps, Volunteers in Service to America (VISTA), and FW-S tutors. Unlike the tutors in the parent program, the tutors in Book Buddies in the South Bronx were not homogeneously white, female, and highly educated. On the contrary, the Retired Senior Volunteer (RSV) AmeriCorps seniors who tutored in the South Bronx Book Buddies project formed a diverse group; fewer than half had attended college at all, and 15% spoke English as a second language. Nearly all of the Book Buddies students in this project spoke Spanish as their primary language. Nevertheless, significant inter-vention effects were obtained with this diverse group of national service volunteers delivering one-on-one instruction in an America Reads site in one of the poorest Congressional districts in America (Meier & Invernizzi, in press).

Not surprisingly, Book Buddies in the South Bronx also had to make some ecological adjustments. Because of contractual obligations with the Corporation for National Service, the South Bronx Book Buddies tutors worked every day. As a result, instead of tutoring twice a week, each child received four tutoring sessions per week. And because so many children needed help, the first first-grade cohort was tutored for 40 sessions be-tween September and January, and a second first-grade cohort was tutored between January and June. Although each first-grade cohort only received half a year of tutoring, all first graders in need of one-on-one assistance received 40 sessions by the end of the school year. Other adaptations included (1) a formalized system for make-up sessions because of the high number of school absences, and (2) weekly small-group tutor-training sessions in addition to the daily supervision. Because so many tutors themselves were not native speakers of English, it was necessary to schedule additional time for direct instruction in pronouncing English letter sounds in isolation and other important linguistic concepts.

THE RESEARCH AND THE LESSONS LEARNED

The effectiveness of the Book Buddies program has been evaluated by several different studies. First, we studied the achievement gains within and across the academic years since the Charlottesville program's inception (Invernizzi et al., 1997). Second, we compared the effects of the Charlottesville Book Buddies intervention with other first-grade interventions in similar school divisions within Virginia (Invernizzi, 1999). Third, we followed children longitudinally to evaluate the program's lasting effects (Invernizzi, 1999). Fourth, we examined the effectiveness of using FW-S students as tutors working with second graders on the early reader plan (Fowler, Lindemann, Thacker-Gwaltney, & Invernizzi, 1999). Lastly, we tested the viability of the Book Buddies program as a model for the America Reads Challenge in a random-assignment, matched-control group setting in the South Bronx (Meier & Invernizzi, in press). Each of these studies has shown that at least two sessions of one-on-one tutoring per week, by trained, supported, and supervised volunteer tutors for a minimum of 20 weeks, can be an effective and affordable alternative intervention for children at risk of reading failure.

In the first study, program evaluations of the first three Charlottesville Book Buddies cohorts reported effect sizes of 1.24 for word recognition, and results showed consistent improvement from one year to the next (Invernizzi et al., 1997). Overall, the results from the first study demonstrate that trained and supervised volunteers can be effective tutors for at-risk first graders. Indeed, effect sizes of that magnitude are "comparable to those found with professionally trained teachers" (Snow et al., 1998, p. 260). Furthermore, when volunteers receive ongoing training over the course of an entire year or longer, they become quite skilled—and, more importantly, they come back! Fifty-eight percent of the Charlottesville community volunteers have tutored for more than 3 years, and 25% have tutored since the program's inception in the early 1990s. The staying power of these supporters of the public schools makes it possible to provide high-quality one-on-one instruction to those who need it most.

In the second study, we learned that the Charlottesville Book Buddies program yields better results than other first-grade interventions in the same geographical region. We compared results for the seventh-year, first-grade Charlottesville Book Buddies cohort to the results of other first-grade interventions occurring in school divisions with similar demographics within Region 5 (the geographical region to which Charlottesville is assigned by the Virginia State Department of Education). Twenty students, or 19%, of the 1998–1999 first graders in the Book Buddies program did not meet the end-of-the-year benchmarks for reading on grade level. Elsewhere in Region 5, over 39% of the first graders who were identified in the fall of the year as at risk remained at risk even after 1 year of intervention. Charlottesville's Book Buddies students fared considerably better in comparison, and this difference was statistically significant ($t = 3.609$, $p < .001$).

We have some indication that these first-grade Book Buddies intervention results have held up to the test of time. For example, of the children listed as reading below grade level on the needs assessment list at the feeder middle school in 1997–1998, only 19% were former participants in Book Buddies. In addition, preliminary analyses of Iowa Test of Basic Skills reading results from the third-year Book Buddies cohort (1994–1995) showed significantly better scores than the scores for a historical control selected from Title I referrals prior to Book Buddies and the Charlottesville Reading Initiative (Invernizzi, 1999).

In the fourth study, we learned that FW-S students can also be effective tutors when trained and given ongoing support like community volunteers. We investigated the effectiveness of FW-S students as tutors within the second-grade Book Buddies program. This small, quasi-experimental pilot study reported encouraging results: The mean scores of second-grade children receiving a second year of Book Buddies intervention through the services of FW-S students were consistently higher than those of matched controls across all literacy measures (Fowler et al., 1999). Most importantly, every child in the tutored group was reading at or above grade level, as measured by word identification and contextual reading by the end of the intervention. The Book Buddies extension into second grade yielded benefits both for the tutored children and for the FW-S students participating in America Reads. FW-S students received systematic training in early reading instruction, and practiced applying their newly acquired skills in the community under the careful supervision of the Book Buddies coordinator. In the words of one FW-S tutor, "I wish I learned as much in my classes as I do tutoring in Book Buddies."

In the South Bronx Book Buddies project, as noted earlier, we tested the Book Buddies model using RSV AmeriCorps, VISTA, and FW-S tutors for high-risk first-grade students in a challenging urban setting. In this matched design with a randomly assigned control group, the results showed that Book Buddies tutoring produced clear effects, regardless of whether the tutoring took place in the fall or spring of first grade. The results from the January testing showed that the children who received 40 Book Buddies lessons significantly surpassed the students in the control group on measures of word reading in context, letter identification, and word reading in isolation. The findings from the June testing revealed that the group of students who received tutoring during the second half of the school year were able to progress to the point where there were no distinguishable differences between the two groups at the end of the year. From these findings, we learned that when the pace of tutoring is intensified, it doesn't matter when tutoring begins during the first-grade year. If 40 sessions of one-on-one tutoring are provided to two different groups of students, twice as many students can be served. We also learned, however, that twice as much work is involved in the supervision and training.

We have also learned many lessons through the Book Buddies adaptations. We have learned that the Book Buddies model can be adjusted to fit many different contexts. Just as we adapted the Howard Street model for the Charlottesville context, surrounding school divisions have adapted Book Buddies to suit their own needs. In some cases, the adaptations have resulted in a better model. By including teachers in the intervention plan to meet the needs of struggling readers, for example, Roosevelt Elementary School stumbled onto a powerful concept. Giving teachers focused time and ongoing professional support while they too participated in a one-on-one early intervention tutoring program changed their perceptions of remedial instruction and of the students they were teaching. In addition, these insights were transferred into classroom practice.

We are currently researching the characteristics of successful tutors and modifying our infrastructure to accommodate more interactions between Book Buddies coordinators and classroom teachers. To date, the consistency of instruction a child receives in the Book Buddies tutoring setting and in the classroom appears to be idiosyncratic to schools and to teachers. Qualitative classroom observation data suggest that a good many of our students are placed in books that are too difficult for them to read in the classroom, and that the phonics instruction they receive is beyond their current understanding of how the written system works. It does no good, for example, to try to teach a child long vowel patterns that involve silent letters if that child is still grappling with basic letter–sound correspondences. Until greater congruence is achieved between intervention programs and classroom instruction, we may be "spinning our wheels" (Walmsley & Allington, 1995).

Despite the fact that the Book Buddies program has been able to achieve effect sizes comparable to those achieved with highly trained professionals, and that the number of children reading below grade level has significantly declined, retention rates and special education placements have not gone down since either Book Buddies or the Charlottesville Reading Initiative was implemented. It may very well be that interventions that do not include the classroom teacher have the negative effect of supplanting effective classroom instruction—the most essential ingredient for long-term success. Research on the Book Buddies volunteer tutorial model indicates that well-trained and supervised volunteers can have an impact on student reading performance. Certainly, however, volunteer tutors should not be expected to take the place of effective classroom reading instruction, or of the important role played by a reading teacher or specialist. Government incentives to provide additional assistance for schools in the form of volunteer or FW-S tutors should be contingent upon a larger vision for intersecting plans, such as staff development for classroom teachers and tutors, program evaluation, and school restructuring efforts to accommodate communication and effective instruction (Walmsley & Allington, 1995). The adaptation of Book Buddies at Roosevelt may just have stumbled on the solution.

Nevertheless, Book Buddies has generated many immeasurable benefits. Community volunteers have gained an appreciation for the diversity of the student population and for the challenges such diversity presents to the classroom teacher. They have begun to understand the ongoing debate between "phonics" and "whole language," and have acquired a deeper sense of how children learn to read. Coordinators, most of whom are graduate students in reading education, have learned to translate their erudition into common sense, and have become skilled in the arts of communication and persuasion. University faculty have learned what it takes to become trusted by a school division. Teachers and other school personnel have learned to reach out to the community for help to accomplish what they cannot do alone. And the children have learned to read.

ACKNOWLEDGMENTS

The work described herein was partially supported under the Educational Research and Development Centers Program, PR/Award No. R305R70004, as administered by the Office of Educational Research and Improvement, U.S. Department of Education. However, the contents do not necessarily represent the positions or policies of the National Institute on Student Achievement, Curriculum and Assessment; or the National Institute on Early Childhood Development; or the U.S. Department of Education.

REFERENCES

Bear, D., Invernizzi, M., Templeton, S., & Johnston F. (1999). *Words their way: Word study for phonics, vocabulary, and spelling instruction.* Upper Saddle River, NJ: Prentice-Hall.

Broaddus, K., & Bloodgood, J. (1999). "We're already supposed to know how to teach reading": Teacher change to support struggling readers. *Reading Research Quarterly, 34*(4), 426–451.

Bruck, M. (1992). Persistence of dyslexics' phonological awareness deficits. *Developmental Psychology, 26,* 439–454.

Charlottesville City Schools (CCS). (1994). *Summary report: 1993–1994 testing program.* Charlottesville, VA: Author.

Clay, M. (1985). *The early detection of reading difficulties.* Auckland, New Zealand: Heinemann.

Dyer, P., & Binkney, R. (1995). Estimating cost-effectiveness and educational outcomes: Retention, remediation, special education, and early intervention. In R. Allington & S. Walmsley (Eds.), *No quick fix* (pp. 61–77). New York: Teachers College Press.

Fowler, M., & Lindemann, L. (2000). *Book Buddies training manual: An interactive approach for tutors of beginning readers.* University of Virginia Curry School of Education McGuffey/TEMPO Reading Outreach and The Center for the Improvement of Early Reading Achievement. Report submitted to the Center for the Improvement of Early Reading Achievement (CIERA), University of Virginia.

Fowler, M., Lindemann, L., Thacker-Gwaltney, S., & Invernizzi, M. (1999). *A second year of one-on-one tutoring: An intervention for second graders with reading difficulties.* Manuscript submitted for publication.

Glass, G., Cahen, L, Smith, M. L., & Filby, N. (1982). *School class size.* Beverly Hills, CA: Sage.

Hiebert, E. (1994). Reading Recovery in the United States: What difference does it make to an age cohort? *Educational Researcher, 23,* 15–25.

Invernizzi, M. (1999, October 21). *1998–1999 Book Buddies results report.* Report submitted to the Charlottesville City School Board.

Invernizzi, M., Juel, C., & Rosemary, C. (1996–1997). A community volunteer tutorial that works. *The Reading Teacher, 50*(4), 304–311.

Invernizzi, M., Rosemary, C., Juel, C., & Richards, H. C. (1997). At-risk readers and community volunteers: A 3-year perspective. *Scientific Studies of Reading, 1,* 277–300.

Iverson, A. J., & Tunmer, W. E. (1993). Phonological processing skills and the Reading Recovery program. *Journal of Educational Psychology, 85,* 112–126.

Johnston, F. R., Invernizzi, M., & Juel, C. (1998). *Book Buddies: Guidelines for volunteer tutors of emergent and early readers.* New York: Guilford Press.

Juel, C. (1988). Learning to read and write: A longitudinal study of fifty-four children from first through fourth grade. *Journal of Educational Psychology, 80,* 437–447.

Juel, C. (1996). What makes tutoring effective? *Reading Research Quarterly, 31*(3), 268–289.

Kennedy, M. M., Birman, B. F., & Demaline, R. E. (1986). *The effectiveness of Chapter 1 services.* Washington, DC: U.S. Department of Education, Office of Educational Research and Improvement.

Lindemann, L., & Fowler, M. (in press). *Tutoring the early reader: Mid-year second grade.* Report submitted to the Center for the Improvement of Early Reading Achievement (CIERA), University of Virginia.

Meier, J., & Invernizzi, M. (in press). Book Buddies in the Bronx: Testing a model for America Reads and national service. *Journal for the Educational Placement of Students Placed at Risk.*

Morris, D. (1995). *First Steps: An early reading intervention program.* (ERIC Documentation Reproduction Service No. ED 388 956)

Morris, D. (1999). *The Howard Street tutoring manual: Teaching at-risk readers in the primary grades.* New York: Guilford Press.

Morris, D., Shaw, B., & Perney, J. (1990). Helping low readers in grades 2 and 3: An after-school volunteer tutoring program. *Elementary School Journal, 91*(2), 133–147.

National Assessment of Educational Progress. (1994). *America's report card.* Washington, DC: U.S. Government Printing Office.

Pinnell, G. S., DeFord, D. E., & Lyons, C. A. (1988). *Reading Recovery: Early intervention for at-risk first graders.* Arlington, VA: Educational Research Service.

Santa, C., & Hoien, T. (1999). An assessment of Early Steps: A program for early intervention of reading problems. *Reading Research Quarterly, 34*(1), 54–73.

Shanahan, T., & Barr, R. (1995). Reading Recovery: An independent evaluation of the effects of an early instructional intervention for at-risk learners. *Reading Research Quarterly, 30*(4), 958–996.

Slavin, R., Madden, N., & Karweit, N. (1989). Effective programs for students at-risk: Conclusions for practice and policy. In R. Slavin, N. Karweit, & N. Madden (Eds.), *Effective programs for students at risk* (pp. 355–372). Needham Heights, MA: Allyn & Bacon.

Slavin, R., Madden, N., Karweit, N., Dolan, L. & Wasik, B. (1994). Success for All: Getting reading right the first time. In E. H. Hiebert & B. M. Taylor (Eds.), *Getting reading right from the start* (pp. 125–148). Needham Heights, MA: Allyn & Bacon.

Snow, C., Burns, M. S., & Griffin, P. (1998). *Preventing reading difficulties in young children.* Washington, DC: National Academy Press.

Spar, M. (1997, November). New poverty estimates for states and local areas. *Spotlight on Virginia, 1*(4), 2–3.

Stanovich, K. E. (1986). Matthew effects in reading: Some consequences of individual differences in the acquisition of literacy. *Reading Research Quarterly, 21*, 360–406.

Staples, C. (1998). *Northumberland reading partners: An after-school community tutorial.* Paper presented at the George Graham Lectures in Reading, Charlottesville, VA.

Torgesen, J. K., & Hecht, S. (1997). Preventive and remedial intervention for children with severe reading disabilities. *Learning Disabilities: A Multidisciplinary Journal, 8*(1), 51–61.

Walmsley, S., & Allington, R. (1995). Redefining and reforming instructional support programs for at-risk students. In R. Allington & S. Walmsley (Eds.), *No quick fix* (pp. 19–44). New York: Teachers College Press.

Chapter 11

READING RECOVERY: A SYSTEMIC APPROACH TO EARLY INTERVENTION

M. Trika Smith-Burke

When educators are asked the question "What is Reading Recovery®?",[1] the responses are reminiscent of the story of the blind men and the elephant. A teacher answers, "A one-to-one tutorial for first graders." Others often comment that it is "hundreds of little books" or "reading strategies." A district-level staff developer considers it "one of the best staff development models she's seen in years." A policy expert sees "an implementation plan" designed to target early intervention as part of a comprehensive literacy plan. And, finally, an assistant superintendent in charge of funding values the "data-driven nature of the program," which allows for finely tuned teaching, program monitoring and evaluation, and research. In fact, like the ending of the fable, the correct answer to the question "What is Reading Recovery?" is *All of the above.*

However, some of the "blind men" refuse to give up common misconceptions, which need clarification. First, Reading Recovery is a *supplemental* program and was *never* meant to function as a comprehensive plan, *nor* as an in-service program for classroom practice. It is *not* aligned with any particular classroom program, *nor* is it a program for small groups of children. Teachers *do* teach children about letters, sounds,

---

1. Reading Recovery® is a registered, trademarked program. The trademark is held by The Ohio State University, which grants royalty free use of the trademark annually to training sites which are in compliance with the *Standards and Guidelines of the Reading Recovery Council of North America* (for more information, contact RRCNA, Columbus, Ohio).

and words in Reading Recovery. And when the program is implemented according to the *Standards and Guidelines of the Reading Recovery Council of North America* (RRCNA, 1998), the lowest-achieving children are served *first*, and children are *not* arbitrarily dropped from the program. (See Askew, Fountas, Lyons, Pinnell, & Schmitt, 1998, for further discussion of these points.)

As part of a comprehensive plan, Reading Recovery is a systemic approach to provide early intervention services for first-grade students in need. It has been designed to accomplish one goal: to dramatically reduce the number of lowest-achieving first graders who are at risk of literacy failure. There are *two positive outcomes* when the program is *fully implemented* (i.e., when service is provided for all children needing service, usually 20–25% of the lowest-achieving first graders):

1. Children are successfully discontinued from the program according to *two criteria*: (a) when they are functioning within average range[2] of first-grade classes; *and* (b) when they have developed a network of perceptual/cognitive strategies that will allow them to continue to learn to write and read progressively more difficult texts, and to benefit from classroom instruction.
2. A small percentage will be identified for further assessment, possibly leading to appropriate, longer-term service.

The purpose of this chapter is to describe Reading Recovery as a systemic approach to early literacy intervention, which focuses on prevention of further difficulty after first grade for the lowest-achieving students. It is the design of its four components—an instructional component for children, a three-tiered staff development component, a monitoring and evaluation component, and an implementation component—that distinguishes it from volunteer tutoring programs and makes it a systemic approach. I begin this chapter by situating Reading Recovery, as a supplement to good classroom teaching, within a prevention model. Next, I review the design of Reading Recovery by explicating the four components that must be in place in order for this preventive approach to be used effectively. Finally, I summarize the research on the program and relate the design of Reading Recovery to a current proposal for improving education and educational reform.

---

2. Clay (1993b) uses the concept of *average band*, defined as plus or minus one half of one standard deviation, as a rigorous test in her research studies. She recommends one standard deviation above and below the mean for local monitoring studies using the rationale that we aim to have children within the band that is addressed by the main thrust of the classroom program.

READING RECOVERY AS SECONDARY PREVENTION

In the late 1960s, the burgeoning caseloads of school psychologists in New Zealand presented Marie Clay with a challenge. Clay (1996/1998, 1998a, 1998b) conceptualized the problem as one of dealing with the diversity of children who, on entering school, are faced with learning from a particular curriculum that may not "have had them in mind" (see H. Levin, quoted in Clay, 1996/1998). Her task was to create a program after 1 year of school to prevent most of this group of the lowest-achieving children from failing to become literate—in other words, to defy predictions about them.

Clay developed her design for early intervention in the late 1970s. Her understanding of the need for prevention (derived from Caplan, 1964; see Clay, 1998c, pp. 210–211) is consistent with a more recent model delineating three levels of prevention—"primary," "secondary," and "tertiary" prevention—proposed by Robert Pianta (1990). His work is part of the current initiative to reduce the numbers of children in special education. The goal of each level of prevention is to significantly reduce the numbers of participants involved at the subsequent level, thus ultimately lowering the number of children needing long-term, more costly special services.

Primary Prevention

Primary prevention provides an important service that is good for all children (e.g., providing vaccinations to all young children). An educational analogue is good classroom literacy instruction, which, if successful, prevents the largest number of students from encountering literacy failure. Based on their work in Australia, Hill and Crevola (Hill & Russell, 1994, cited in Crevola & Hill, 1998; Hill & Crevola, 1999) have hypothesized that good classroom instruction should reach approximately 80% of children, leaving 20% who will need further services even when provided with exceptional classroom teaching.

Secondary Prevention

Because certain populations can be identified as high-risk through correlational research, Pianta (1990) proposes a second level of service, or secondary prevention. This level should be targeted as early intervention to further reduce the number of participants who would qualify for more costly long-term services.

Reading Recovery is a "second-chance" program and does exactly this. In sites where the program is fully implemented[3] and is meeting the

3. "Full coverage" in Reading Recovery is usually defined as enough Reading Recovery teachers trained to provide service to the lowest-achieving children in first grade, depending on level of need and available resources—usually from 20% to 30% of the first-grade cohort.

needs of the lowest-achieving children, Reading Recovery is also functioning as "prereferral screening" for special education placement related to literacy. In other words, in these schools it is considered prudent and cost-effective to provide Reading Recovery instruction before allowing a child to be referred, tested, and placed in the costly and oversubscribed special education system. No assessment by a psychologist is required to provide Reading Recovery services to a child; this eliminates the cost of testing associated with entry into special education.

Clay (1991, 1993b) stresses the need for excellent classroom teaching (i.e., primary prevention). However, she argues that given the broad diversity of children entering school, there will be a group who need further service for a variety of reasons (Clay, 1996/1998, 1998b). She provides a rationale for her position:

> The mismatch between what schools require and the individual diversity
> of learners has been accepted as inevitable and institutionalized in schools
> systems. The delivery system for education is group or whole-class instruc
> tion because societies believe they cannot afford to instruct individuals, so
> classes are instructed. *But classes do not learn. Only individuals learn.* (1996/
> 1998, p. 223; emphasis added)

Clay (1993b) designed Reading Recovery for those children, in all their diversity, who need an alternative to retention, or an extra transitional year, or long-term remedial or special education services—the most common, yet less than successful, existing solutions to this problem (Allington & McGill-Franzen, 1995; Dyer & Binkley, 1995; Shepard, 1991). Since these are the lowest-achieving children, Clay also makes a strong case that these children—who are most at risk of failure and are the hardest to teach—need to be taught in a manner that will help them to transfer their new learning to classroom tasks and to sustain their gains after the intervention. Only highly skilled teachers can fulfill this task if the service is to be short-term and cost-effective.

In addition, because research has shown that deficits are difficult to overcome after third grade (Allington & Walmsley, 1995; Juel, 1988), it is imperative to intervene early in order to break the cycle of the "Matthew effect"—the rich getting richer and the poor getting poorer (Stanovich, 1986). However, an intensive first-grade tutorial is not enough (Allington & Walmsley, 1995). It is important to remember that particularly in low-achieving schools, *both* intensive, primary, instructional strategies in classrooms (see Hall, Prevatte, & Cunningham, 1995, and Taylor, Short, Shearer, & Frye, 1995) *and* an effective tutorial program to work with the hardest-to-teach children are needed to decrease literacy failure (see Crevola & Hill, 1998, Slavin, Madden, Karweit, Livermon, & Dolan, 1990, and Stringfield, Ross, & Smith, 1996, for discussions of comprehensive literacy plans).

Tertiary Prevention

Tertiary prevention requires identification through testing by "experts" in order to provide services (Pianta, 1990). Special education in the United States is the educational analogue of tertiary prevention, providing services for children whose learning does not fit within the regular education system.

Policy makers are currently reviewing the unimpressive, costly results of these services. For example, often after many years in a resource room in elementary school, children no longer receive special education services on entry to high school (Dyer & Binkney, 1995) but still lag far behind their peers. Allington and Walmsley (1995) have pointed out that entry–exit testing adds substantially to the cost of special education, as do smaller class size and specialist assistance; yet special education does not produce the desired results for many children. Examining referrals to special education, McGill-Franzen (1987) has attributed the dramatic increase of referrals to the change in legislation when funding became available under the federal law P.L. 94-142.

Reform efforts are looking to early intervention to reduce the numbers of children eligible for special education. Wilson and Daviss (1994) suggest that this will not happen unless the reform is carefully designed and well-trained teachers are available to work with the lowest-achieving students. School reformers (Sarason, 1982, 1990; Fullan, 1999; Hill & Crevola, 1999; Crevola & Hill, 1998) also remind us that for change to occur, any specialized services must be provided in the context of a comprehensive school plan. In examining factors influencing change in literacy instruction, Hill and Rowe (1996) found that classroom-related factors may be more important than more remote factors (i.e., those at the school, district, or state levels). Fullan (1999) also stresses the importance of intervening at multiple levels, and emphasizes the need to include staff development for teachers as well as principals. In the context of comprehensive reform, Reading Recovery with its systemic design provides an effective secondary prevention strategy, if implemented according to the *Standards and Guidelines of the RRCNA* (RRCNA, 1998).

THE DESIGN OF READING RECOVERY: THE FOUR COMPONENTS

When Clay (1987, 1990, 1992/1994) first designed Reading Recovery, she was aware that in order to disseminate a program cross-culturally to countries with different governmental and educational systems, providing only an instructional framework and teacher training would not be enough. The design also had to allow for continual growth in understanding by program professionals, school and district personnel, researchers, and governmental administrators. Clay (1987) suggested that changes would need to occur across four dimensions: "behavioural change on the part of teachers; child behaviour change achieved by teaching; organisational changes in schools achieved by teachers and administrators; social/political changes in funding by controlling authorities" (p. 38).

Turning to systems theory,[4] Clay (1987) realized that she had to address a variety of issues beyond the one-to-one tutorial:

- Providing depth in training for different levels, yet maintaining a common focus on the individual child's learning.
- Providing continual feedback to teachers and teacher trainers about their success, and/or providing information to help them become more successful and refine their teaching of children and teachers, respectively.
- Building in enough flexibility that Reading Recovery could function as part of different educational structures across countries.
- Ongoing data collection to answer persistent questions; to evaluate/test whether new information from theory, research, and practice should be incorporated into the model; and to monitor the effectiveness, integrity, and quality of the service (feeding information back into all the components to improve service, if necessary).

With these factors in mind, she created four basic components in her design:

- An instructional component, based on her theory of how children learn to read and write continuous text.
- A three-tiered staff development component.
- A monitoring, research, and evaluation component.
- An implementation component.

A brief description of each component, which highlights the significant contribution of each, follows. (See Jones & Smith-Burke, 1999, for a more detailed discussion of the theory, research, and practice that led to the development of Reading Recovery.)

---

4. Clay drew from the work of Dalin (cited in Clay, 1987) and Goodlad (1977).

The Instructional Component

Clay's research led to the development of a theory and model of how children learn to read and write continuous text (Clay, 1982, 1991, 1993a, 1993b, 1998a). New Zealand teachers asked Clay to develop a way to identify children who were likely to encounter difficulty learning to read and write after a year at school. Based on her model, Clay selected six tasks—letter identification, a list of high frequency words for word recognition, Concepts about Print, writing vocabulary, hearing and recording sounds in words, and text reading. These six tasks are described in her book *An Observation Survey of Early Literacy Achievement* (Clay, 1993a), designed for use by classroom teachers. Given the diversity of the children, Clay found that using just one task did not give an adequate picture of a child's "emergent literacy" (see Teale & Sulzby, 1986, for a discussion of this concept); nor did it provide enough information from which to begin an instructional program. *All six measures were necessary.* Once teachers could identify these children, they found them very difficult to teach. This led them to request the development of a program for these children by Clay.

The instructional component in Reading Recovery is based on Clay's theoretical model, developed with the assistance of experienced teachers. Field-based trials were conducted in order to determine that the instructional framework was "user-friendly" to teachers (Clay & Watson, 1982; Clay, 1993b; Jones & Smith-Burke, 1999), thus ensuring the feasibility as well as the effectiveness of the methodology. Instruction is (1) short-term (usually 12 to 20 weeks); (2) daily (30-minute lessons); (3) individual; (4) supplemental to classroom instruction; (5) provided by well-trained teachers; and (6) serves the lowest-achieving first-grade children, working from the bottom up. Children are successfully discontinued from the program according to two criteria: (1) being within the average range of the class;[5] *and* (2) having a "self-extending system" of perceptual/cognitive strategies (see Clay, 1991, 1993b) that permits them to problem solve and continue to learn to write and read in instructional-level texts of increasing difficulty over time.

Before lessons start, there are 10 sessions of "roaming around the known"—a period during which teachers build rapport with the children and help them develop fluency and flexibility in using whatever knowledge they have. By the end of this period, teachers have a much more thorough understanding of children's item knowledge (e.g., words, letter–sound correspondences) and their strategic ability to use this information during reading and writing. It is on this foundation that a

5. See footnote 2.

teacher builds a highly individualized program for each child. Then the teacher gradually moves into instruction to incorporate the essential parts of a Reading Recovery lesson:[6]

- Rereading of familiar books.
- Taking of a "running record"[7] (on the new book from the previous day).
- Letter and/or word work.
- Composing and writing a story (including hearing and recording sounds in words, and the use of spelling patterns).
- Assembling the cut-up story.
- Introduction and reading of a new book.

The structured nature of the set of tasks in the lesson framework can be misleading. No two lessons are the same—in the book selection, the prompts and procedures used, or in what becomes the primary focus for each part of the lesson. Each lesson is tailored to each individual child. There are four significant emphases: (1) never teaching what children already know and know how to do; (2) teaching children some items and a strategy for "how to learn" more, so that learning becomes generative; (3) assisting children in understanding the reciprocity between reading and writing, and ways to link and use information across these tasks; and (4) teaching for perceptual/cognitive strategies (e.g., how to use information to self-monitor, figure out an unknown word, and/or self-correct) in order to problem solve while reading and writing continuous text. These emphases foster accelerated learning, independent problem solving, and ongoing learning. Children are successfully discontinued from the program in approximately 12 to 20 weeks on average—the first positive outcome. A small number of children are referred for further assessment and possibly longer-term service—the second positive outcome.

The Three-Tiered Staff Development Component

There are three different roles within the Reading Recovery program: the university trainer of teacher leaders; district teacher leaders (i.e., teacher trainers); and Reading Recovery teachers. Each role is defined in terms of the different expertise brought to each role, and of the differential training to prepare them for the responsibilities in each role.

6. For a detailed description of the lesson, please see Clay's (1993b) *Reading Recovery: A Guidebook for Teachers in Training.*

7. For information on "running records," see Clay's (1993a) *An Observation Survey of Early Literacy Achievement.*

University trainers[8] provide initial training and ongoing professional development for the teacher trainers or teacher leaders; teach one or two children; help maintain, analyze, and disseminate information about the national data base; problem solve with teacher leaders, their administrators, and teachers at the training site level; consider new, related research and conduct studies for possible changes in the program; conduct basic research with colleagues (e.g., see the work of Hopkins, Schmitt, Nierstheimer, Dixey, and Younts [1995], which examined a model for preservice teacher education based on the professional development model in Reading Recovery); attend professional development sessions; organize and present at regional and national conferences; establish policies for instruction, staff development, and implementation of the program nationally within RRCNA; and disseminate general information to legislators and the public about Reading Recovery.

Teacher leaders[9] teach children; provide the intial training and ongoing continuing education for Reading Recovery teachers; attend professional development sessions; work with principals in setting up and maintaining the program; assist schools in creating school Reading Recovery teams or advisory groups to implement the program, according to the *Standards and Guidelines of the RRCNA* (RRCNA, 1998); assist teachers in problem solving with the hardest-to-teach children; collect, analyze, and report data at the training site level; work at the district level to help plan and coordinate the program with other district literacy initiatives; disseminate information within their site to recruit teachers and inform school staff and the public about the program; and give presentations at national and regional conferences.

Reading Recovery teachers[10] teach a minimum of four Reading Recovery children each, but also serve in another role during the other part of the day. During the year a Reading Recovery teacher is expected to serve

8. The trainer role requires a doctorate in education, literacy, or a related field, as well as evidence of leadership, superior ability to teach young children *and* adults, knowledge of and experience in public schools, and familiarity with research and data analysis.

9. Teacher leaders must minimally hold a master's degree in education, literacy, or a related field; have at least 5 years of successful teaching (including some primary experience) with a major interest in literacy; and show evidence of leadership within their district. In addition, they usually have the ability to work with adults, to collaborate with colleagues, to organize materials and/or people, to analyze data and write reports, and to communicate.

10. Reading Recovery teachers usually have three years of successful teaching experience, preferably at the primary level; see themselves as lifelong learners and love problem solving; believe that all children can learn, and have a commitment to teaching the lowest-achieving children; enjoy collaboration and communicating with fellow teachers; and have served as leaders within their own school.

two students for every 30-minute slot that he/she teaches (usually four slots, discontinuing approximately six to eight children per year after the training year). After their training year, they are also required to attend continuing education sessions to refine their teaching. After 4 or 5 years in Reading Recovery, they also may rotate out of the position in order to allow other teachers to be trained, thus building depth of expertise and flexibility in the school staff. In addition, they may serve on the school Reading Recovery team or advisory group, to ensure effective implementation of the program for each particular school.

Staff members in all three roles are required to teach children and participate in ongoing professional development sessions. When implemented according to the *Standards and Guidelines of the RRCNA* (RRCNA, 1998), the design of Reading Recovery fosters the ongoing development of expertise in teaching, the use of data to inform decision making, and the support for reflective practice and growth at all levels.

The Monitoring, Research, and Evaluation Component

Success in Reading Recovery is measured by student achievement. Even the staff development component is evaluated in this manner. As a dissemination mechanism, the staff development system is in place so that there is also a way to support teachers and teacher leaders to improve instruction and the delivery of services and implement changes.

All aspects of this program are informed by data. This provides an opportunity for refinement, as well as a year-end evaluation of the program's effect on student achievement. For example, at the teacher level, a Reading Recovery teacher selects an instructional focus and a new book for the next lesson only after analyzing the running record, the story written by the child, the lesson record, the writing vocabulary chart, and the book graph.[11] At the school program level, the decision to discontinue a child from the program is based on Observation Survey data administered by another teacher, as well as a discussion with the classroom teacher about the child's ability to apply his/her learning in the classroom setting independently. At the training site level, the teacher leaders examine data to understand which teachers need support and which schools need to train one or more additional Reading Recovery teachers in order to reach full implementation, so that the real impact of the program can be experienced across the school district. At the university training center level, trainers use data to examine sites individually and re-

---

11. For a dicussion of these data collection procedures during a child's program, see *Reading Recovery: A Guidebook for Teachers in Training* (Clay, 1993b).

gionally. Trainers can also use this data collection system when trialing possible changes in procedures with a small group of schools/districts.

Tasks from the Observation Survey are given at the beginning and the end of the year, and on entry and exit from the program (sometimes these coincide), for every child. The National Data and Evaluation Center for Reading Recovery in Ohio feeds the results back to the university training centers and the training sites, so that they can monitor, solve problems, and report progress. Often districts supplement Observation Survey data with standardized testing and continue to collect data on their students who have been successfully discontinued from the program over subsequent years, to make sure that they are maintaining their gains.

Since using a traditional control group was inconsistent with the concept of providing service to the lowest-achieving children first, Clay devised another way to demonstrate the success of the program with enough flexibility to be used across educational systems in different countries. She did so through the use of an alternative comparison group: a random sample of children who scored higher than the Reading Recovery children initially and therefore did not qualify for the program. Reading Recovery children must meet the two criteria discussed previously to leave the program. In other words, the goal is to have successful Reading Recovery children disappear into the average range of the class. They do not differ significantly from the comparison group, as in a traditional design, but instead function like readers and writers making good progress in the average range of this group. Provided with good classroom instruction in subsequent primary grades, most Reading Recovery children who have successfully completed the program maintain their gains and fall within the average band of a random sample drawn from their cohort.

The Implementation Component

Clay (1987, 1990, 1992/1994, 1998c) included an implementation component to address the problems surrounding the introduction of an innovation into an educational system, at both the school and district levels. In creating her design of Reading Recovery, Clay built in checks and balances at all levels to ensure successful implementation, including the following:

- Effective and efficient instruction of children.
- Productive training and ongoing education of Reading Recovery teachers, teacher leaders, and trainers.
- Collaboration at school, district, and university levels.
- Data collection for monitoring and evaluating all aspects of the program by teachers, teacher leaders, trainers, schools, and districts.

- A mechanism to synthesize and/or conduct research to modify the program when needed.
- An information system to acquire information about effective practice or particular difficulties, and/or to feed information back into the different aspects of the program to improve the delivery of services to children.

The checks and balances are built into the roles and responsibilities of the three-tiered staffing model. For example, at the teacher level, another teacher does the final testing of a student to determine whether he/she can be discontinued successfully from the program. Clay (1987) envisioned the role of the teacher leader as a "redirecting system,"[12] who provides information, training, and the ability to solve instructional and implementation problems, and who collects and analyzes data at school and district levels. Teacher leaders are key to the successful introduction and growth of this innovative program as part of a comprehensive plan in the overall system. At the regional and state levels, university trainers uncover problems such as missed instructional time or a low discontinuing rate by analyzing data across sites. Trainers then design professional development sessions for teacher leaders who, in turn, provide in-service sessions for their trained Reading Recovery teachers to improve instruction and/or implementation. Teacher leaders intervene with principals and school teams to support the delivery of instruction according to the *Standards and Guidelines of the RRCNA* (RRCNA, 1998).

Staff members at all three levels—Reading Recovery teachers, teacher leaders, and trainers—work with school and district personnel to foster collaboration, coordination, cooperation, communication, and comprehensive planning at both the school and district levels (Smith-Burke, 1999). Their ultimate goal is to institutionalize Reading Recovery as an early intervention system—an important piece of the fabric of a comprehensive educational plan for literacy instruction.

RESEARCH ON READING RECOVERY

When one is considering research on Reading Recovery, it is extremely important to ask about variables that often go unmentioned in many articles and research reports but may have a serious impact on results.

---

12. Clay based this aspect of the implementation on systems theory—particularly on the work of Dalin (1978, cited in Clay, 1987), who stressed developing skill at all levels of the organization, and Goodlad (1977), who stressed a network of colleagues to provide support and coined the term "redirecting system."

Some key factors to consider when reviewing studies on Reading Recovery are these:

- Stage of implementation in each school within a district.
- Level of coverage.
- Understanding and support of the program by principal and staff in each school.
- Selection of the lowest-achieving children for service.
- Daily teaching of children.
- Availability of the teacher leader to solve instructional and implementation problems.
- Monitoring progress of successfully discontinued children in subsequent years.
- Reading Recovery teachers', teacher leaders', and trainers' attendance at professional development sessions.
- Ongoing data collection, analysis, and dissemination.
- Support of the district-level administrators and the local school board.

Without consideration of these factors, it is extremely difficult to interpret the results of a study.

The progress of Reading Recovery children has been documented nationally in the United States since 1985 (Lyons, 1998). Lyons suggests that two types of replication are evident in the evaluation of Reading Recovery's effectiveness: systematic and simultaneous replication (Frymier, Barber, Gansneider, & Robertson, 1989). There is little doubt that Reading Recovery is successful with children. From 1985 to 1997 a total of 436,249 children were served. Of this total group,[13] 60% were successfully discontinued from the program. Of the 313,848 who received a complete program, 81% were successfully discontinued. Historically, there is a national pattern of increasing success for this group over the first 4 years of initial implementation in the United States. Since 1987–1988, the percentage for this group has remained consistently in the 81–88% range nationally (Askew et al., 1998).

Although some researchers have raised questions about design and/or reporting, other researchers who have reviewed the results of Reading Recovery (Wasik & Slavin, 1993; Hiebert, 1994; Frater & Staniland, 1994; Shanahan & Barr, 1995; Herman & Stringfield, 1997; and Pinnell, 1997) agree that Reading Recovery has demonstrated its instructional effectiveness.

13. This group included all children who participated for even 1 day of involvement in the program, including those who moved, those who were withdrawn from the program, and those who had insufficient time to complete the program.

Askew et al. (1998) provide a useful summary in table form of the results of many studies on Reading Recovery, including two studies that reported initial-year and following-year achievement (Pinnell, 1989; Rowe, 1995).

In addition, Askew et al. (1998) summarize studies examining the development of particular factors, such as phonological awareness (see Iverson & Tunmer, 1993; Sylva & Hurry, 1995; Stahl, Stahl, & McKenna, 1999), metalinguistic skill (Center, Wheldall, Freeman, Outhred, & McNaught, 1995), and scaffolding (Hobsbaum, Peters, & Sylva, 1996). Additional studies look at Reading Recovery from a Vygotskian perspective (Cox, Fang, & Schmitt, 1998) and in terms of the training model and its possible modification and transfer to undergraduate teacher training (Schmitt, Younts, & Hopkins, 1994; Hopkins et al., 1995). In all these studies, Reading Recovery has proven effective (for a more detailed discussion, see Askew et al., 1998). Two studies (Kelly, Gomez-Valdez, Klein, & Neal, 1994; Ashdown & Simic, in press) have examined the achievement of English as a Second Language (ESL) children in Reading Recovery; both of these studies have demonstrated that ESL students make good progress in Reading Recovery. One study reported the successful progress of bilingual students in Descubriendo La Lectura (DLL),[14] the redevelopment of Reading Recovery in Spanish (Escamilla, 1994). Since then, Escamilla, Loera, Ruiz, and Rodriguez (1998) have also reported successful follow-up results from DLL.

Askew et al. (1998) have also analyzed cross-sectional studies and longitudinal studies to answer this question: "Do Reading Recovery students maintain their gains?" (See their report for a full list of the studies they examined, which included research from Ohio, Massachusetts, New York (Jaggar & Smith-Burke, 1994; Jaggar & Simic, 1996), and Texas (Askew, Kaye, Wickstrom, & Frasier, 2000), as well as Clay's [1993b] own research.) A common pattern in several studies using both Reading Recovery and standardized measures is that Reading Recovery students who have successfully completed the program are just within or a bit below the average band in second grade, but move to within the average band in third and fourth grades, continuing to progress and maintain their gains. Students' scores on average are comparable with those of their randomly sampled peers in these grades.

An article recently published in *Spectrum* describes a 5-year study of the implementation of Reading Recovery as part of a comprehensive lit-

14. Descubriendo La Lectura (DLL) is the Spanish redevelopment of Reading Recovery in which the lowest-achieving first graders who are learning to read and write in Spanish in bilingual classrooms are provided with supplemental daily, one-on-one instruction in Spanish. In other words, DLL is the Spanish version of Reading Recovery that was redeveloped and modified to reflect linguistic characteristics of the Spanish language.

eracy plan in the San Luis Coastal Unified District in California (Brown, Denton, Kelly, & Neal, 1999). This is one of the few studies probing the systemic impact of Reading Recovery in a school district. The comprehensive plan included an emphasis on good primary classroom teaching, a well-resourced Reading Recovery program fully implemented in all schools, and a 5-year study design, collecting data from the *Observation Survey of Early Literacy Achievement* during first grade and standardized test data at the end of each year.

The authors reported that at the end of first grade in each of the five years of the study, between 81% to 85% of first graders receiving a full instructional program in Reading Recovery reached average proficiency levels on the Observation Survey tasks, and most scored at average level on the *Iowa Test of Basic Skills* (ITBS). To answer their second research question (i.e., whether successfully discontinued students maintained their gains over the next four years), the authors provided end-of-year data from the ITBS and the *Standford Achievement Test, Ninth Edition* (SAT-9) for those successfully discontinued students who remained in the district in grades 2–5. These data demonstrated that in each year, more than 75% of these students scored at or above average levels—a remarkable achievement since they had started within the lowest 20% of their first-grade classes. Using Reading Recovery as a systemic approach to early intervention in first grade within a comprehensive literacy plan, the district has demonstrated that (1) it is possible to significantly reduce the number of first graders at-risk of literacy failure and (2) that a significant proportion of these children can maintain their gains in subsequent years. The district team is using the ongoing monitoring data to continue to problem solve in order to improve results.

CONCLUSION

In their book, *Redesigning Education*, Kenneth Wilson, a Nobel-prize-winning physicist, and Bennett Daviss call for American education to utilize "the redesign process" that exists in industry (but not in education) as a way to bring about significant reform in education and make it more effective. They state:

> The redesign process is the integration of research, development, dissemination, and refinement by which innovations and the procedures that create them are originated, improved, and made affordable. But its usefulness reaches far beyond the laboratory or marketplace. In essence, the redesign process is an institutionalized method of strategic, systemic change that works unceasingly to enact a vision of excellence as well as to redefine excellence itself when changing conditions make it necessary. (p. 22)

They point out that this redesign process requires an ongoing conversation across professional levels—what they call "a continuous circuit of information through which researchers, development engineers, marketing executives, salespeople, and consumers discuss their needs and goals" (p. 23). They have identified critical aspects related to success in industry: use of current research, differentiated kinds of training, and expertise within roles and across administrative levels that complement each other. There must be an integrated approach to solving a given problem, carried out in interdisciplinary teams, with continuous, ongoing learning to improve and refine an existing "product." These authors argue that to bring about significant change in education, an innovation must embody this redesign process. From their perspective, *"Reading Recovery offers US education its first real demonstration of the power of a process combining research, development (including ongoing teacher education), marketing, and technical support in an orchestrated system of change"* (Wilson & Daviss, 1994, p. 76, emphasis added).

Wilson and Daviss (1994) point out that the design of the components is what makes Reading Recovery unique. They also emphasize that a key factor in continued success of any program is provision for identifying problematic areas and introducing changes into all components of the program. This can be accomplished in Reading Recovery through the use of the data collection system and the three-tiered staff development system, as a tool for dissemination of information and training. Changes may be derived from research (i.e., from existing data collection) and/or practice (e.g., from Reading Recovery teachers or teacher leaders) within the framework of Reading Recovery, or from the larger field of literacy work, including related research or practical suggestions that must be trialed in a Reading Recovery context before any changes can be made to the overall program.

One recent example of this type of change came from questions from researchers (Hiebert, 1994) about the reporting of the data, and from school districts and university training centers about implementation factors. As a result, during 1997–1998 the data collection and reporting system was redesigned to make every student's data visible in the reporting. Additional data are being collected to explore questions about implementation factors, such as percentage of coverage, years of Reading Recovery teaching experience, average number of weeks in program, average number of students served/discontinued, reasons for missed instructional time, and average number of students retained in grade or referred to/placed in special education.

Two other recent shifts in thinking include practical considerations that were implemented some time ago in New Zealand but were introduced only later (about 1995) in the United States: the concepts of (1) school

Reading Recovery teams or advisory groups, and (2) the rotation of Reading Recovery teachers out of the program after 4 or 5 years, even though these teachers may return to the program at a later date. These two concepts strengthen the educational effort in several ways. A school Reading Recovery team allows a school, utilizing the *Standards and Guidelines of the RRCNA* (RRCNA, 1998), to implement the program in the best way for its own needs. Through rotation, Reading Recovery teachers bring understanding from their experience in the program to whatever other jobs they take on (e.g., administration, staff development), particularly a strong belief that all children can learn with good instruction. They also add to their own professional repertoire, benefiting Reading Recovery when and if they return to the program.

A word of caution is in order here, however. District 2 in New York City found that rotation of Reading Recovery teachers into primary classroom teaching can be a powerful strategy, *only if adequate in-service support is provided to these teachers in their new role as classroom teachers.* Due to the narrow focus of Reading Recovery and the individual nature of instruction, these teachers were not able to translate their knowledge easily or directly into classroom instruction. Classroom instruction is group instruction, which must meet the needs of children with a much greater range of abilities, has a broader set of goals and objectives, and may differ instructionally from Reading Recovery. In addition, literacy is embedded in many other subject areas that must be taught (e.g., social studies, math, etc.). District 2 had to provide additional classroom in-service support to help Reading Recovery teachers who returned to the classroom to build new knowledge, routines, and procedures for class teaching, and to learn when their Reading Recovery understandings were useful (A. Alvarado, personal communication, 1995) and when they were not. Clay (1993b) also warns us that she would not consider it wise to use methodology designed for the lowest-achieving children with children possessing the wide range of abilities evident in any classroom.

Wilson and Daviss (1994) state that Reading Recovery is a program that does a specific job well; however, it is a subsystem that must work within a more comprehensive reform plan. They conclude:

> The program does incorporate several key features of a successful redesign process. It has shaped its methods according to the results of its own and others' research. It has tested and honed its techniques through years of trials and refinements. (p. 54)

As in the fable mentioned at the beginning of this chapter, when the parts did not allow the blind men to comprehend the whole elephant, so too an individual component is not Reading Recovery, even though each component is critical to the success of the endeavor. Utilizing just one part in isolation from the others is bound to fail (Pinnell, Lyons, DeFord, Bryk, & Seltzer, 1994; Shanahan & Barr, 1995).

With a sense of community in schools and a commitment to children's literacy learning, the possibility of success is great. With new awareness of the importance of the design and systemic nature of the Reading Recovery as an early intervention component in a comprehensive plan, perhaps now there will be incentive for teachers, educators, and parents to unite and work together to provide *both* good classroom teaching *and* Reading Recovery to ensure that *all children* learn to read and write.

REFERENCES

Allington, R. L., & McGill-Franzen, A. (1995). Flunking: Throwing good money after bad. In R. L. Allington & S. A. Walmsley (Eds.), *No quick fix: Rethinking literacy programs in America's elementary schools* (pp. 45–60). New York: Teachers College Press.

Allington, R., & Walmsley, S. (Eds.). (1995). *No quick fix: Rethinking literacy programs in America's elementary schools.* New York: Teachers College Press.

Ashdown, J., & Simic, O. (in press). Is early literacy intervention effective for ESL students?: Evidence from Reading Recovery. *Literacy Teaching and Learning.*

Askew, B. J., Fountas, I. C., Lyons, C. A., Pinnell, G. S., & Schmitt, M. C. (1998). *Reading Recovery review: Understandings, outcomes and implications.* Columbus, OH: Reading Recovery Council of North America.

Askew, B. J., Kaye, B., Wickstrom, C., & Frasier, D. (2000). *Subsequent progress of former Reading Recovery children: Two longitudinal studies.* Manuscript in preparation.

Brown, W., Denton, E., Kelly, P., & Neal, J. (1999). Reading Recovery effectiveness: A five-year success story in San Luis Coastal Unified School District. *Spectrum, 17*(1), 3–12.

Caplan, G. (1964). *Principles of preventive psychiatry.* London: Tavistock Publications.

Center, Y., Wheldall, K., Freeman, L., Outhred, L., & McNaught, M. (1995). An experimental evaluation of Reading Recovery. *Reading Research Quarterly, 30*, 240–263.

Clay, M. M. (Ed.). (1982). *Observing young readers: Selected papers.* Portsmouth, NH: Heinemann.

Clay, M. M. (1987). Systemic adaptations to an educational innovation. *New Zealand Journal of Educational Studies, 22*(1), 35–58.

Clay, M. M. (1990). The Reading Recovery programme, 1984–1988: Coverage, outcomes and Education Board district figures. *New Zealand Journal of Educational Studies, 25*(1), 61–70.

Clay, M. M. (1991). *Becoming literate: The construction of inner control.* Portsmouth, NH: Heinemann.

Clay, M. M. (1993a). *An observation survey of early literacy achievement.* Portsmouth, NH: Heinemann.

Clay, M. M. (1993b). *Reading Recovery: A guidebook for teachers in training.* Portsmouth, NH: Heinemann.

Clay, M. M. (1994). Reading Recovery: The wider implications of an educational innovation. *Literacy Teaching and Learning, 1*(1), 121–194. (Original work published 1992)

Clay, M. M. (1998). Accommodating diversity in early literacy learning. In M. M. Clay, *By different paths to common outcomes* (pp. 223–247). York, ME: Stenhouse. (Original work published 1996)

Clay, M. M. (1998a). *By different paths to common outcomes.* York, ME: Stenhouse.

Clay, M. M. (1998b). Children come to school by different paths. In M. M. Clay, *By different paths to common outcomes* (pp. 1–4). York, ME: Stenhouse.

Clay, M. M. (1998c). The challenge of literacy improvement. In M. M. Clay, *By different paths to common outcomes* (pp. 197–219). York, ME: Stenhouse.

Clay, M. M., & Watson, B. (1982). An inservice program for Reading Recovery teachers. In M. M. Clay (Ed.), *Observing young readers: Selected papers* (pp. 192–200). Portsmouth, NH: Heinemann.

Cox, B. E., Fang, Z., & Schmitt, M. C. (1998). At-risk children's metacognitive growth during the Reading Recovery experience: A Vygotskian interpretation. *Literacy Teaching and Learning, 3,* 55–76.

Crevola, C. A., & Hill, P. W. (1998). Evaluation of a whole-school approach to prevention and intervention in early literacy. *Journal of Education for Students Placed at Risk, 3*(2), 133–157.

Dyer, P., & Binkney, R. (1995). Estimating cost-effectiveness and educational outcomes: Retention, remediation, special education, and early intervention. In R. L. Allington & S. A. Walmsley (Eds.), *No quick fix: Rethinking literacy programs in America's elementary schools* (pp. 61–77). New York: Teachers College Press.

Escamilla, K. (1994). Descubriendo La Lectura: An early intervention literacy program in Spanish. *Literacy Teaching and Learning, 1,* 57–85.

Escamilla, K., Loera, M., Ruiz, O., & Rodriguez, Y. (1998). An examination of sustaining effects in Descubriendo La Lectura programs. *Literacy Teaching and Learning, 3,* 59–81.

Frater, G., & Staniland, B. (1994). Reading Recovery from New Zealand: A report from the Office of Her Majesty's Chief Inspector of Schools. *Literacy Teaching and Learning, 1,* 143–162.

Frymier, J., Barber, L., Gansneider, B., & Robertson, N. (1989). Simultaneous replication: A technique for large-scale research. *Phi Delta Kappan, 71*(3), 228–231.

Fullan, M. (1999). *Change forces: The sequel.* Philadelphia: Falmer Press.

Goodlad, J. I. (1977). *Networking and educational improvement: Reflections on strategy.* Washington, DC: National Institute of Education.

Hall, D. R., Prevatte, C., & Cunningham, P. (1995). Eliminating ability grouping and reducing failure in primary grades. In R. L. Allington & S. E. Walmsley (Eds.), *No quick fix: Rethinking literacy programs in America's elementary schools* (pp. 137–158). New York: Teachers College Press.

Herman, R., & Stringfield, S. (1997). *Ten promising programs for educating all children: Evidence of impact.* Arlington, VA: Educational Research Service.

Hiebert, E. H. (1994). Reading Recovery in the United States: What difference does it make to an age cohort? *Educational Researcher, 23,* 15–25.

Hill, P. W., & Crevola, C. A. (1999). The role of standards in educational reform for the 21st century. In D. Marsh (Ed.), *Preparing our schools for the 21st century* (pp. 117–142). Arlington, VA: Association for Supervision and Curriculum Development.

Hill, P. W., & Rowe, K. J. (1996). Multilevel modeling in school effectiveness research. *School Effectiveness and School Improvement, 7*(1), 1–34.

Hobsbaum, A., Peters, S., & Sylva, K. (1996). Scaffolding in Reading Recovery. *Oxford Review of Education, 22,* 17–35.

Hopkins, C. J., Schmitt, M. C., Nierstheimer, S. J., Dixey, B. P., & Younts, T. (1995). Infusing features of the Reading Recovery professional development model into the experiences of preservices teachers. In K. A. Hinchman, D. J. Leu, & C. K. Kinzer (Eds.), *Perspectives on literacy research and methods* (pp. 349–367). Chicago: National Reading Conference.

Iverson, S. J., & Tunmer, W. E. (1993). Phonological processing skills and the Reading Recovery program. *Journal of Educational Psychology, 85,* 112–126.

Jaggar, A. M., & Simic, O. (1996). *A four-year follow-up study of Reading Recovery children in New York state: Preliminary report.* New York: Reading Recovery Project, School of Education, New York University.

Jaggar, A. M., & Smith-Burke, M. T. (1994). *Follow-up study of Reading Recovery children in Community School District #2, New York City.* New York: Reading Recovery Project, School of Education, New York University.

Jones, N. K., & Smith-Burke, M. T. (1999). Forging a relationship among research, theory and practice: Clay's research design and methodology. In J. Gaffney & B. J. Askew (Eds.), *Stirring the waters: The influence of Marie Clay* (pp. 261–285). Portsmouth, NH: Heinemann.

Juel, C. (1988). Learning to read and write: A longitudinal study of 54 children from first through fourth grade. *Journal of Educational Psychology, 80,* 437–447.

Kelly, P. R., Gomez-Valdez, C., Klein, A., & Neal, J. (1994). *Progress of first and second language learners in an early intervention program.* Paper presented at the meeting of the American Educational Research Association, San Francisco.

Lyons, C. A. (1998). Reading Recovery in the United States: More than a decade of data. *Literacy Teaching and Learning, 3*(1), 77–92.

McGill-Franzen, A. (1987). Failure to learn to read: Formulating a policy problem. *Reading Research Quarterly, 22,* 475–490.

Pianta, R. C. (1990). Widening the debate on educational reform: Prevention as a viable alternative. *Exceptional Children, 56*(4), 306–313.

Pinnell, G. S. (1989). Reading Recovery: Helping at-risk children learn to read. *The Elementary School Journal, 90*(2), 161–183.

Pinnell, G. S. (1997). Reading Recovery: A summary of research. In J. Flood, S. B. Heath, & D. Lapp (Eds.), *Handbook of research on teaching literacy through the communicative and visual arts* (pp. 638–654). New York: Macmillan.

Pinnell, G. S., Lyons, C. A., DeFord, D. E., Bryk, A., & Seltzer, M. (1994). Comparing instructional models for the literacy education of high risk first graders. *Reading Research Quarterly, 29,* 8–39.

Rowe, K. J. (1995). Factors affecting students' progress in reading: Key findings from a longitudinal study. *Literacy Teaching and Learning, 1,* 57–110.

RRCNA. (Reading Recovery Council of North America). (1998). *Standards and guidelines of the reading recovery council of North America.* Columbus, OH: Author.

Sarason, S. B. (1982). *The culture of schools and the problem of change* (2nd ed.). Boston: Allyn & Bacon.

Sarason, S. B. (1990). *The predictable failure of educational reform.* San Francisco: Jossey-Bass.

Schmitt, M. C., Younts, T., & Hopkins, C. J. (1994, December). *From at-risk to strategic, self-regulated learners: Reading Recovery from Vygotskian and metacognitive perspectives.* Paper presented at the National Reading Conference, San Diego, CA.

Shanahan, T., & Barr, R. (1995). A synthesis of research on Reading Recovery. *Reading Research Quarterly, 30,* 958–996.

Shepard, L. (1991). Negative policies for dealing with diversity: When does assessment and diagnosis turn into sorting and segregation? In E. Hiebert (Ed.), *Literacy for a diverse society: Perspectives, practices and policies* (pp. 279–298). New York: Teachers College Press.

Slavin, R. E., Madden, N., Karweit, N., Livermon, B., & Dolan, L. (1990). Success for All: First-year outcomes of a comprehensive plan for reforming urban education. *American Educational Research Journal, 27,* 255–278.

Smith-Burke, M. T. (1999). *Reading Recovery as part of a comprehensive approach to literacy instruction.* Paper presented at the Northeast Early Literacy Conference, Boston.

Stahl, K. A. D., Stahl, S., & McKenna, M. C. (1999). The development of phonological awareness and orthographic processing in Reading Recovery. *Literacy Teaching and Learning, 3*(2), 27–42.

Stanovich, K. E. (1986). Matthew effects in reading: Some consequences of individual differences in the acquisition of literacy. *Reading Research Quarterly, 21,* 360–407.

Stringfield, S., Ross, S., & Smith, L. (Eds.). (1996). *Bold plans for school restructuring: The new American Schools designs.* Mahwah, NJ: Erlbaum.

Sylva, K., & Hurry, J. (1995). Early intervention in children with reading difficulties: An evaluation of Reading Recovery and phonological training. *Literacy Teaching and Learning, 2*(2), 49–68.

Taylor, B., Short, R., Shearer, B., & Frye, B. (1995). First grade teachers provide early reading intervention in the classroom. In R. L. Allington & S. E. Walmsley (Eds.), *No quick fix: Rethinking literacy programs in America's elementary schools* (pp. 159–176). New York: Teachers College Press.

Teale, W., & Sulzby, E. (Eds.). (1986). *Emergent literacy: Writing and reading.* Norwood, NJ: Ablex.

Wasik, B. A., & Slavin, R. E. (1993). Preventing early reading failure with one-to-one tutoring: A review of five programs. *Reading Research Quarterly, 28,* 179–200.

Wilson, K. G., & Daviss, B. (1994). *Redesigning education.* New York: Henry Holt.

INDEX

Writing
  assessment of, 121
  early reader plan, 205
  modeling of, 18–19
  reading and, 6
  shared and supported, 125–126
  for sound, 202, 204
  strategies for, 136
  University of Maryland–College
    Park program, 165
  University of North Carolina–
    Chapel Hill program, 142, 150
Written communication, 19

Y

Yale University program
  community service ethos and, 86–
    87
  Dwight Central Management
    Team and, 89
  Dwight neighborhood, 88–89
  effectiveness of, 97

evaluation and expansion of, 95–96
factors in success of, 97–98
focus of, 91–92
Greater Dwight Development
  Corporation (GDDC), 90
Homebuyer Program, 89
institutional urban citizenship and,
  87–88, 98–99
Joint Community Development
  Program grant, 89–90
overview of, 9, 92, 94
scheduling issues, 96
student selection, 92, 93
Timothy Dwight Elementary
  School, 90–91, 96–97
training for, 93–94
tutors for, 92, 93
weekend tutoring sessions, 94–95
Youth Reading Survey, 42–43, 44

Z

"Zone of proximal development," 21